The Healthy
Mediterranean

Cookbook for Beginners

2000+ Days Super Simple and Mouthwatering Mediterranean Diet
Recipes with a BONUS 30-Day Meal Plan for Easy Weight Loss,
Eating Well, and Lifelong Health | Ready in 30 Minutes or Less

Karolyn T. Lopez

TABLE OF
CONTENTS

Introduction

Basics of the Mediterranean diet

The Mediterranean diet is a unique diet choice, as I've come to see that it is continuously picking up traction with the times. The Mediterranean diet has captivated my attention for its unique approach to dining and its growing popularity. This diet, rich in culture and history, offers a plethora of benefits alongside a refreshing change to one's usual meal plan. My journey into the heart of the Mediterranean diet began with curiosity and led to an extensive exploration of its origins, nutrient-dense recipes, and ultimately, to this guide designed to navigate you through the enticing world of Mediterranean cuisine.

Diving into the Mediterranean diet reveals a world where nutrition meets tradition, gaining popularity for its health benefits and unique culinary approach. Originating across the Mediterranean Sea's diverse countries, this diet emphasizes plant-based foods like nuts, veggies, fruits, whole grains, and legumes, rich in omega-3s, fiber, and healthy fats. Red meat, certain dairies, sugars, and processed foods are minimized, making room for vegetables and lean proteins to shine. Studies have shown that following this diet can reduce the risk of heart disease, stroke, and certain types of cancer. The diet is also associated with a longer lifespan and improved cognitive function.

One of the key principles of the Mediterranean diet is to focus on plant-based foods. This means consuming plenty of fruits, vegetables, whole grains, legumes, nuts, and seeds. These foods are rich in fiber, vitamins, minerals, and antioxidants, which are essential for good health.

Another important aspect of the Mediterranean diet is to limit the consumption of red meat and dairy products. Instead, people are encouraged to eat fish, poultry, and eggs in moderation. This helps to reduce the intake of saturated fats, which can increase the risk of heart disease.

Olive oil is a staple in the Mediterranean diet and is considered a healthy source of fat. It is used in cooking, dressings, and as a dip for bread. Other healthy fats found in the diet include nuts, seeds, and avocado.

The Mediterranean diet also emphasizes the importance of eating meals with family and friends. This not only promotes social interaction but also helps to control portion sizes and encourages the consumption of healthier foods.

In conclusion, the Mediterranean diet is a delicious and healthy way of eating that can improve overall health and wellbeing. By focusing on plant-based foods, healthy fats, and whole foods, people can reduce their risk of chronic diseases and live a longer, happier life.

Why Choose The Mediterranean Diet?

Here's a distilled overview of the compelling reasons to choose the Mediterranean diet, each highlighted under its own spotlight for clarity and emphasis.

Plant-Based Focus

At its core, the Mediterranean diet prioritizes plant-based foods, including vegetables, fruits, nuts, seeds, legumes, whole grains, and olive oil. This focus ensures a diet rich in dietary fiber, antioxidants, and essential nutrients, contributing to a diverse and enjoyable eating experience. The abundance of fresh, whole foods supports physical health and vitality, laying the groundwork for a nutritious lifestyle.

Heart Health

A standout benefit of the Mediterranean diet is its profound positive impact on heart health. Characterized by high levels of omega-3 fatty acids and monounsaturated fats, with minimal intake of red meat, the diet is linked to reduced risks of cardiovascular diseases. It aids in maintaining healthy blood pressure and cholesterol levels, offering a protective shield against heart-related conditions.

Broad Health Benefits

Beyond cardiovascular wellness, the Mediterranean diet is associated with a lower risk of type 2 diabetes, certain cancers, and neurodegenerative diseases. Its nutrient-dense profile supports overall bodily health, fostering longevity and decreasing the likelihood of chronic diseases. The emphasis on whole, minimally processed foods also aids in weight management and digestive health.

The Mediterranean Lifestyle

Integral to the diet's allure is the Mediterranean lifestyle, which emphasizes meals as communal,

social events. This approach promotes slower eating, mindfulness, and the pleasure of food in the company of loved ones. The lifestyle encourages moderate physical activity, aligning with a comprehensive perspective on health and well-being.

Culinary Adventure

Adopting the Mediterranean diet opens the door to a vast culinary adventure, celebrating the diverse flavors, ingredients, and cooking traditions of the Mediterranean region. From savory dishes enriched with herbs and spices to sweet delicacies featuring fresh fruits and honey, the diet showcases the rich and vibrant essence of Mediterranean cuisine.

In sum, choosing the Mediterranean diet is not merely about adopting a set of eating habits; it's about embracing a lifestyle that cherishes health, community, and the joy of culinary exploration. The diet's proven health benefits, coupled with its focus on flavor and communal dining, render it an unparalleled choice for those seeking a balanced and fulfilling approach to living.

Health Benefits Of The Mediterranean Diet

The Mediterranean diet is a way of eating that emphasizes whole, unprocessed foods and includes an abundance of fruits, vegetables, legumes, nuts, and healthy fats. It also includes moderate amounts of fish, poultry, and dairy products. The health benefits of the Mediterranean diet include:

Reduced risk of heart disease: Studies have shown that following a Mediterranean diet can help reduce the risk of heart disease by lowering blood pressure, cholesterol levels, and inflammation.

Improved brain health: The Mediterranean diet is rich in antioxidants and other nutrients that can help protect brain cells from damage and improve cognitive function.

Lowered risk of diabetes: The diet is associated with lower rates of type 2 diabetes due to its emphasis on whole, unprocessed foods and limited intake of refined carbohydrates.

Weight management: The Mediterranean diet is a balanced, low-calorie diet that can help promote weight loss and maintenance of a healthy weight.

Improved gut health: The diet is rich in prebiotics and probiotics that can help support a healthy gut microbiome and improve digestive health.

Reduced risk of certain cancers: Studies have shown that following a Mediterranean diet may be associated with a reduced risk of certain types of cancer, including breast, colorectal, and prostate cancer.

Improved mood and mental health: The diet is associated with lower rates of depression and anxiety due to its emphasis on whole, unprocessed foods and limited intake of processed foods high in added sugars and unhealthy fats.

The Mediterranean Diet Food Pyramid

The Mediterranean-style Diet Pyramid is a widely accepted guide to healthy eating that provides a healthy lifestyle based on the traditional eating habits of countries around the Mediterranean. The pyramid has nine levels, each representing a different food category that is an integral part of our daily diet.

First of all, the first layer is fruits and vegetables. This is the bottom of the pyramid and the most important layer. It is recommended to eat a lot of vegetables and fruits every day to get rich vitamins, minerals and dietary fiber. These nutrients are essential for maintaining the health of our bodies, and they can help us prevent various diseases such as heart disease, diabetes, and certain types of cancer.

The second layer is whole grains. This includes unrefined grains such as oats, brown rice and whole wheat bread. They are high in fiber and B vitamins, which help maintain a healthy digestive system and energy levels. Whole grains also help us control our weight because they help us feel full, which reduces our intake of other high-calorie foods.

The third layer is beans and nuts. These foods are good sources of protein and also contain healthy fats and fiber. They can help us control our blood sugar levels and reduce our risk of heart disease. In addition, beans

and nuts are also rich in antioxidants, which can help us resist free radical damage.

The fourth floor is fish and seafood. These foods are rich in omega-3 fatty acids, which are good for heart health. At the same time, they are also a source of high-quality protein. Fish and seafood are also rich in vitamins D and B12, which are essential for the health of our nervous system and blood.

The fifth layer is poultry and eggs. These foods are good sources of protein and also contain a variety of vitamins and minerals. Poultry is lower in fat than red meat, making it more suitable for a healthy diet.

The sixth layer is cheese and yogurt. These foods are rich in calcium and protein, which are beneficial to bone health. Calcium is the main component of our bones and teeth, while protein is the main building block of our body.

The seventh layer is milk and other dairy products. These foods are a great source of calcium and vitamin D, which are good for bone health. Vitamin D helps our bodies absorb calcium, which in turn helps maintain our bones and teeth healthy.

The eighth layer is meat and meat substitutes. Foods in this layer should be consumed in moderation, as they are usually higher in saturated fat and cholesterol. While meat is an important source of high-quality protein, excessive intake may increase the risk of heart disease and other chronic diseases.

Finally, the ninth layer is sweet food, snacks and alcohol. These foods should be eaten as little as possible because they usually contain more sugar, salt and unhealthy fat. Excessive consumption of these foods may lead to weight gain and increase the risk of heart disease, diabetes and other health problems.

Foods To Eat And Avoid

The Mediterranean diet consists of traditional foods from countries bordering the Mediterranean sea, such as Greece, France, and Italy. The diet typically contains fruits, vegetables, whole grains, lentils, nuts, and seeds. Extra-virgin olive oil is a typical source of healthy fats. The diet does not contain heavily processed foods, products with added sugar, or large amounts of unhealthy fats as found in butter, red meat, and cheese.

Foods to eat:

Embrace: Plant-Based Staples

The Mediterranean diet is renowned for its emphasis on whole, plant-based foods. Fill your plate with a vibrant array of vegetables, fruits, nuts, seeds, legumes, and whole grains. These foods are not only the cornerstone of the diet but also provide essential nutrients, fiber, and antioxidants that support overall health. Olive oil, celebrated for its heart-healthy fats, should be the primary fat source, enhancing dishes with its rich flavor.

Include: Seafood and Poultry

Seafood and poultry are key protein sources within the Mediterranean diet, enjoyed in moderation. Aim for at least two servings of seafood per week, focusing on fatty fish like salmon, mackerel, and sardines, rich in omega-3 fatty acids. Poultry, eaten in smaller quantities than plant-based proteins, offers a lean alternative to red meat, perfectly complementing the diet's plant-forward approach.

Foods to avoid:

Limit: Red Meat and Dairy

Red meat is consumed sparingly in the Mediterranean diet, reserved for special occasions rather than daily meals. When choosing dairy, opt for fermented or lower-fat options like yogurt and cheese, which can provide probiotics and calcium without the saturated fat content of their full-fat counterparts.

Avoid: Processed Foods and Sugars

Central to the Mediterranean diet's philosophy is the minimization of processed foods and added sugars. Instead of reaching for sugary snacks or heavily processed meals, the diet encourages whole foods and natural sweeteners like fruits and honey. This shift not only aligns with the diet's health principles but also with its emphasis on enjoying the natural tastes and textures of food.

By focusing on these dietary guidelines, you can fully embrace the Mediterranean way of eating, enjoying a diet that's not only delicious but also rich in nutrients and health benefits.

Chapter 1 Breakfasts

Cauliflower Avocado Toast

Prep time: 15 minutes / Cook time: 8 minutes / Serves 2

- 1 (12 ounces / 340 g) steamer bag cauliflower
- 1 large egg
- ½ cup shredded Mozzarella cheese
- 1 ripe medium avocado
- ½ teaspoon garlic powder
- ¼ teaspoon ground black pepper

1. Cook cauliflower according to package instructions. Remove from bag and place into cheesecloth or clean towel to remove excess moisture.
2. Place cauliflower into a large bowl and mix in egg and Mozzarella. Cut a piece of parchment to fit your air fryer basket. Separate the cauliflower mixture into two, and place it on the parchment in two mounds. Press out the cauliflower mounds into a ¼-inch-thick rectangle. Place the parchment into the air fryer basket.
3. Adjust the temperature to 400ºF (204ºC) and set the timer for 8 minutes.
4. Flip the cauliflower halfway through the cooking time.
5. When the timer beeps, remove the parchment and allow the cauliflower to cool 5 minutes.
6. Cut open the avocado and remove the pit. Scoop out the inside, place it in a medium bowl, and mash it with garlic powder and pepper. Spread onto the cauliflower. Serve immediately.

Per Serving:calories: 321 / fat: 22g / protein: 16g / carbs: 19g / fiber: 10g / sodium: 99mg

Avocado Toast with Smoked Trout

Prep time: 10 minutes / Cook time: 0 minutes / Serves 2

- 1 avocado, peeled and pitted
- 2 teaspoons lemon juice, plus more for serving
- ¾ teaspoon ground cumin
- ¼ teaspoon kosher salt
- ¼ teaspoon red pepper flakes, plus more for sprinkling
- ¼ teaspoon lemon zest
- 2 pieces whole-wheat bread, toasted
- 1 (3.75-ounce / 106-g) can smoked trout

1. In a medium bowl, mash together the avocado, lemon juice, cumin, salt, red pepper flakes, and lemon zest.
2. Spread half the avocado mixture on each piece of toast. Top each piece of toast with half the smoked trout. Garnish with a pinch of red pepper flakes (if desired), and/or a sprinkle of lemon juice (if desired).

Per Serving:calories: 300 / fat: 20g / protein: 11g / carbs: 21g / fiber: 6g / sodium: 390mg

Greek Yogurt and Berries

Prep time: 5 minutes / Cook time: 30 minutes / Serves 4

- 4 cups plain full-fat Greek yogurt
- 1 cup granola
- ½ cup blackberries
- 2 bananas, sliced and frozen
- 1 teaspoon chia seeds, for topping
- 1 teaspoon chopped fresh mint leaves, for topping
- 4 teaspoons honey, for topping (optional)

1. Evenly divide the yogurt among four bowls. Top with the granola, blackberries, bananas, chia seeds, mint, and honey (if desired), dividing evenly among the bowls. Serve.

Per Serving:calories: 283 / fat: 9g / protein: 12g / carbs: 42g / fiber: 5g / sodium: 115mg

Tiropita (Greek Cheese Pie)

Prep time: 15 minutes / Cook time: 45 minutes / Serves 12

- 1 tablespoon extra virgin olive oil plus 3 tablespoons for brushing
- 1 pound (454 g) crumbled feta
- 8 ounces (227g) ricotta cheese
- 2 tablespoons chopped fresh mint, or 1 tablespoon dried mint
- 2 tablespoons chopped fresh dill, or 1 tablespoon dried dill
- ¼ teaspoon freshly ground black pepper
- 3 eggs
- 12 phyllo sh eets, defrosted
- 1 teaspoon white sesame seeds

1. Preheat the oven to 350°F (180 C). Brush a 9 × 13-inch (23 × 33cm) casserole dish with olive oil.
2. Combine the feta and ricotta in a large bowl, using a fork to mash the ingredients together. Add the mint, dill, and black pepper, and mix well. In a small bowl, beat the eggs and then add them to the cheese mixture along with 1 tablespoon olive oil. Mix well.
3. Carefully place 1 phyllo sheet in the bottom of the prepared dish. (Keep the rest of the dough covered with a damp towel.) Brush the sheet with olive oil, then place a second phyllo sheet on top of the first and brush with olive oil. Repeat until you have 6 layers of phyllo.
4. Spread the cheese mixture evenly over the phyllo and then fold the excess phyllo edges in and over the mixture. Cover the mixture with 6 more phyllo sheets, repeating the process by placing a single phyllo sheet in the pan and brushing it with olive oil. Roll the excess phyllo in to form an edge around the pie.

5. Brush the top phyllo layer with olive oil and then use a sharp knife to score it into 12 pieces, being careful to cut only through the first 3–4 layers of the phyllo dough. Sprinkle the sesame seeds and a bit of water over the top of the pie.

6. Place the pie on the middle rack of the oven. Bake for 40 minutes or until the phyllo turns a deep golden color. Carefully lift one side of the pie to ensure the bottom crust is baked. If it's baked, move the pan to the bottom rack and bake for an additional 5 minutes.

7. Remove the pie from the oven and set aside to cool for 15 minutes. Use a sharp knife to cut the pie into 12 pieces. Store covered in the refrigerator for up to 3 days.

Per Serving:calories: 230 / fat: 15g / protein: 11g / carbs: 13g / fiber: 1g / sodium: 510mg

Spiced Scrambled Eggs

Prep time: 15 minutes / Cook time: 28 minutes / Serves 4
- 2 tablespoons olive oil
- 1 small red onion, chopped
- 1 medium green pepper, cored, seeded, and finely chopped
- 1 red Fresno or jalapeño chili pepper, seeded and cut into thin strips
- 3 medium tomatoes, chopped
- Sea salt and freshly ground pepper, to taste
- 1 tablespoon ground cumin
- 1 teaspoon ground coriander
- 4 large eggs, lightly beaten

1. Heat the olive oil in a large, heavy skillet over medium heat.
2. Add the onion and cook until soft and translucent, 6–7 minutes.
3. Add the peppers and continue to cook until soft, another 4–5 minutes. Add in the tomatoes and season to taste.
4. Stir in the cumin and coriander.
5. Simmer for 10 minutes over medium-low heat.
6. Add the eggs, stirring them into the mixture to distribute.
7. Cover the skillet and cook until the eggs are set but still fluffy and tender, about 5–6 minutes more.
8. Divide between 4 plates and serve immediately.

Per Serving:calories: 169 / fat: 12g / protein: 8g / carbs: 8g / fiber: 2g / sodium: 81mg

Turkish Egg Bowl

Prep time: 10 minutes / Cook time: 15 minutes / Serves 2
- 2 tablespoons ghee
- ½–1 teaspoon red chile flakes
- 2 tablespoons extra-virgin olive oil
- 1 cup full-fat goat's or sheep's milk yogurt
- 1 clove garlic, minced
- 1 tablespoon fresh lemon juice
- Salt and black pepper, to taste

- Dash of vinegar
- 4 large eggs
- Optional: pinch of sumac
- 2 tablespoons chopped fresh cilantro or parsley

1. In a skillet, melt the ghee over low heat. Add the chile flakes and let it infuse while you prepare the eggs. Remove from the heat and mix with the extra-virgin olive oil. Set aside. Combine the yogurt, garlic, lemon juice, salt, and pepper.

2. Poach the eggs. Fill a medium saucepan with water and a dash of vinegar. Bring to a boil over high heat. Crack each egg individually into a ramekin or a cup. Using a spoon, create a gentle whirlpool in the water; this will help the egg white wrap around the egg yolk. Slowly lower the egg into the water in the center of the whirlpool. Turn off the heat and cook for 3 to 4 minutes. Use a slotted spoon to remove the egg from the water and place it on a plate. Repeat for all remaining eggs.

3. To assemble, place the yogurt mixture in a bowl and add the poached eggs. Drizzle with the infused oil, and garnish with cilantro. Add a pinch of sumac, if using. Eat warm.

Per Serving:calories: 576 / fat: 46g / protein: 27g / carbs: 17g / fiber: 4g / sodium: 150mg

Spinach and Feta Frittata

Prep time: 10 minutes / Cook time: 26 minutes / Serves 4
- 1 tablespoon olive oil
- ½ medium onion, peeled and chopped
- ½ medium red bell pepper, seeded and chopped
- 2 cups chopped fresh baby spinach
- 1 cup water
- 1 cup crumbled feta cheese
- 6 large eggs, beaten
- ¼ cup low-fat plain Greek yogurt
- ½ teaspoon salt
- ½ teaspoon ground black pepper

1. Press the Sauté button on the Instant Pot® and heat oil. Add onion and bell pepper, and cook until tender, about 8 minutes. Add spinach and cook until wilted, about 3 minutes. Press the Cancel button and transfer vegetables to a medium bowl to cool. Wipe out inner pot.

2. Place the rack in the Instant Pot® and add water. Spray a 1.5-liter baking dish with nonstick cooking spray. Drain excess liquid from spinach mixture, then add to dish with cheese.

3. In a separate medium bowl, mix eggs, yogurt, salt, and black pepper until well combined. Pour over vegetable and cheese mixture. Cover dish tightly with foil, then gently lower into machine.

4. Close lid, set steam release to Sealing, press the Manual button, and set time to 15 minutes. When the timer beeps, let pressure release naturally for 10 minutes, then quick-release any remaining pressure until the float

valve drops. Press the Cancel button and open lid. Let stand for 10–15 minutes before carefully removing dish from pot.

5. Run a thin knife around the edge of the frittata and turn it out onto a serving platter. Serve warm.

Per Serving:calories: 259 / fat: 19g / protein: 16g / carbs: 6g / fiber: 1g / sodium: 766mg

Herb & Cheese Fritters

Prep time: 10 minutes / Cook time: 15 minutes / Serves 5

- 3 medium zucchini
- 8 ounces (227 g) frozen spinach, thawed and squeezed dry (weight excludes water squeezed out)
- 4 large eggs
- ½ teaspoon salt
- ¼ teaspoon black pepper
- 3 tablespoons flax meal or coconut flour
- ¼ cup grated Pecorino Romano
- 2 cloves garlic, minced
- ¼ cup chopped fresh herbs, such as parsley, basil, oregano, mint, chives, and/or thyme
- ¼ cup extra-virgin avocado oil or ghee

1. Grate the zucchini and place in a bowl lined with cheesecloth. Set aside for 5 minutes, then twist the cheesecloth around the zucchini and squeeze out as much liquid as you can. You should end up with about 13 ounces (370 g) of drained zucchini.

2. In a mixing bowl, combine the zucchini, spinach, eggs, salt, and pepper. Add the flax meal and Pecorino and stir again. Add the garlic and herbs and mix through.

3. Heat a large pan greased with 1 tablespoon of ghee over medium heat. Once hot, use a ¼-cup measuring cup to make the fritters (about 57 g/2 ounces each). Place in the hot pan and shape with a spatula. Cook in batches for 3 to 4 minutes per side, until crisp and golden. Grease the pan between each batch until all the ghee has been used.

4. Eat warm or cold, as a breakfast, side, or snack. Store in the fridge for up to 4 days or freeze for up to 3 months.

Per Serving:calories: 239 / fat: 20g / protein: 10g / carbs: 8g / fiber: 3g / sodium: 426mg

Hearty Berry Breakfast Oats

Prep time: 5 minutes / Cook time: 0 minutes / Serves 2

- 1½ cups whole-grain rolled or quickcooking oats (not instant)
- ¾ cup fresh blueberries, raspberries, or blackberries, or a combination
- 2 teaspoons honey
- 2 tablespoons walnut pieces

1. Prepare the whole-grain oats according to the package directions and divide between 2 deep bowls.

2. In a small microwave-safe bowl, heat the berries and honey for 30 seconds. Top each bowl of oatmeal with

the fruit mixture. Sprinkle the walnuts over the fruit and serve hot.

Per Serving:calories: 556 / fat: 13g / protein: 22g / carbs: 92g / fiber: 14g / sodium: 3mg

Black Olive Toast with Herbed Hummus

Prep time: 5 minutes / Cook time: 5 minutes / Serves 2

- ¼ cup store-bought plain hummus
- 2 tablespoons finely chopped fresh flat-leaf parsley
- 1 tablespoon finely chopped fresh dill
- 1 tablespoon finely chopped fresh mint
- 1 teaspoon finely grated lemon peel
- 2 slices (½" thick) black olive bread
- 1 clove garlic, halved
- 1 tablespoon extra-virgin olive oil

1. In a small bowl, combine the hummus, herbs, and lemon peel.

2. Toast the bread. Immediately rub the warm bread with the garlic.

3. Spread half the hummus over each slice of bread and drizzle with the oil.

Per Serving:calories: 197 / fat: 11g / protein: 6g / carbs: 20g / fiber: 4g / sodium: 177mg

Spiced Antioxidant Granola Clusters

Prep time: 10 minutes / Cook time: 1 hour 10 minutes / Serves 10

- 1 cup unsweetened fine coconut flakes
- 1 cup unsweetened large coconut flakes
- ¼ cup packed flax meal
- ¼ cup chia seeds
- ½ cup pecans, chopped
- 1 cup blanched almonds, roughly chopped, or flaked almonds
- 2 teaspoons cinnamon
- 1 teaspoon ground anise seed
- ½ teaspoon ground nutmeg
- ½ teaspoon ground cloves
- 1 tablespoon fresh lemon zest
- ¼ teaspoon black pepper
- ¼ teaspoon salt
- ⅓ cup light tahini
- ¼ cup virgin coconut oil
- 2 large egg whites
- Optional: unsweetened almond milk, coconut cream, coconut yogurt, or full-fat goat's yogurt, to serve

1. Preheat the oven to 265°F (130°C) conventional or 230°F (110°C) fan assisted convection. Line a baking tray with parchment paper.

2. Place all of the dry ingredients, including the lemon zest, in a large bowl. Stir to combine. In a small bowl, mix the tahini with the coconut oil, then add to the dry ingredients. Add the egg whites and mix to combine.

3. Spoon onto the lined baking tray and crumble all

over. Bake for 1 hour and 10 minutes to 1 hour and 20 minutes, until golden. Remove from the oven and let cool completely; it will crisp up as it cools. Serve on its own or with almond milk, coconut cream or coconut yogurt, or full-fat goat's yogurt. Store in a jar at room temperature for up to 2 weeks or freeze for up to 3 months.

Per Serving:calories: 291 / fat: 25g / protein: 6g / carbs: 15g / fiber: 6g / sodium: 128mg

Spanish Tortilla with Potatoes and Peppers

Prep time : 5 minutes / Cook time: 50 minutes / Serves 6

- ½ cup olive oil, plus 2 tablespoons, divided
- 2 pounds (907 g) baking potatoes, peeled and cut into ¼-inch slices
- 2 onions, thinly sliced
- 1 roasted red pepper, drained and cut into strips
- 6 eggs
- 2 teaspoons salt
- 1 teaspoon freshly ground black pepper

1. In a large skillet over medium heat, heat ½ cup of the olive oil. Add the potatoes and cook, stirring occasionally, until the potatoes are tender, about 20 minutes. Remove the potatoes from the pan with a slotted spoon and discard the remaining oil.
2. In a medium skillet over medium heat, heat the remaining 2 tablespoons of olive oil. Add the onions and cook, stirring frequently, until softened and golden brown, about 10 minutes. Remove the onions from the pan with a slotted spoon, leaving the oil in the pan, and add them to the potatoes. Add the pepper slices to the potatoes as well.
3. In a large bowl, whisk together the eggs, salt, and pepper. Add the cooked vegetables to the egg mixture and gently toss to combine.
4. Heat the medium skillet over low heat. Add the egg-vegetable mixture to the pan and cook for about 10 minutes, until the bottom is lightly browned. Use a spatula to loosen the tortilla and transfer the whole thing to a large plate, sliding it out of the pan so that the browned side is on the bottom. Invert the skillet over the tortilla and then lift the plate to flip it back into the skillet with the browned side on top. Return to the stove and continue to cook over low heat until the tortilla is fully set in the center, about 5 more minutes.
5. Serve the tortilla warm or at room temperature.

Per Serving:calories: 370 / fat: 26g / protein: 9g / carbs: 29g / fiber: 5g / sodium: 876mg

Nuts and Fruit Oatmeal

Prep time: 10 minutes / Cook time: 7 minutes / Serves 2

- 1 cup rolled oats
- 1¼ cups water
- ¼ cup orange juice

- 1 medium pear, peeled, cored, and cubed
- ¼ cup dried cherries
- ¼ cup chopped walnuts
- 1 tablespoon honey
- ¼ teaspoon ground ginger
- ¼ teaspoon ground cinnamon
- ⅛ teaspoon salt

1. Place oats, water, orange juice, pear, cherries, walnuts, honey, ginger, cinnamon, and salt in the Instant Pot®. Stir to combine.
2. Close lid, set steam release to Sealing, press the Manual button, and set time to 7 minutes. When the timer beeps, let pressure release naturally, about 20 minutes. Press the Cancel button, open lid, and stir well. Serve warm.

Per Serving:calories: 362 / fat: 8g / protein: 7g / carbs: 69g / fiber: 8g / sodium: 164mg

Peachy Green Smoothie

Prep time: 10 minutes / Cook time: 0 minutes / Serves 2

- 1 cup almond milk
- 3 cups kale or spinach
- 1 banana, peeled
- 1 orange, peeled
- 1 small green apple
- 1 cup frozen peaches
- ¼ cup vanilla Greek yogurt

1. Put the ingredients in a blender in the order listed and blend on high until smooth.
2. Serve and enjoy.

Per Serving:calories: 257 / fat: 5g / protein: 9g / carbs: 50g / fiber: 7g / sodium: 87mg

Amaranth Breakfast Bowl with Chocolate and Almondsy

Prep time: 10 minutes / Cook time: 6 minutes / Serves 6

- 2 cups amaranth, rinsed and drained
- 2 cups almond milk
- 2 cups water
- ¼ cup maple syrup
- 3 tablespoons cocoa powder
- 1 teaspoon vanilla extract
- ¼ teaspoon salt
- ½ cup toasted sliced almonds
- ⅓ cup miniature semisweet chocolate chips

1. Place amaranth, almond milk, water, maple syrup, cocoa powder, vanilla, and salt in the Instant Pot®. Stir to combine. Close lid, set steam release to Sealing, press the Rice button, and set time to 6 minutes. When the timer beeps, quick-release the pressure until the float valve drops, press the Cancel button, open lid, and stir well.
2. Serve hot, topped with almonds and chocolate chips.

Per Serving:calories: 263 / fat: 12g / protein: 5g / carbs: 35g / fiber: 5g / sodium: 212mg

Buffalo Egg Cups

Prep time: 10 minutes / Cook time: 15 minutes / Serves 2

- 4 large eggs
- 2 ounces (57 g) full-fat cream cheese
- 2 tablespoons buffalo sauce
- ½ cup shredded sharp Cheddar cheese

1. Crack eggs into two ramekins.
2. In a small microwave-safe bowl, mix cream cheese, buffalo sauce, and Cheddar. Microwave for 20 seconds and then stir. Place a spoonful into each ramekin on top of the eggs.
3. Place ramekins into the air fryer basket.
4. Adjust the temperature to 320ºF (160ºC) and bake for 15 minutes.
5. Serve warm.

Per Serving:calories: 354 / fat: 29g / protein: 21g / carbs: 3g / fiber: 0g / sodium: 343mg

Strawberry Basil Honey Ricotta Toast

Prep time: 10 minutes / Cook time: 0 minutes / Serves 2

- 4 slices of whole-grain bread
- ½ cup ricotta cheese (whole milk or low-fat)
- 1 tablespoon honey
- Sea salt
- 1 cup fresh strawberries, sliced
- 4 large fresh basil leaves, sliced into thin shreds

1. Toast the bread.
2. In a small bowl, combine the ricotta, honey, and a pinch or two of sea salt. Taste and add additional honey or salt if desired.
3. Spread the mixture evenly over each slice of bread (about 2 tablespoons per slice).
4. Top each piece with sliced strawberries and a few pieces of shredded basil.

Per Serving:calories: 275 / fat: 8g / protein: 15g / carbs: 41g / fiber: 5g / sodium: 323mg

Savory Cottage Cheese Breakfast Bowl

Prep time: 10 minutes / Cook time: 0 minutes / Serves 4

- 2 cups low-fat cottage cheese
- 2 tablespoons chopped mixed fresh herbs, such as basil, dill, flat-leaf parsley, and oregano
- ½ teaspoon ground black pepper
- 1 large tomato, chopped
- 1 small cucumber, peeled and chopped
- ¼ cup pitted kalamata olives, halved
- 1 tablespoon extra-virgin olive oil

1. In a medium bowl, combine the cottage cheese, herbs, and pepper. Add the tomato, cucumber, and olives and gently stir to combine. Drizzle with the oil to serve.

Per Serving:calories: 181 / fat: 10g / protein: 15g / carbs: 8g / fiber: 1g / sodium: 788mg

Baked Ricotta with Pears

Prep time: 5 minutes /Cook time: 25 minutes/ Serves: 4

- Nonstick cooking spray
- 1 (16-ounce / 454-g) container whole-milk ricotta cheese
- 2 large eggs
- ¼ cup white whole-wheat flour or whole-wheat pastry flour
- 1 tablespoon sugar
- 1 teaspoon vanilla extract
- ¼ teaspoon ground nutmeg
- 1 pear, cored and diced
- 2 tablespoons water
- 1 tablespoon honey

1. Preheat the oven to 400°F(205ºC). Spray four 6-ounce ramekins with nonstick cooking spray.
2. In a large bowl, beat together the ricotta, eggs, flour, sugar, vanilla, and nutmeg. Spoon into the ramekins. Bake for 22 to 25 minutes, or until the ricotta is just about set. Remove from the oven and cool slightly on racks.
3. While the ricotta is baking, in a small saucepan over medium heat, simmer the pear in the water for 10 minutes, until slightly softened. Remove from the heat, and stir in the honey.
4. Serve the ricotta ramekins topped with the warmed pear.

Per Serving:calories: 306 / fat: 17g / protein: 17g / carbs: 21g / fiber: 1g / sodium: 131mg

Berry Baked Oatmeal

Prep time: 10 minutes / Cook time: 45 to 50 minutes / Serves 8

- 2 cups gluten-free rolled oats
- 2 cups (10-ounce / 283-g bag) frozen mixed berries (blueberries and raspberries work best)
- 2 cups plain, unsweetened almond milk
- 1 cup plain Greek yogurt
- ¼ cup maple syrup
- 2 tablespoons extra-virgin olive oil
- 2 teaspoons ground cinnamon
- 1 teaspoon baking powder
- 1 teaspoon vanilla extract
- ½ teaspoon kosher salt
- ¼ teaspoon ground nutmeg
- ⅛ teaspoon ground cloves

1. Preheat the oven to 375ºF (190ºC).
2. Mix all the ingredients together in a large bowl. Pour into a 9-by-13-inch baking dish. Bake for 45 to 50 minutes, or until golden brown.

Per Serving:calories: 180 / fat: 6g / protein: 6g / carbs: 28g / fiber: 4g / sodium: 180mg

Almond Butter Banana Chocolate Smoothie

Prep time: 5 minutes / Cook time: 0 minutes / Serves 1

- ¾ cup almond milk
- ½ medium banana, preferably frozen
- ¼ cup frozen blueberries
- 1 tablespoon almond butter
- 1 tablespoon unsweetened cocoa powder
- 1 tablespoon chia seeds

1. In a blender or Vitamix, add all the ingredients. Blend to combine.

Per Serving:calories: 300 / fat: 16g / protein: 8g / carbs: 37g / fiber: 10g / sodium: 125mg

Mediterranean-Inspired White Smoothie

Prep time: 5 minutes / Cook time: 0 minutes / Serves

- ½ medium apple (any variety), peeled, halved, and seeded
- 5 roasted almonds
- ½ medium frozen banana, sliced (be sure to peel the banana before freezing)
- ¼ cup full-fat Greek yogurt
- ½ cup low-fat 1% milk
- ¼ teaspoon ground cinnamon
- ½ teaspoon honey

1. Combine all the ingredients in a blender. Process until smooth.
2. Pour into a glass and serve promptly. (This recipe is best consumed fresh.)

Per Serving:calories: 236 / fat: 7g / protein: 8g / carbs: 40g / fiber: 5g / sodium: 84mg

Spiced Potatoes with Chickpeas

Prep time: 10 minutes / Cook time: 10 minutes / Serves 4

- ¼ cup olive oil
- 3 medium potatoes, peeled and shredded
- 2 cups finely chopped baby spinach
- 1 medium onion, finely diced
- 1 tablespoon minced fresh ginger
- 1 teaspoon ground cumin
- 1 teaspoon ground coriander
- ½ teaspoon ground turmeric
- ½ teaspoon salt
- 1 (15-ounce / 425-g) can chickpeas, drained and rinsed
- 1 medium zucchini, diced
- ¼ cup chopped cilantro
- 1 cup plain yogurt

1. Heat the olive oil in a large skillet over medium heat. Add the potatoes, spinach, onions, ginger, cumin, coriander, turmeric, and salt and stir to mix well. Spread the mixture out into an even layer and let cook, without stirring, for about 5 minutes until the potatoes are crisp and browned on the bottom.

2. Add the chickpeas and zucchini and mix to combine, breaking up the layer of potatoes. Spread the mixture out again into an even layer and continue to cook, without stirring, for another 5 minutes or so, until the potatoes are crisp on the bottom.
3. To serve, garnish with cilantro and yogurt.

Per Serving:calories: 679 / fat: 20g / protein: 28g / carbs: 100g / fiber: 24g / sodium: 388mg

Harissa Shakshuka with Bell Peppers and Tomatoes

Prep time: 10 minutes / Cook time: 20 minutes / Serves 4

- 1½ tablespoons extra-virgin olive oil
- 2 tablespoons harissa
- 1 tablespoon tomato paste
- ½ onion, diced
- 1 bell pepper, seeded and diced
- 3 garlic cloves, minced
- 1 (28-ounce / 794-g) can no-salt-added diced tomatoes
- ½ teaspoon kosher salt
- 4 large eggs
- 2 to 3 tablespoons fresh basil, chopped or cut into ribbons

1. Preheat the oven to 375ºF (190ºC).
2. Heat the olive oil in a 12-inch cast-iron pan or ovenproof skillet over medium heat. Add the harissa, tomato paste, onion, and bell pepper; sauté for 3 to 4 minutes. Add the garlic and cook until fragrant, about 30 seconds. Add the diced tomatoes and salt and simmer for about 10 minutes.
3. Make 4 wells in the sauce and gently break 1 egg into each. Transfer to the oven and bake until the whites are cooked and the yolks are set, 10 to 12 minutes.
4. Allow to cool for 3 to 5 minutes, garnish with the basil, and carefully spoon onto plates.

Per Serving:calories: 190 / fat: 10g / protein: 9g / carbs: 15g / fiber: 4g / sodium: 255mg

Smoky Sausage Patties

Prep time: 30 minutes / Cook time: 9 minutes / Serves 8

- 1 pound (454 g) ground pork
- 1 tablespoon coconut aminos
- 2 teaspoons liquid smoke
- 1 teaspoon dried sage
- 1 teaspoon sea salt
- ½ teaspoon fennel seeds
- ½ teaspoon dried thyme
- ½ teaspoon freshly ground black pepper
- ¼ teaspoon cayenne pepper

1. In a large bowl, combine the pork, coconut aminos, liquid smoke, sage, salt, fennel seeds, thyme, black pepper, and cayenne pepper. Work the meat with your hands until the seasonings are fully incorporated.

2. Shape the mixture into 8 equal-size patties. Using your thumb, make a dent in the center of each patty. Place the patties on a plate and cover with plastic wrap. Refrigerate the patties for at least 30 minutes.
3. Working in batches if necessary, place the patties in a single layer in the air fryer, being careful not to overcrowd them.
4. Set the air fryer to 400°F (204°C) and air fry for 5 minutes. Flip and cook for about 4 minutes more.

Per Serving:calories: 70 / fat: 2g / protein: 12g / carbs: 0g / fiber: 0g / sodium: 329mg

Jalapeño Popper Egg Cups

Prep time: 10 minutes / Cook time: 10 minutes / Serves 2
- 4 large eggs
- ¼ cup chopped pickled jalapeños
- 2 ounces (57 g) full-fat cream cheese
- ½ cup shredded sharp Cheddar cheese

1. In a medium bowl, beat the eggs, then pour into four silicone muffin cups.
2. In a large microwave-safe bowl, place jalapeños, cream cheese, and Cheddar. Microwave for 30 seconds and stir. Take a spoonful, approximately ¼ of the mixture, and place it in the center of one of the egg cups. Repeat with remaining mixture.
3. Place egg cups into the air fryer basket.
4. Adjust the temperature to 320°F (160°C) and bake for 10 minutes.
5. Serve warm.

Per Serving:calories: 375 / fat: 30g / protein: 23g / carbs: 3g / fiber: 0g / sodium: 445mg

Greek Yogurt Parfait

Prep time: 5 minutes / Cook time: 0 minutes / Serves 1
- ½ cup plain whole-milk Greek yogurt
- 2 tablespoons heavy whipping cream
- ¼ cup frozen berries, thawed with juices
- ½ teaspoon vanilla or almond extract (optional)
- ¼ teaspoon ground cinnamon (optional)
- 1 tablespoon ground flaxseed
- 2 tablespoons chopped nuts (walnuts or pecans)
- 1. In a small bowl or glass, combine the yogurt, heavy whipping cream, thawed berries in their juice, vanilla or almond extract (if using), cinnamon (if using), and flaxseed and stir well until smooth. Top with chopped nuts and enjoy.

Per Serving:calories: 333 / fat: 27g / protein: 10g / carbs: 15g / fiber: 4g / sodium: 71mg

Green Spinach & Salmon Crepes

Prep time: 10 minutes / Cook time: 5 minutes / Serves 1
- Green Spinach Crepe:
- 1 cup fresh spinach or thawed and drained frozen spinach

- 1 small bunch fresh parsley
- ½ teaspoon fresh thyme leaves or ¼ teaspoon dried thyme
- 1 tablespoon nutritional yeast
- 1 tablespoon flax meal
- Salt and black pepper, to taste
- 2 large eggs
- 2 teaspoons extra-virgin avocado oil or ghee for cooking
- Salmon Filling:
- 3 ounces (85 g) wild smoked salmon
- ½ large avocado, sliced
- 2 tablespoons crumbled goat's cheese or feta
- 1 teaspoon fresh lemon or lime juice
- Optional: fresh herbs or microgreens, to taste

1. Make the green spinach crepe: 1. Place the spinach, herbs, nutritional yeast, flax meal, salt, and pepper in a food processor or blender. Process well until the spinach is finely chopped. Add the eggs and process on low speed until the mixture is just combined.
2. Heat half of the oil in a large skillet and add half of the mixture. Swirl the pan so the mixture completely covers the bottom. Cook for about 3 minutes or until just set, then add the salmon and avocado. Sprinkle the crepe with the goat's cheese and drizzle with the lemon juice. Slide onto a plate and optionally garnish with fresh herbs or microgreens. Serve warm.

Per Serving:calories: 673 / fat: 48g / protein: 44g / carbs: 23g / fiber: 15g / sodium: 762mg

Oatmeal with Apple and Cardamom

Prep time: 10 minutes / Cook time: 7 minutes / Serves 4
- 1 tablespoon light olive oil
- 1 large Granny Smith, Honeycrisp, or Pink Lady apple, peeled, cored, and diced
- ½ teaspoon ground cardamom
- 1 cup steel-cut oats
- 3 cups water
- ¼ cup maple syrup
- ½ teaspoon salt

1. Press the Sauté button on the Instant Pot® and heat oil. Add apple and cardamom and cook until apple is just softened, about 2 minutes. Press the Cancel button.
2. Add oats, water, maple syrup, and salt to pot, and stir well. Close lid, set steam release to Sealing, press the Manual button, and set time to 5 minutes.
3. When the timer beeps, let pressure release naturally for 10 minutes, then quick-release the remaining pressure until the float valve drops. Press the Cancel button, open lid, and stir well. Serve hot.

Per Serving:calories: 249 / fat: 6g / protein: 6g / carbs: 48g / fiber: 5g / sodium: 298mg

Veggie Hash with Eggs

Prep time: 20 minutes / Cook time: 6¼ hours / Serves 2
- Nonstick cooking spray

- 1 onion, chopped
- 2 garlic cloves, minced
- 1 red bell pepper, chopped
- 1 yellow summer squash, chopped
- 2 carrots, chopped
- 2 Yukon Gold potatoes, peeled and chopped
- 2 large tomatoes, seeded and chopped
- ¼ cup vegetable broth
- ½ teaspoon salt
- ⅛ teaspoon freshly ground black pepper
- ½ teaspoon dried thyme leaves
- 3 or 4 eggs
- ½ teaspoon ground sweet paprika

1. Spray the slow cooker with the nonstick cooking spray.
2. In the slow cooker, combine all the ingredients except the eggs and paprika, and stir.
3. Cover and cook on low for 6 hours.
4. Uncover and make 1 indentation in the vegetable mixture for each egg. Break 1 egg into a small cup and slip the egg into an indentation. Repeat with the remaining eggs. Sprinkle with the paprika.
5. Cover and cook on low for 10 to 15 minutes, or until the eggs are just set, and serve.

Per Serving:calories: 381 / fat: 8g / protein: 17g / carbs: 64g / net carbs: 52g / sugars: 17g / fiber: 12g / sodium: 747mg / cholesterol: 246mg

Heart-Healthy Hazelnut-Collagen Shake

Prep time: 5 minutes / Cook time: 0 minutes / Serves 1
- 1½ cups unsweetened almond milk
- 2 tablespoons hazelnut butter
- 2 tablespoons grass-fed collagen powder
- ½–1 teaspoon cinnamon
- ⅛ teaspoon LoSalt or pink Himalayan salt
- ⅛ teaspoon sugar-free almond extract
- 1 tablespoon macadamia oil or hazelnut oil

1. Place all of the ingredients in a blender and pulse until smooth and frothy. Serve immediately.

Per Serving:calories: 507 / fat: 41g / protein: 3g / carbs: 35g / fiber: 12g / sodium: 569mg

Broccoli-Mushroom Frittata

Prep time: 10 minutes / Cook time: 20 minutes / Serves 2
- 1 tablespoon olive oil
- 1½ cups broccoli florets, finely chopped
- ½ cup sliced brown mushrooms
- ¼ cup finely chopped onion
- ½ teaspoon salt
- ¼ teaspoon freshly ground black pepper
- 6 eggs
- ¼ cup Parmesan cheese

1. In a nonstick cake pan, combine the olive oil, broccoli, mushrooms, onion, salt, and pepper. Stir until the vegetables are thoroughly coated with oil. Place the

cake pan in the air fryer basket and set the air fryer to 400°F (204°C). Air fry for 5 minutes until the vegetables soften.
2. Meanwhile, in a medium bowl, whisk the eggs and Parmesan until thoroughly combined. Pour the egg mixture into the pan and shake gently to distribute the vegetables. Air fry for another 15 minutes until the eggs are set.
3. Remove from the air fryer and let sit for 5 minutes to cool slightly. Use a silicone spatula to gently lift the frittata onto a plate before serving.

Per Serving:calories: 329 / fat: 23g / protein: 24g / carbs: 6g / fiber: 0g / sodium: 793mg

Red Pepper and Feta Egg Bites

Prep time: 5 minutes / Cook time: 8 minutes / Serves 6
- 1 tablespoon olive oil
- ½ cup crumbled feta cheese
- ¼ cup chopped roasted red peppers
- 6 large eggs, beaten
- ¼ teaspoon ground black pepper
- 1 cup water

1. Brush silicone muffin or poaching cups with oil. Divide feta and roasted red peppers among prepared cups. In a bowl with a pour spout, beat eggs with black pepper.
2. Place rack in the Instant Pot® and add water. Place cups on rack. Pour egg mixture into cups. Close lid, set steam release to Sealing, press the Manual button, and set time to 8 minutes.
3. When the timer beeps, quick-release the pressure until the float valve drops and open lid. Remove silicone cups carefully and slide eggs from cups onto plates. Serve warm.

Per Serving:calories: 145 / fat: 11g / protein: 10g / carbs: 3g / fiber: 1g / sodium: 294mg

Breakfast Panini with Eggs, Olives, and Tomatoes

Prep time: 5 minutes / Cook time: 0 minutes / Serves 4
- 1 (12-ounce / 340-g) round whole-wheat pagnotta foggiana or other round, crusty bread
- 2 tablespoons olive oil
- ½ cup sliced pitted cured olives, such as Kalamata
- 8 hard-boiled eggs, peeled and sliced into rounds
- 2 medium tomatoes, thinly sliced into rounds
- 12 large leaves fresh basil

1. Split the bread horizontally and brush the cut sides with the olive oil.
2. Arrange the sliced olives on the bottom half of the bread in a single layer. Top with a layer of the egg slices, then the tomato slices, and finally the basil leaves. Cut the sandwich into quarters and serve immediately.

Per Serving:calories: 427 / fat: 21g / protein: 23g / carbs: 39g / fiber: 7g / sodium: 674mg

Greek Eggs and Potatoes

Prep time: 5 minutes / Cook time: 30 minutes / Serves 4

- 3 medium tomatoes, seeded and coarsely chopped
- 2 tablespoons fresh chopped basil
- 1 garlic clove, minced
- 2 tablespoons plus ½ cup olive oil, divided
- Sea salt and freshly ground pepper, to taste
- 3 large russet potatoes
- 4 large eggs
- 1 teaspoon fresh oregano, chopped

1. Put tomatoes in a food processor and purée them, skins and all.
2. Add the basil, garlic, 2 tablespoons olive oil, sea salt, and freshly ground pepper, and pulse to combine.
3. Put the mixture in a large skillet over low heat and cook, covered, for 20–25 minutes, or until the sauce has thickened and is bubbly.
4. Meanwhile, dice the potatoes into small cubes. Put ½ cup olive oil in a nonstick skillet over medium-low heat.
5. Fry the potatoes for 5 minutes until crisp and browned on the outside, then cover and reduce heat to low. Steam potatoes until done.
6. Carefully crack the eggs into the tomato sauce. Cook over low heat until the eggs are set in the sauce, about 6 minutes.
7. Remove the potatoes from the pan and drain them on paper towels, then place them in a bowl.
8. Sprinkle with sea salt and freshly ground pepper to taste and top with the oregano.
9. Carefully remove the eggs with a slotted spoon and place them on a plate with the potatoes. Spoon sauce over the top and serve.

Per Serving:calories: 548 / fat: 32g / protein: 13g / carbs: 54g / fiber: 5g / sodium: 90mg

MOZZARELLA & FRUIT PLATTER

Serving Portions: 8/Preparation: 15 mins.

- 8 oz. of container fresh mozzarella salad pearls . 8 oz. of container marinated fresh mozzarella balls
- 3 oz. of prosciutto
- 4 oz. of salami
- 2 oz. of Kalamata olives
- 4 C. of cherry tomatoes
- 2 ripe peaches, pitted and slivered
- ½ of medium cantaloupe melon, peel removed and cubed
- 1 baguette, cut into cubes
- 4 C. of fresh baby arugula
- 3 oz. of almonds, roasted
- ¼ C. of balsamic glaze

1. Lay out a large-sized serving platter in the middle of a wooden board. Put it aside.

2. XE "icing sugar" Lay out mozzarella and remnant ingredients except for balsamic glaze onto the platter over wooden board.
3. Dribble with balsamic glaze and enjoy immediately.

Per Serving:Calories: 410/ Fat: 20.8g/ Carbs: 30.9g/ Fiber: 4.3g/ Protein: 27.6g

BAGELS PLATTER

Serving Portions: 6/Preparation: 15 mins.

- For Whipped Cream Cheese:
- 1 C. of cream cheese, softened
- ¼ C. of scallions, cut up
- 1 tsp. of lemon juice
- Pinch of salt
- For Platter:
- 6 bagels, cut in half
- 6 tbsp. of butter, softened
- ½ lb. cooked bacon slices
- ½ lb. smoked salmon
- 2 avocados, peel removed, pitted and slivered . 1 cucumber, slivered
- 2 radishes, slivered
- 1 large-sized tomato, slivered
- 6 hard-boiled eggs, peel removed and slivered

1. XE "icing sugar" Lay out a large-sized serving platter in the middle of a wooden board. Put it aside.
2. For whipped cream cheese: in a medium-sized basin, put the cream cheese and with a hand mingleer, whip until fluffy and light.
3. Put in the scallion, lemon juice and salt and stir to blend.
4. Spread the butter over each bagel half evenly.
5. Lay out the basin of whipped cream cheese onto the platter over wooden board.
6. Lay out the bagel halves and remnant ingredients around the basin and enjoy.

Per Serving:Calories: 957/ Fat: 61.6g/ Carbs: 61.6g/ Fiber: 7.4g/

WAFFLE PLATTER

Serving Portions: 4/Preparation: 15 mins. / Cooking: 16 minutes

- For Waffles:
- ¼ C. of butter, melted and cooled
- 4 large-sized eggs
- 4 oz. of cream cheese, softened
- ½ C. of powdered sugar
- 2 tsp. of vanilla extract
- Pinch of salt
- ½ C. of almond flour
- ¼ C. of coconut flour
- 2 tsp. of baking powder
- For Platter:
- ½ C. of plain yogurt

- ¼ C. of strawberry jam
- ¼ C. of maple syrup
- 4 hard-boiled eggs, peel removed and halved
- 8 cooked bacon slices
- ¼ C. of fresh strawberries
- ¼ C. of fresh blueberries

1. In a large-sized basin, put in the butter and eggs and whisk until creamy.
2. Put in the cream cheese, sugar, vanilla extract and salt and whisk until incorporated thoroughly.
3. Put in the flours and baking powder and whisk until incorporated thoroughly.
4. Place ¼ of the mixture into preheated waffle iron and cook for around 4 minutes.
5. Cook the remnant waffles in the same manner.
6. Lay out a large-sized serving platter in the middle of a wooden board. Put it aside.
7. In 3 small-sized basins, put the yogurt, jam and maple syrup respectively.
8. Lay out the basins of yogurt, jam and maple syrup onto the platter over wooden board.
9. Lay out the waffles, eggs, bacon and berries around the basins and enjoy.

Per Serving:Calories: 069/ Fat: 64.2g/ Carbs: 56.6g/ Fiber: 5g/Protein: 41.6g

PEPPERONI & CHICKPEAS PLATTER
Serving Portions: 12/Preparation: 15 mins.
- 1 (3½-oz.) package slivered pepperoni
- 1 (24-oz.) jar pepperoncini, liquid removed . 1 (15-oz.) can chickpeas, liquid removed
- 2 C. of fresh mushrooms, halved
- 2 C. of cherry tomatoes, halved
- 1 (6-oz.) can pitted ripe olives, liquid removed . ½ lb. provolone cheese, cubed
- 1 (8-oz.) bottle Italian vinaigrette dressing . 12 C. of lettuce, torn

1. XE "icing sugar" Lay out a large-sized serving platter in the middle of a wooden board. Put it aside.
2. In a large-sized basin, put in pepperoni and remnant ingredients except for lettuce and toss it all to mingle nicely.
3. Put in your refrigerator for at least 30 minutes.
4. Lay out the lettuce onto the platter over wooden board and top with pepperoni mixture.
5. Enjoy immediately.

Per Serving:Calories: 302/ Fat: 14.9g/ Carbs: 30.3g/ Fiber: 7.5g/ Protein: 14.6g

DELI MEAT & CHEESESPLATTER
Serving Portions: 12
- Preparation: 15 mins.
- 6 oz. of prosciutto, slivered
- 6 oz. of salami, slivered thinly
- 3 oz. of pepperoni, slivered thinly
- 8 oz. of bocconcini
- 1 tbsp. of olive oil
- 1 tbsp. of fresh parsley leaves, cut up
- Pinch of red pepper flakes
- 8 oz. of Parmesan cheese, cubed
- 8 oz. of provolone cheese, slivered thinly
- 8 oz. of Asiago cheese, slivered thinly
- 1 C. of marinated artichokes, liquid removed . 1 C. of mixed olives, pitted and slivered
- ½ C. of peppadew peppers
- ½ C. of almonds
- 1 focaccia bread loaf, toasted and slivered

1. XE "icing sugar" Lay out a large-sized serving platter in the middle of a wooden board. Put it aside.
2. Lay out prosciutto and remnant ingredients onto the platter over wooden board and enjoy immediately.

Per Serving:Calories: 506/ Fat: 31.8g/ Carbs: 24.8g/ Fiber: 2.7g/ Protein: 31.1g

Chapter 2 Beans and Grains

Puréed Red Lentil Soup

Prep time: 15 minutes / Cook time: 21 minutes / Serves 6

- 2 tablespoons olive oil
- 1 medium yellow onion, peeled and chopped
- 1 medium carrot, peeled and chopped
- 1 medium red bell pepper, seeded and chopped
- 1 clove garlic, peeled and minced
- 1 bay leaf
- ½ teaspoon ground black pepper
- ¼ teaspoon salt
- 1 (15-ounce / 425-g) can diced tomatoes, drained
- 2 cups dried red lentils, rinsed and drained
- 6 cups low-sodium chicken broth

1. Press the Sauté button on the Instant Pot® and heat oil. Add onion, carrot, and bell pepper. Cook until just tender, about 5 minutes. Add garlic, bay leaf, black pepper, and salt, and cook until fragrant, about 30 seconds. Press the Cancel button.
2. Add tomatoes, lentils, and broth, then close lid, set steam release to Sealing, press the Manual button, and set time to 15 minutes. When the timer beeps, let pressure release naturally, about 15 minutes. Open lid, remove and discard bay leaf, and purée with an immersion blender or in batches in a blender. Serve warm.

Per Serving:calories: 289 / fat: 6g / protein: 18g / carbs: 39g / fiber: 8g / sodium: 438mg

Farro Salad with Tomatoes and Olives

Prep time: 10 minutes / Cook time: 20 minutes / Serves 6

- 10 ounces (283 g) farro, rinsed and drained
- 4 cups water
- 4 Roma tomatoes, seeded and chopped
- 4 scallions, green parts only, thinly sliced
- ½ cup sliced black olives
- ¼ cup minced fresh flat-leaf parsley
- ¼ cup extra-virgin olive oil
- 2 tablespoons balsamic vinegar
- ¼ teaspoon ground black pepper

1. Place farro and water in the Instant Pot®. Close lid and set steam release to Sealing. Press the Multigrain button and set time to 20 minutes. When the timer beeps, let pressure release naturally, about 30 minutes.
2. Open lid and fluff with a fork. Transfer to a bowl and cool 30 minutes. Add tomatoes, scallions, black olives, and parsley and mix well.
3. In a small bowl, whisk together oil, balsamic vinegar, and pepper. Pour over salad and toss to evenly coat. Refrigerate for at least 4 hours before serving. Serve chilled or at room temperature.

Per Serving:calories: 288 / fat: 14g / protein: 7g / carbs: 31g / fiber: 3g / sodium: 159mg

Spiced Quinoa Salad

Prep time: 15 minutes / Cook time: 17 minutes / Serves 6

- 2 tablespoons vegetable oil
- 1 medium white onion, peeled and chopped
- 2 cloves garlic, peeled and minced
- ½ teaspoon ground cumin
- ½ teaspoon ground coriander
- ½ teaspoon smoked paprika
- ½ teaspoon salt
- ¼ teaspoon ground black pepper
- 1½ cups quinoa, rinsed and drained
- 2 cups vegetable broth
- 1⅓ cups water
- 2 cups fresh baby spinach leaves
- 2 plum tomatoes, seeded and chopped

1. Press the Sauté button on the Instant Pot® and heat oil. Add onion and cook until tender, about 3 minutes. Add garlic, cumin, coriander, paprika, salt, and pepper, and cook 30 seconds until garlic and spices are fragrant.
2. Add quinoa and toss to coat in spice mixture. Cook 2 minutes to lightly toast quinoa. Add broth and water, making sure to scrape bottom and sides of pot to loosen any brown bits. Press the Cancel button.
3. Close lid and set steam release to Sealing. Press the Rice button and set time to 12 minutes.
4. When the timer beeps, let pressure release naturally, about 20 minutes. Open lid, add spinach and tomatoes, and fluff quinoa with a fork. Serve warm, at room temperature, or cold.

Per Serving:calories: 215 / fat: 7g / protein: 7g / carbs: 32g / fiber: 4g / sodium: 486mg

Garlicky Split Chickpea Curry

Prep time: 10 minutes / Cook time: 4 to 6 hours / Serves 6

- 1½ cups split gram
- 1 onion, finely chopped
- 2 tomatoes, chopped
- 1 tablespoon freshly grated ginger
- 1 teaspoon cumin seeds, ground or crushed with a mortar and pestle
- 2 teaspoons turmeric
- 2 garlic cloves, crushed
- 1 hot green Thai or other fresh chile, thinly sliced
- 3 cups hot water
- 1 teaspoon salt
- 2 tablespoons rapeseed oil
- 1 teaspoon cumin seeds, crushed

- 1 garlic clove, sliced
- 1 fresh green chile, sliced
1. Heat the slow cooker to high. Add the split gram, onion, tomatoes, ginger, crushed cumin seeds, turmeric, crushed garlic, hot chile, water, and salt, and then stir.
2. Cover and cook on high for 4 hours, or on low for 6 hours, until the split gram is tender.
3. Just before serving, heat the oil in a saucepan. When the oil is hot, add the cumin seeds with the sliced garlic. Cook until the garlic is golden brown, and then pour it over the dhal.
4. To serve, top with the sliced green chile.

Per Serving:calories: 119 / fat: 5g / protein: 4g / carbs: 15g / net carbs: 12g / sugars: 7g / fiber: 3g / sodium: 503mg / cholesterol: 1mg

Barley and Vegetable Casserole

Prep time: 10 minutes / Cook time: 6 to 8 hours / Serves 6
- 1 cup raw barley (not the quick-cooking type)
- 3 cups low-sodium vegetable broth
- 3 garlic cloves, minced
- 2 bell peppers, any color, seeded and chopped
- 1 small onion, chopped
- 2 ounces (57 g) mushrooms, sliced
- 1 teaspoon extra-virgin olive oil
- 2 tablespoons Italian seasoning
- 1 teaspoon sea salt
- ¼ teaspoon freshly ground black pepper
1. In a slow cooker, combine the barley, vegetable broth, garlic, bell peppers, onion, mushrooms, olive oil, Italian seasoning, salt, and black pepper. Stir to mix well.
2. Cover the cooker and cook for 6 to 8 hours on Low heat.

Per Serving:calories: 147 / fat: 2g / protein: 5g / carbs: 30g / fiber: 8g / sodium: 464mg

Greek-Style Black-Eyed Pea Soup

Prep time: 10 minutes / Cook time: 26 minutes / Serves 8
- 2 tablespoons light olive oil
- 2 stalks celery, chopped
- 1 medium white onion, peeled and chopped
- 2 cloves garlic, peeled and minced
- 2 tablespoons chopped fresh oregano
- 1 teaspoon fresh thyme leaves
- 1 pound (454 g) dried black-eyed peas, soaked overnight and drained
- ¼ teaspoon salt
- 1 teaspoon ground black pepper
- 4 cups water
- 1 (15-ounce / 425-g) can diced tomatoes
1. Press the Sauté button on the Instant Pot® and heat oil. Add celery and onion, and cook until just tender, about 5 minutes. Add garlic, oregano, and thyme, and cook until fragrant, about 30 seconds. Press the Cancel button.
2. Add black-eyed peas, salt, pepper, water, and tomatoes to the Instant Pot® and stir well. Close lid, set steam

release to Sealing, press the Manual button, and set time to 20 minutes. When the timer beeps, let pressure release naturally, about 20 minutes.
3. Open lid and stir well. Serve hot.

Per Serving:calories: 153 / fat: 3g / protein: 8g / carbs: 25g / fiber: 5g / sodium: 189mg

Sweet Potato and Chickpea Moroccan Stew

Prep time: 10 minutes / Cook time: 40 minutes / Serves 4
- 6 tablespoons extra virgin olive oil
- 2 medium red or white onions, finely chopped
- 6 garlic cloves, minced
- 3 medium carrots (about 8 ounces /227 g), peeled and cubed
- 1 teaspoon ground cumin
- 1 teaspoon ground coriander
- ½ teaspoon smoked paprika
- ½ teaspoon ground turmeric
- 1 cinnamon stick
- ½ pound (227 g) butternut squash, peeled and cut into ½-inch cubes
- 2 medium sweet potatoes, peeled and cut into ½-inch cubes
- 4 ounces (113 g) prunes, pitted
- 4 tomatoes (any variety), chopped, or 20 ounces (567g) canned chopped tomatoes
- 14 ounces (397 g) vegetable broth
- 14 ounces (397 g) canned chickpeas
- ½ cup chopped fresh parsley, for serving
1. Place a deep pan over medium heat and add the olive oil. When the oil is shimmering, add the onions and sauté for 5 minutes, then add the garlic and carrots, and sauté for 1 more minute.
2. Add the cumin, coriander, paprika, turmeric, and cinnamon stick. Continue cooking, stirring continuously, for 1 minute, then add the squash, sweet potatoes, prunes, tomatoes, and vegetable broth. Stir, cover, then reduce the heat to low and simmer for 20 minutes, stirring occasionally and checking the water levels, until the vegetables are cooked through. (If the stew appears to be drying out, add small amounts of hot water until the stew is thick.)
3. Add the chickpeas to the pan, stir, and continue simmering for 10 more minutes, adding more water if necessary. Remove the pan from the heat, discard the cinnamon stick, and set the stew aside to cool for 10 minutes.
4. When ready to serve, sprinkle the chopped parsley over the top of the stew. Store covered in the refrigerator for up to 4 days.

Per Serving:calories: 471 / fat: 23g / protein: 9g / carbs: 63g / fiber: 12g / sodium: 651mg

Amaranth Salad

Prep time: 5 minutes / Cook time: 6 minutes / Serves 4

- 2 cups water
- 1 cup amaranth
- 1 teaspoon dried Greek oregano
- ½ teaspoon salt
- ½ teaspoon ground black pepper
- 1 tablespoon extra-virgin olive oil
- 2 teaspoons red wine vinegar

1. Add water and amaranth to the Instant Pot®. Close lid, set steam release to Sealing, press the Manual button, and set time to 6 minutes. When the timer beeps, quick-release the pressure until the float valve drops.
2. Open lid and fluff amaranth with a fork. Add oregano, salt, and pepper. Mix well. Drizzle with olive oil and wine vinegar. Serve hot.

Per Serving:calories: 93 / fat: 5g / protein: 3g / carbs: 12g / fiber: 3g / sodium: 299mg

Lentil Chili

Prep time: 15 minutes / Cook time: 30 minutes / Serves 6
- 2 tablespoons olive oil
- 1 medium yellow onion, peeled and chopped
- 1 large poblano pepper, seeded and chopped
- ¼ cup chopped fresh cilantro
- 2 cloves garlic, peeled and minced
- 1 tablespoon chili powder
- ½ teaspoon ground cumin
- ½ teaspoon ground black pepper
- ¼ teaspoon salt
- 2 cups dried red lentils, rinsed and drained
- 6 cups vegetable broth
- 1 (10-ounce / 283-g) can tomatoes with green chilies, drained
- 1 (15-ounce / 425-g) can kidney beans, drained and rinsed
- 1 tablespoon lime juice

1. Press the Sauté button on the Instant Pot® and heat oil. Add onion and poblano pepper, and cook until just tender, about 3 minutes. Add cilantro, garlic, chili powder, cumin, black pepper, and salt, and cook until fragrant, about 30 seconds. Press the Cancel button.
2. Add lentils and broth, close lid, set steam release to Sealing, press the Manual button, and set time to 25 minutes. When the timer beeps, let pressure release naturally, about 15 minutes.
3. Open lid and stir in tomatoes, beans, and lime juice. Let stand uncovered on the Keep Warm setting for 10 minutes. Serve warm.

Per Serving:calories: 261 / fat: 6g / protein: 15g / carbs: 42g / fiber: 9g / sodium: 781mg

Asparagus-Spinach Farro

Prep time: 5 minutes / Cook time: 16 minutes / Serves 4
- 2 tablespoons olive oil
- 1 cup quick-cooking farro
- ½ shallot, finely chopped
- 4 garlic cloves, minced
- Sea salt
- Freshly ground black pepper
- 2½ cups water, vegetable broth, or chicken broth
- 8 ounces (227 g) asparagus, woody ends trimmed, cut into 2-inch pieces
- 3 ounces (85 g) fresh baby spinach
- ½ cup grated Parmesan cheese

1. In a large skillet, heat the olive oil over medium-high heat. Add the farro, shallot, and garlic, season with salt and pepper, and cook for about 4 minutes. Add the water and bring the mixture to a boil. Reduce the heat to low, cover, and simmer for 10 minutes (or for the time recommended on the package of farro).
2. Add the asparagus and cook until tender, about 5 minutes. Add the spinach and cook for 30 seconds more, or until wilted.
3. Top with the Parmesan and serve.

Per Serving:calories: 277 / fat: 11g / protein: 10g / carbs: 38g / fiber: 7g / sodium: 284mg

Lentils with Spinach

Prep time: 10 minutes / Cook time: 20 minutes / Serves 4
- 1 cup dried yellow lentils, rinsed and drained
- 4 cups water
- 1 tablespoon olive oil
- ½ medium yellow onion, peeled and chopped
- 1 clove garlic, peeled and minced
- ½ teaspoon smoked paprika
- ½ teaspoon ground black pepper
- 1 (15-ounce / 425-g) can diced tomatoes, drained
- 10 ounces (283 g) baby spinach leaves
- ½ cup crumbled feta cheese

1. Add lentils and water to the Instant Pot®. Close lid, set steam release to Sealing, press the Manual button, and set time to 6 minutes. When the timer beeps, quick-release the pressure. Press the Cancel button and open lid. Drain lentils and set aside. Clean pot.
2. Press the Sauté button and heat oil. Add onion and cook until just tender, about 3 minutes. Add garlic, smoked paprika, and pepper, and cook for an additional 30 seconds. Stir in tomatoes, spinach, and lentils. Simmer for 10 minutes. Top with feta and serve.

Per Serving:calories: 289 / fat: 8g / protein: 21g / carbs: 31g / fiber: 10g / sodium: 623mg

Quinoa Salad in Endive Boats

Prep time: 10 minutes / Cook time: 3 minutes / Serves 4
- 1 tablespoon walnut oil
- 1 cup quinoa, rinsed and drained
- 2½ cups water
- 2 cups chopped jarred artichoke hearts
- 2 cups diced tomatoes
- ½ small red onion, peeled and thinly sliced
- 2 tablespoons olive oil
- 1 tablespoon balsamic vinegar

- 4 large Belgian endive leaves
- 1 cup toasted pecans

1. Press the Sauté button on the Instant Pot® and heat walnut oil. Add quinoa and toss for 1 minute until slightly browned. Add water and stir. Press the Cancel button.
2. Close lid, set steam release to Sealing, press the Manual button, and set time to 2 minutes. When the timer beeps, let pressure release naturally for 10 minutes. Quick-release any remaining pressure until the float valve drops and open lid. Drain liquid and transfer quinoa to a serving bowl.
3. Add artichoke hearts, tomatoes, onion, olive oil, and vinegar to quinoa and stir to combine. Cover and refrigerate mixture for 1 hour or up to overnight.
4. Place endive leaves on four plates. Top each with ¼ cup quinoa mixture. Sprinkle toasted pecans over the top of each endive boat and serve.

Per Serving:calories: 536 / fat: 35g / protein: 13g / carbs: 46g / fiber: 13g / sodium: 657mg

Venetian-Style Pasta E Fagioli

Prep time: 15 minutes / Cook time: 50 minutes / Serves 2

- 1 cup uncooked borlotti (cranberry) beans or pinto beans
- 3 tablespoons extra virgin olive oil, divided
- 1 small carrot, finely chopped
- ½ medium onion (white or red), finely chopped
- 1 celery stalk, finely chopped
- 1 bay leaf
- 1 tablespoon tomato paste
- 2 cups cold water
- 1 rosemary sprig plus ½ teaspoon chopped fresh rosemary needles
- ¼ teaspoon fine sea salt
- ¼ teaspoon freshly ground black pepper plus more to taste
- 1½ ounces (43 g) uncooked egg fettuccine or other egg noodles
- 1 garlic clove, peeled and finely sliced
- ¼ teaspoon red pepper flakes
- 2 teaspoons grated Parmesan cheese
- Pinch of coarse sea salt, for serving

1. Place the beans in a large bowl and cover with cold water by 3 inches (7.5cm) to allow for expansion. Soak for 12 hours or overnight, then drain and rinse.
2. Add 2 tablespoons of the olive oil to a medium pot over medium heat. When the oil begins to shimmer, add the carrot, onions, celery, and bay leaf. Sauté for 3 minutes, then add the tomato paste and continue sautéing and stirring for 2 more minutes.
3. Add the beans, cold water, and rosemary sprig. Cover, bring to a boil, then reduce the heat to low and simmer for 30–40 minutes or until the beans are soft, but not falling apart. Remove the rosemary sprig and bay leaf.

Use a slotted spoon to remove about 1 cup of the beans. Set aside.

4. Using an immersion blender, blend the remaining beans in the pot, then add the whole beans back to the pot along with the sea salt and ¼ teaspoon of the black pepper. Increase the heat to medium. When the mixture begins to bubble, add the pasta and cook until done, about 3 minutes.
5. While the pasta is cooking, heat 1 teaspoon of the olive oil in a small pan over medium heat. Add the garlic, red pepper flakes, and chopped rosemary needles. Sauté for 2 minutes, then transfer the mixture to the beans and stir.
6. When the pasta is done cooking, remove from the heat and set aside to cool for 5 minutes before dividing between 2 plates. Drizzle 1 teaspoon of the olive oil and sprinkle 1 teaspoon of the grated Parmesan over each serving. Season with freshly ground pepper to taste and a pinch of coarse sea salt. This dish is best served promptly, but can be stored in the refrigerator for up to 2 days.

Per Serving:calories: 409 / fat: 22g / protein: 12g / carbs: 42g / fiber: 11g / sodium: 763mg

Black-Eyed Peas with Olive Oil and Herbs

Prep time: 15 minutes / Cook time: 20 minutes / Serves 8

- ¼ cup extra-virgin olive oil
- 4 sprigs oregano, leaves minced and stems reserved
- 2 sprigs thyme, leaves stripped and stems reserved
- 4 sprigs dill, fronds chopped and stems reserved
- 1 pound (454 g) dried black-eyed peas, soaked overnight and drained
- ¼ teaspoon salt
- 1 teaspoon ground black pepper
- 4 cups water

1. In a small bowl, combine oil, oregano leaves, thyme leaves, and dill fronds, and mix to combine. Cover and set aside.
2. Tie herb stems together with butcher's twine. Add to the Instant Pot® along with black-eyed peas, salt, pepper, and water. Close lid, set steam release to Sealing, press the Manual button, and set time to 20 minutes. When the timer beeps, let pressure release naturally, about 20 minutes.
3. Open lid, remove and discard herb stem bundle, and drain off any excess liquid. Stir in olive oil mixture. Serve hot.

Per Serving:calories: 119 / fat: 7g / protein: 6g / carbs: 9g / fiber: 3g / sodium: 76mg

Lebanese Rice and Broken Noodles with Cabbage

Prep time: 5 minutes / Cook time: 25 minutes / Serves: 6

- 1 tablespoon extra-virgin olive oil
- 1 cup (about 3 ounces / 85 g) uncooked vermicelli or thin spaghetti, broken into 1- to 1½-inch pieces

- 3 cups shredded cabbage (about half a 14-ounce package of coleslaw mix or half a small head of cabbage)
- 3 cups low-sodium or no-salt-added vegetable broth
- ½ cup water
- 1 cup instant brown rice
- 2 garlic cloves
- ¼ teaspoon kosher or sea salt
- ⅛ to ¼ teaspoon crushed red pepper
- ½ cup loosely packed, coarsely chopped cilantro
- Fresh lemon slices, for serving (optional)

1. In a large saucepan over medium-high heat, heat the oil. Add the pasta and cook for 3 minutes to toast, stirring often. Add the cabbage and cook for 4 minutes, stirring often. Add the broth, water, rice, garlic, salt, and crushed red pepper, and bring to a boil over high heat. Stir, cover, and reduce the heat to medium-low. Simmer for 10 minutes.
2. Remove the pan from the heat, but do not lift the lid. Let sit for 5 minutes. Fish out the garlic cloves, mash them with a fork, then stir the garlic back into the rice. Stir in the cilantro. Serve with the lemon slices (if using).

Per Serving:calories: 150 / fat: 4g / protein: 3g / carbs: 27g / fiber: 3g / sodium: 664mg

Greek Chickpeas and Rice with Tahini and Lemon

Prep time: 10 minutes / Cook time: 1 hour 45 minutes / Serves 2

- ¾ cup uncooked chickpeas
- 1 tablespoon tahini
- 3 tablespoon fresh lemon juice plus juice of 1 lemon for serving
- 4 tablespoon water
- 2 tablespoon extra virgin olive oil
- 1 medium onion (any variety), chopped
- 1 garlic clove, minced
- ¾ cup uncooked medium-grain rice
- ¾ teaspoon fine sea salt
- ½ teaspoon freshly ground black pepper
- 1 bay leaf
- 2½ cups reserved cooking water
- 4 teaspoons chopped fresh parsley

1. Place the chickpeas in a large bowl and cover with cold water by 3 inches to allow for expansion. Soak overnight or for 12 hours.
2. In a small bowl, combine the tahini with the lemon juice and 4 tablespoons of water. Whisk with a fork. Set aside.
3. When ready to cook, drain and rinse the chickpeas. Fill a large pot with cold water, place it over high heat, and add the chickpeas. Bring to a boil (removing any foam with a slotted spoon), then reduce the heat to medium-low and simmer until the chickpeas are tender but not falling apart, about 60–90 minutes. (Some chickpeas will cook faster, so begin checking after 30 minutes.)

Reserve 2½ cups of the cooking water and then drain the chickpeas. Set aside.
4. Add the olive oil to a medium pot placed over medium heat. When the oil begins to shimmer, add the onions and sauté for 4–5 minutes or until the onions are soft. Add the garlic and sauté for more 1 minute, then add the rice and stir until the rice is coated in the oil.
5. Add the tahini-lemon juice mixture to the pot, followed by the sea salt, black pepper, bay leaf, and 1½ cups of the cooking water (if using canned chickpeas, use 1½ cups tap water instead). Reduce the heat to medium-low and simmer for about 10 minutes, then add the chickpeas and continue simmering until the rice is cooked and the water has been absorbed, about 10 minutes, then remove the pot from the heat. (Add more hot water in small amounts if the mixture appears to be too dry.) Remove the pot from the heat.
6. Discard the bay leaf and transfer the mixture to two bowls. Squeeze half a lemon over each serving, then sprinkle 2 teaspoons of the parsley over each serving. Store covered in the refrigerator for up to 3 days.

Per Serving:calories: 842 / fat: 25g / protein: 25g / carbs: 134g / fiber: 27g / sodium: 863mg

Two-Bean Bulgur Chili

Prep time: 10 minutes / Cook time: 30 minutes / Serves 4

- 2 tablespoons olive oil
- 1 onion, diced
- 2 celery stalks, diced
- 1 carrot, diced
- 1 jalapeño pepper, seeded and chopped
- 3 garlic cloves, minced
- 1 (28-ounce/ 794-g) can diced tomatoes
- 1 tablespoon tomato paste
- 1½ teaspoons chili powder
- 2 teaspoons dried oregano
- 2 teaspoons ground cumin
- 1 (15-ounce/ 425-g) can black beans, drained and rinsed
- 1 (15-ounce/ 425-g) can cannellini beans, drained and rinsed
- ¾ cup dried bulgur
- 4 cups chicken broth
- Sea salt
- Freshly ground black pepper

1. In a Dutch oven, heat the olive oil over medium-high heat. Add the onion, celery, carrot, jalapeño, and garlic and sauté until the vegetables are tender, about 4 minutes.
2. Reduce the heat to medium and add the diced tomatoes, tomato paste, chili powder, oregano, and cumin. Cook for 3 minutes, then add the black beans, cannellini beans, bulgur, and broth.
3. Increase the heat to high, cover, and bring to a boil. Reduce the heat to low and simmer until the chili is

cooked to your desired thickness, about 30 minutes. Season with salt and black pepper and serve.

Per Serving:calories: 385 / fat: 9g / protein: 16g / carbs: 64g / fiber: 20g / sodium: 325mg

Creamy Yellow Lentil Soup

Prep time: 15 minutes / Cook time: 20 minutes / Serves 6

- 2 tablespoons olive oil
- 1 medium yellow onion, peeled and chopped
- 1 medium carrot, peeled and chopped
- 2 cloves garlic, peeled and minced
- 1 teaspoon ground cumin
- ½ teaspoon ground black pepper
- ¼ teaspoon salt
- 2 cups dried yellow lentils, rinsed and drained
- 6 cups water

1. Press the Sauté button on the Instant Pot® and heat oil. Add onion and carrot and cook until just tender, about 3 minutes. Add garlic, cumin, pepper, and salt and cook until fragrant, about 30 seconds. Press the Cancel button.
2. Add lentils and water, close lid, set steam release to Sealing, press the Manual button, and set time to 15 minutes. When the timer beeps, let pressure release naturally, about 15 minutes. Open lid and purée with an immersion blender or in batches in a blender. Serve warm.

Per Serving:calories: 248 / fat: 5g / protein: 15g / carbs: 35g / fiber: 8g / sodium: 118mg

Lemon Orzo with Fresh Herbs

Prep time: 10 minutes / Cook time: 10 minutes / Serves 4

- 2 cups orzo
- ½ cup fresh parsley, finely chopped
- ½ cup fresh basil, finely chopped
- 2 tablespoons lemon zest
- ½ cup extra-virgin olive oil
- ⅓ cup lemon juice
- 1 teaspoon salt
- ½ teaspoon freshly ground black pepper

1. Bring a large pot of water to a boil. Add the orzo and cook for 7 minutes. Drain and rinse with cold water. Let the orzo sit in a strainer to completely drain and cool.
2. Once the orzo has cooled, put it in a large bowl and add the parsley, basil, and lemon zest.
3. In a small bowl, whisk together the olive oil, lemon juice, salt, and pepper. Add the dressing to the pasta and toss everything together. Serve at room temperature or chilled.

Per Serving:calories: 568 / fat: 29g / protein: 11g / carbs: 65g / fiber: 4g / sodium: 586mg

Quinoa, Broccoli, and Baby Potatoes

Prep time: 10 minutes / Cook time: 5 minutes / Serves 4

- 2 tablespoons olive oil
- 1 cup baby potatoes, cut in half
- 1 cup broccoli florets
- 2 cups cooked quinoa
- Zest of 1 lemon
- Sea salt and freshly ground pepper, to taste

1. Heat the olive oil in a large skillet.
2. Add the potatoes and cook until tender and golden brown. Add the broccoli and cook until soft, about 3 minutes.
3. Remove from heat and add the quinoa and lemon zest. Season and serve.

Per Serving:calories: 204 / fat: 9g / protein: 5g / carbs: 27g / fiber: 4g / sodium: 12mg

Quinoa with Artichokes

Prep time: 10 minutes / Cook time: 26 minutes / Serves 4

- 2 tablespoons light olive oil
- 1 medium yellow onion, peeled and diced
- 2 cloves garlic, peeled and minced
- ½ teaspoon salt
- ½ teaspoon ground black pepper
- 1 cup quinoa, rinsed and drained
- 2 cups vegetable broth
- 1 cup roughly chopped marinated artichoke hearts
- ½ cup sliced green olives
- ½ cup minced fresh flat-leaf parsley
- 2 tablespoons lemon juice

1. Press the Sauté button on the Instant Pot® and heat oil. Add onion and cook until tender, about 5 minutes. Add garlic, salt, and pepper, and cook until fragrant, about 30 seconds. Press the Cancel button.
2. Stir in quinoa and broth. Close lid, set steam release to Sealing, press the Manual button, and set time to 20 minutes. When the timer beeps, let pressure release naturally, about 20 minutes, then open lid. Fluff quinoa with a fork, then stir in remaining ingredients. Serve immediately.

Per Serving:calories: 270 / fat: 13g / protein: 6g / carbs: 33g / fiber: 4g / sodium: 718mg

Brown Rice Vegetable Bowl with Roasted Red Pepper Dressing

Prep time: 10 minutes / Cook time: 22 minutes / Serves 2

- ¼ cup chopped roasted red bell pepper
- 2 tablespoons extra-virgin olive oil
- 1 tablespoon red wine vinegar
- 1 teaspoon honey
- 2 tablespoons light olive oil
- 2 cloves garlic, peeled and minced
- ½ teaspoon ground black pepper
- ¼ teaspoon salt
- 1 cup brown rice
- 1 cup vegetable broth

- ¼ cup chopped fresh flat-leaf parsley
- 2 tablespoons chopped fresh chives
- 2 tablespoons chopped fresh dill
- ½ cup diced tomato
- ½ cup chopped red onion
- ½ cup diced cucumber
- ½ cup chopped green bell pepper

1. Place roasted red pepper, extra-virgin olive oil, red wine vinegar, and honey in a blender. Purée until smooth, about 1 minute. Refrigerate until ready to serve.
2. Press the Sauté button on the Instant Pot® and heat light olive oil. Add garlic and cook until fragrant, about 30 seconds. Add black pepper, salt, and rice and stir well. Press the Cancel button.
3. Stir in broth. Close lid, set steam release to Sealing, press the Manual button, and set time to 22 minutes.

Per Serving:calories: 561 / fat: 23g / protein: 10g / carbs: 86g / fiber: 5g / sodium: 505mg

Wheat Berry Salad

Prep time: 20 minutes / Cook time: 50 minutes / Serves 12
- 1½ tablespoons vegetable oil
- 6¾ cups water
- 1½ cups wheat berries
- 1½ teaspoons Dijon mustard
- 1 teaspoon sugar
- 1 teaspoon salt
- ½ teaspoon ground black pepper
- ¼ cup white wine vinegar
- ½ cup extra-virgin olive oil
- ½ small red onion, peeled and diced
- 1⅓ cups frozen corn, thawed
- 1 medium zucchini, trimmed, grated, and drained
- 2 stalks celery, finely diced
- 1 medium red bell pepper, seeded and diced
- 4 scallions, diced
- ¼ cup diced sun-dried tomatoes
- ¼ cup chopped fresh parsley

1. Add vegetable oil, water, and wheat berries to the Instant Pot®. Close lid, set steam release to Sealing, press the Manual button, and set time to 50 minutes. When the timer beeps, quick-release the pressure until the float valve drops and open lid. Fluff wheat berries with a fork. Drain any excess liquid, transfer to a large bowl, and set aside to cool.
2. Purée mustard, sugar, salt, black pepper, vinegar, olive oil, and onion in a blender. Stir dressing into wheat berries. Stir in rest of ingredients. Serve.

Per Serving:calories: 158 / fat: 10g / protein: 2g / carbs: 16g / fiber: 2g / sodium: 268mg

Lentil and Spinach Curry

Prep time: 10 minutes / Cook time: 17 minutes / Serves 4
- 1 tablespoon olive oil

- ½ cup diced onion
- 1 clove garlic, peeled and minced
- 1 cup dried yellow lentils, rinsed and drained
- 4 cups water
- ½ teaspoon ground coriander
- ½ teaspoon ground turmeric
- ½ teaspoon curry powder
- ½ cup diced tomatoes
- 5 ounces (142 g) baby spinach leaves

1. Press the Sauté button on the Instant Pot® and heat oil. Add onion and cook until translucent, about 5 minutes. Add garlic and cook for 30 seconds. Add lentils and toss to combine. Press the Cancel button.
2. Pour in water. Close lid, set steam release to Sealing, press the Manual button, and set time to 6 minutes. When the timer beeps, quick-release the pressure until the float valve drops and open lid. Press the Cancel button. Drain any residual liquid. Stir in coriander, turmeric, curry powder, tomatoes, and spinach.
3. Press the Sauté button, press the Adjust button to change the heat to Less, and simmer uncovered until tomatoes are heated through and spinach has wilted, about 5 minutes.
4. Transfer to a dish and serve.

Per Serving:calories: 195 / fat: 4g / protein: 13g / carbs: 26g / fiber: 8g / sodium: 111mg

Pilaf with Eggplant and Raisins

Prep time: 10 minutes / Cook time: 30 minutes / Serves 4
- 4 eggplant (preferably thinner, about 6 ounces/170g each) cut into ¼-inch (.5cm) thick slices (if the slices are too large, cut them in half)
- 1½ teaspoons fine sea salt, divided
- ½ cup extra virgin olive oil
- 1 medium onion (any variety), diced
- 4 garlic cloves, thinly sliced
- ¼ cup white wine
- 1 cup uncooked medium-grain rice
- 1 (15-ounce / 425-g) can crushed tomatoes
- 3 cups hot water
- 4 tablespoons black raisins
- 4 teaspoons finely chopped fresh parsley
- 4 teaspoons finely chopped fresh mint
- ¼ teaspoon freshly ground black pepper to serve

1. Place the eggplant in a colander and sprinkle with ½ teaspoon of the sea salt. Set aside to rest for 10 minutes, then rinse well and squeeze to remove any remaining water.
2. Add the olive oil to a medium pot placed over medium heat. When the oil begins to shimmer, add the eggplant and sauté for 7 minutes or until soft, moving the eggplant continuously, then add the onions and continue sautéing and stirring for 2 more minutes.
3. Add the garlic and sauté for 1 additional minute, then add the white wine and deglaze the pan. After about 1 minute,

add the rice and stir until the rice is coated with the oil.

4. Add the crushed tomatoes, hot water, and remaining sea salt. Stir and bring to a boil, then reduce the heat to low and simmer for 20 minutes.Add more hot water, ¼ cup at a time, if the water level gets too low.

5. Add the raisins, stir, then cover the pot and remove from the heat. Set aside to cool for 15 minutes.

6. To serve, sprinkle 1 teaspoon of the mint and 1 teaspoon of the parsley over each serving, then season each serving with black pepper. Store covered in the refrigerator for up to 3 days.

Per Serving:calories: 612 / fat: 29g / protein: 11g / carbs: 84g / fiber: 21g / sodium: 859mg

BEANS, POTATO & KALE SOUP

Serving Portions: 4/Preparation: 15 mins. / Cooking: 55 mins.

- 2 tsp. of olive oil
- 1 medium onion, cut up
- 4 cloves garlic, cut up finely
- 2 tsp. of fresh rosemary leaves, cut up finely
- 1 lb. white potatoes, peel removed and cut into
- small cubes
- 4 C. of water
- Salt and powdered black pepper, as desired
- 1 (15-oz.) can white beans, liquid removed
- 3 C. of fresh kale, tough ribs removed and cut up
- roughly

1. In a large-sized saucepan, sizzle the oil on burner at around medium heat.
2. Cook the onions for around 7-9 minutes, mixing frequently.
3. Put in the garlic and rosemary and cook for around 1 minute.
4. Put in the potatoes, water, salt and pepper.
5. Cook the mixture until boiling.
6. Immediately turn the heat at around low and cook, uncovered for around 30-35 minutes.
7. With the back of a spoon, mash some of the potatoes roughly.
8. Putinthebeans and kale and cook for around4-7minutes.
9. Enjoy hot.

Per Serving:Calories: 289/ Fat: 3.2g/ Carbs: 54.7g/ Fiber: 15.5g/ Protein: 12.7g

BEANS & POTATO STEW

Serving Portions: 6/Preparation: 15 mins. / Cooking: 50 mins.

- 2 tbsp. of olive oil
- 1 large onion, cut up
- 2 tsp. of red chili powder
- 1 tsp. of cumin powder
- 1 large bell pepper, seeded and cut up
- 2 medium poblano peppers, seeded and cut up . 2 cloves garlic, cut up finely
- Salt, as desired
- 1½ lb. Yukon Gold potatoes, scrubbed and cut into 1-inch chunks

- 1 C. of water
- 30 oz. of canned pinto beans, liquid removed . 1 (15-oz.) can diced tomatoes with juices
- 2 tbsp. of lime juice
- Powdered black pepper, as desired

1. In a Dutch oven, sizzle the oil on burner at around medium heat.
2. Cook the onion, chili powder and cumin for around 5 minutes.
3. Put in the bell pepper, poblano peppers, garlic and salt and cook for around 5 minutes, mixing time to time.
4. Put in the potatoes and stir to blend.
5. Immediately turn the heat at around low and cook with a cover for around 5 minutes, mixing time to time.
6. Put in the water and cook with a cover for around 20-30 minutes.
7. Put in the beans and tomatoes with juices and gently stir to blend.
8. Immediately turn the heat at around medium-high.
9. Cook the mixture until boiling.
10. Immediately turn the heat at around medium-low.
11. Cook for around 5 minutes.
12. Put in the lime juice, salt and pepper and take off from burner.
13. Enjoy hot.

Per Serving:Calories: 316/ Fat: 6.1g/ Carbs: 53.8g/ Fiber: 15.6g/ Protein: 15.3g

BEANS WITH MUSHROOMS

Serving Portions: 2/Preparation: 10 mins. / Cooking: 25 mins.

- 1 tbsp. of olive oil
- 1 onion, cut up
- 6 oz. of fresh button mushrooms, slivered . ¼ C. of sun-dried tomatoes, cut up roughly
- 1 (14-oz.) can kidney beans
- 2 tbsp. of tomato paste
- ½ tbsp. of red chili powder
- ½ tbsp. of cumin powder
- Salt and powdered black pepper, as desired . 1 tbsp. of fresh parsley, cut up

1. In a large-sized saucepan, sizzle the oil on burner at around medium heat.
2. Cook the onion for around 4-5 minutes.
3. Put in the mushrooms and sundried tomatoes and cook for around 5 minutes.
4. Put in kidney beans with liquid, tomato paste and spices.
5. Cook the mixture until boiling.
6. Immediately turn the heat at around low and cook for around 10 minutes.
7. Put in the salt and pepper and takeoff from burner.
8. Enjoy hot with the decoration of parsley.

Per Serving:Calories: 313/ Fat: 8.1g/ Carbs: 45.7g/ Fiber: 19.1g/ Protein: 16.9g

Chicken Gyros with Grilled Vegetables and Tzatziki Sauce

Prep time: 15 minutes / Cook time: 15 minutes / Serves 2

- For the chicken
- 2 tablespoons freshly squeezed lemon juice
- 2 tablespoons olive oil, divided, plus extra for oiling the grill
- 1 teaspoon minced fresh oregano, or ½ teaspoon dry oregano
- ½ teaspoon garlic powder
- ½ teaspoon salt, divided, plus more to season vegetables
- 8 ounces (227 g) chicken tenders
- 1 small zucchini, cut into ½-inch strips lengthwise
- 1 small eggplant, cut into 1-inch strips lengthwise
- ½ red pepper, seeded and cut in half lengthwise
- ¾ cup plain Greek yogurt
- ½ English cucumber, peeled and minced
- 1 tablespoon minced fresh dill
- 2 (8-inch) pita breads

1. In a medium bowl, combine the lemon juice, 1 tablespoon of olive oil, the oregano, garlic powder, and ¼ teaspoon of salt. Add the chicken and marinate for 30 minutes.
2. Place the zucchini, eggplant, and red pepper in a large mixing bowl and sprinkle liberally with salt and the remaining 1 tablespoon of olive oil. Toss them well to coat. Let the vegetables rest while the chicken is marinating.
3. In a medium bowl, combine the yogurt, the cucumber, the remaining salt, and the dill. Stir well to combine and set aside in the refrigerator.
4. When ready to grill, heat the grill to medium-high and oil the grill grate.
5. Drain any liquid from the vegetables and place them on the grill. Remove the chicken tenders from the marinade and place them on the grill.
6. Cook chicken and vegetables for 3 minutes per side, or until the chicken is no longer pink inside and the vegetables have grill marks.
7. Remove the chicken and vegetables from the grill and set aside. On the grill, heat the pitas for about 30 seconds, flipping them frequently so they don't burn.
8. Divide the chicken tenders and vegetables between the pitas and top each with ¼ cup of the tzatziki sauce. Roll the pitas up like a cone to eat.

Per Serving:calories: 584 / fat: 21g / protein: 38g / carbs: 64g / fiber: 12g / sodium: 762mg

Seared Duck Breast with Orange Ouzo Sauce

Prep time: 10 minutes / Cook time: 15 minutes / Serves 4

- 2 duck breast halves
- 1 teaspoon salt, plus a pinch
- 1 tablespoon olive oil
- 1 shallot, minced
- 1 Thai chile, or other small, hot chile, halved lengthwise
- ½ cup chopped fennel bulb, plus a handful of the minced fronds for garnish
- ¼ cup ouzo
- 1 cup chicken broth
- Juice of one orange, about ½ cup
- Freshly ground black pepper

1. Using a very sharp knife, score a cross-hatch pattern into the skin of each duck breast, cutting through the skin and the fat layer, but not into the meat. Sprinkle the salt evenly over them and let stand at room temperature for about 15 minutes.
2. Heat the olive oil in a large skillet over medium-high heat. Add the duck breasts, skin-side down, and cook over medium heat until the skin is nicely browned and a good amount of fat has been rendered, about 8 to 10 minutes. Turn the breasts over and cook until the meat is medium-rare, about 3 more minutes. Remove the breasts from the pan, tent with foil, and let rest for about 10 minutes.
3. While the duck is resting, make the sauce. In the same skillet over medium heat, cook the shallot, chile, and fennel bulb, until the vegetables begin to soften, about 3 minutes. Remove the pan from the heat and add the ouzo (be careful not to let it catch fire). Cook, scraping up any browned bits from the pan, until the liquid is reduced by half.
4. Add the broth and orange juice, along with a pinch of salt, and bring to a boil. Let the sauce boil until it is thick and syrupy, about 5 minutes more. Remove from the heat.
5. Slice the duck breast against the grain into ⅛-inch-thick slices. Arrange the slices onto 4 serving plates and drizzle the sauce over the top. Garnish with the chopped fennel fronds and serve immediately.

Per Serving:calories: 229 / fat: 9g / protein: 27g / carbs: 7g / fiber: 1g / sodium: 781mg

Jerk Chicken Thighs

Prep time: 30 minutes / Cook time: 15 to 20 minutes / Serves 6

- 2 teaspoons ground coriander
- 1 teaspoon ground allspice
- 1 teaspoon cayenne pepper
- 1 teaspoon ground ginger
- 1 teaspoon salt
- 1 teaspoon dried thyme
- ½ teaspoon ground cinnamon
- ½ teaspoon ground nutmeg
- 2 pounds (907 g) boneless chicken thighs, skin on
- 2 tablespoons olive oil

1. In a small bowl, combine the coriander, allspice, cayenne, ginger, salt, thyme, cinnamon, and nutmeg. Stir until thoroughly combined.
2. Place the chicken in a baking dish and use paper towels to pat dry. Thoroughly coat both sides of the chicken with the spice mixture. Cover and refrigerate for at least 2 hours, preferably overnight.
3. Preheat the air fryer to 360ºF (182ºC).
4. Working in batches if necessary, arrange the chicken in a single layer in the air fryer basket and lightly coat with the olive oil. Pausing halfway through the cooking time to flip the chicken, air fry for 15 to 20 minutes, until a thermometer inserted into the thickest part registers 165ºF (74ºC).

Per Serving:calories: 227 / fat: 11g / protein: 30g / carbs: 1g / fiber: 0g / sodium: 532mg

calorie: 377 / fat: 24g / protein: 35g / carbs: 3g / sugars: 0g / fiber: 1g / sodium: 583mg

Mediterranean Roasted Turkey Breast

Prep time: 15 minutes / Cook time: 6 to 8 hours / Serves 4
- 3 garlic cloves, minced
- 1 teaspoon sea salt
- 1 teaspoon dried oregano
- ½ teaspoon freshly ground black pepper
- ½ teaspoon dried basil
- ½ teaspoon dried parsley
- ½ teaspoon dried rosemary
- ½ teaspoon dried thyme
- ¼ teaspoon dried dill
- ¼ teaspoon ground nutmeg
- 2 tablespoons extra-virgin olive oil
- 2 tablespoons freshly squeezed lemon juice
- 1 (4- to 6-pound / 1.8- to 2.7-kg) boneless or bone-in turkey breast
- 1 onion, chopped
- ½ cup low-sodium chicken broth
- 4 ounces (113 g) whole Kalamata olives, pitted
- 1 cup sun-dried tomatoes (packaged, not packed in oil), chopped

1. In a small bowl, stir together the garlic, salt, oregano, pepper, basil, parsley, rosemary, thyme, dill, and nutmeg.
2. Drizzle the olive oil and lemon juice all over the turkey breast and generously season it with the garlic-spice mix.
3. In a slow cooker, combine the onion and chicken broth. Place the seasoned turkey breast on top of the onion. Top the turkey with the olives and sun-dried tomatoes.
4. Cover the cooker and cook for 6 to 8 hours on Low heat.
5. Slice or shred the turkey for serving.

Per Serving:calories: 676 / fat: 19g / protein: 111g / carbs: 14g / fiber: 3g / sodium: 626mg

Gingery Quinoa Chicken

Prep time: 15 minutes / Cook time: 6 to 8 hours / Serves 2
- 1 teaspoon extra-virgin olive oil
- ½ cup quinoa
- ½ cup low-sodium chicken broth
- ½ cup coconut milk
- 1 teaspoon minced fresh ginger
- 1 teaspoon minced garlic
- Zest of 1 lime
- ½ teaspoon ground coriander
- 2 bone-in, skinless chicken thighs
- ⅛ teaspoon sea salt
- Freshly ground black pepper
- Juice of 1 lime, for garnish

1. Grease the inside of the slow cooker with the olive oil.
2. Put the quinoa, broth, coconut milk, ginger, garlic, zest, and coriander in the crock. Stir thoroughly.
3. Season the chicken thighs with the salt and a few grinds of the black pepper. Place them on top of the quinoa.
4. Cover and cook for 6 to 8 hours, until the quinoa has absorbed all the liquid and the chicken is cooked through.
5. Drizzle each portion with lime juice just before serving.

Per Serving:calories: 571 /fat: 27g / protein: 47g/carbs: 36g / sugars: 3g / fiber: 5g/sodium: 369mg

Easy Turkey Tenderloin

Prep time: 20 minutes / Cook time: 30 minutes / Serves 4
- Olive oil
- ½ teaspoon paprika
- ½ teaspoon garlic powder
- ½ teaspoon salt
- ½ teaspoon freshly ground black pepper
- Pinch cayenne pepper
- 1½ pounds (680 g) turkey breast tenderloin

1. Spray the air fryer basket lightly with olive oil.
2. In a small bowl, combine the paprika, garlic powder, salt, black pepper, and cayenne pepper. Rub the mixture all over the turkey.
3. Place the turkey in the air fryer basket and lightly spray with olive oil.
4. Air fry at 370ºF (188ºC) for 15 minutes. Flip the turkey over and lightly spray with olive oil. Air fry until the

internal temperature reaches at least 170ºF (77ºC) for an additional 10 to 15 minutes.

5. Let the turkey rest for 10 minutes before slicing and serving.

Per Serving:calories: 196 / fat: 3g / protein: 40g / carbs: 1g / fiber: 0g / sodium: 483mg

Rosemary Baked Chicken Thighs

Prep time: 20 minutes / Cook time: 20 minutes / Serves 4 to 6

- 5 tablespoons extra-virgin olive oil, divided
- 3 medium shallots, diced
- 4 garlic cloves, peeled and crushed
- 1 rosemary sprig
- 2 to 2½ pounds (907 g to 1.1 kg) bone-in, skin-on chicken thighs (about 6 pieces)
- 2 teaspoons kosher salt
- ¼ teaspoon freshly ground black pepper
- 1 lemon, juiced and zested
- ⅓ cup low-sodium chicken broth

1. In a large sauté pan or skillet, heat 3 tablespoons of olive oil over medium heat. Add the shallots and garlic and cook for about a minute, until fragrant. Add the rosemary sprig.
2. Season the chicken with salt and pepper. Place it in the skillet, skin-side down, and brown for 3 to 5 minutes.
3. Once it's cooked halfway through, turn the chicken over and add lemon juice and zest.
4. Add the chicken broth, cover the pan, and continue to cook for 10 to 15 more minutes, until cooked through and juices run clear. Serve.

Per Serving:calories: 294 / fat: 18g / protein: 30g / carbs: 3g / fiber: 1g / sodium: 780mg

Greek-Style Roast Turkey Breast

Prep time: 10 minutes / Cook time: 7½ hours / Serves 8

- 1 (4-pound / 1.8-kg) turkey breast, trimmed of fat
- ½ cup chicken stock
- 2 tablespoons fresh lemon juice
- 2 cups chopped onions
- ½ cup pitted kalamata olives
- ½ cup oil-packed sun-dried tomatoes, drained and thinly sliced
- 1 clove garlic, minced
- 1 teaspoon dried oregano
- ½ teaspoon ground cinnamon
- ½ teaspoon ground dill
- ¼ teaspoon ground nutmeg
- ¼ teaspoon cayenne pepper
- 1 teaspoon sea salt
- ¼ teaspoon black pepper
- 3 tablespoons all-purpose flour

1. Place the turkey breast, ¼ cup of the chicken stock, lemon juice, onions, Kalamata olives, garlic, and sun-

dried tomatoes into the slow cooker. Sprinkle with the oregano, cinnamon, dill, nutmeg, cayenne pepper, salt, and black pepper. Cover and cook on low for 7 hours.
2. Combine the remaining ¼ cup chicken stock and the flour in a small bowl. Whisk until smooth. Stir into the slow cooker. Cover and cook on low for an additional 30 minutes.
3. Serve hot over rice, pasta, potatoes, or another starch of your choice.

Per Serving:calories: 386 / fat: 7g / protein: 70g / carbs: 8g / fiber: 2g / sodium: 601mg

Classic Whole Chicken

Prep time: 5 minutes / Cook time: 50 minutes / Serves 4

- Oil, for spraying
- 1 (4-pound / 1.8-kg) whole chicken, giblets removed
- 1 tablespoon olive oil
- 1 teaspoon paprika
- ½ teaspoon granulated garlic
- ½ teaspoon salt
- ½ teaspoon freshly ground black pepper
- ¼ teaspoon finely chopped fresh parsley, for garnish

1. Line the air fryer basket with parchment and spray lightly with oil.
2. Pat the chicken dry with paper towels. Rub it with the olive oil until evenly coated.
3. In a small bowl, mix together the paprika, garlic, salt, and black pepper and sprinkle it evenly over the chicken.
4. Place the chicken in the prepared basket, breast-side down.
5. Air fry at 360ºF (182ºC) for 30 minutes, flip, and cook for another 20 minutes, or until the internal temperature reaches 165ºF (74ºC) and the juices run clear.
6. Sprinkle with the parsley before serving.

Per Serving:calories: 549 / fat: 11g / protein: 105g / carbs: 0g / fiber: 0g / sodium: 523mg

Turkey Meatloaf

Prep time: 10 minutes / Cook time: 50 minutes / Serves 4

- 8 ounces (227 g) sliced mushrooms
- 1 small onion, coarsely chopped
- 2 cloves garlic
- 1½ pounds (680 g) 85% lean ground turkey
- 2 eggs, lightly beaten
- 1 tablespoon tomato paste
- ¼ cup almond meal
- 2 tablespoons almond milk
- 1 tablespoon dried oregano
- 1 teaspoon salt
- ½ teaspoon freshly ground black pepper
- 1 Roma tomato, thinly sliced

1. Preheat the air fryer to 350ºF (177ºC). Lightly coat a round pan with olive oil and set aside.

2. In a food processor fitted with a metal blade, combine the mushrooms, onion, and garlic. Pulse until finely chopped. Transfer the vegetables to a large mixing bowl.

3. Add the turkey, eggs, tomato paste, almond meal, milk, oregano, salt, and black pepper. Mix gently until thoroughly combined. Transfer the mixture to the prepared pan and shape into a loaf. Arrange the tomato slices on top.

4. Air fry for 50 minutes or until the meatloaf is nicely browned and a thermometer inserted into the thickest part registers 165ºF (74ºC). Remove from the air fryer and let rest for about 10 minutes before slicing.

Per Serving:calories: 353 / fat: 20g / protein: 38g / carbs: 7g / fiber: 2g / sodium: 625mg

Roast Chicken

Prep time: 20 minutes / Cook time: 55 minutes / Serves 4
- ¼ cup white wine
- 2 tablespoons olive oil, divided
- 1 tablespoon Dijon mustard
- 1 garlic clove, minced
- 1 teaspoon dried rosemary
- Juice and zest of 1 lemon
- Sea salt and freshly ground pepper, to taste
- 1 large roasting chicken, giblets removed
- 3 large carrots, peeled and cut into chunks
- 1 fennel bulb, peeled and cut into ½-inch cubes
- 2 celery stalks, cut into chunks

1. Preheat the oven to 400ºF (205ºC).
2. Combine the white wine, 1 tablespoon of olive oil, mustard, garlic, rosemary, lemon juice and zest, sea salt, and freshly ground pepper in a small bowl.
3. Place the chicken in a shallow roasting pan on a roasting rack.
4. Rub the entire chicken, including the cavity, with the wine and mustard mixture.
5. Place the chicken in the oven and roast for 15 minutes.
6. Toss the vegetables with the remaining tablespoon of olive oil, and place around the chicken.
7. Turn the heat down to 375ºF (190ºC).
8. Roast an additional 40–60 minutes, basting the chicken every 15 minutes with the drippings in the bottom of the pan.
9. Cook chicken until internal temperature reaches 180ºF (82ºC) in between the thigh and the body of the chicken. When you remove the instant-read thermometer, the juices should run clear.
10. Let the chicken rest for at least 10–15 minutes before serving.

Per Serving:calories: 387 / fat: 14g / protein: 50g / carbs: 12g / fiber: 4g / sodium: 306mg

Balsamic Chicken Thighs with Tomato and Basil

Prep time: 15 minutes / Cook time: 17 minutes / Serves 6

- 1 pound (454 g) boneless, skinless chicken thighs
- ¼ teaspoon salt
- ¼ teaspoon ground black pepper
- ¼ teaspoon Italian seasoning
- 3 tablespoons olive oil
- 1 medium white onion, peeled and chopped
- 1 medium red bell pepper, seeded and chopped
- 2 cloves garlic, peeled and minced
- 4 medium tomatoes, seeded and diced
- ½ cup red wine
- ¼ cup balsamic vinegar
- ½ cup grated Parmesan cheese
- ¼ cup chopped fresh basil

1. Season chicken on both sides with salt, black pepper, and Italian seasoning. Press the Sauté button on the Instant Pot® and heat oil. Add chicken and brown well on both sides, about 4 minutes per side. Transfer chicken to a plate and set aside.
2. Add onion and bell pepper to the Instant Pot®. Cook until just tender, about 2 minutes. Add garlic and cook until fragrant, about 30 seconds. Stir in tomatoes and wine, and scrape any brown bits from the bottom of the pot. Press the Cancel button.
3. Stir in chicken and balsamic vinegar. Close lid, set steam release to Sealing, press the Manual button, and set time to 6 minutes. When the timer beeps, let pressure release naturally, about 15 minutes. Press the Cancel button and open lid. Top with cheese and basil, and serve hot.

Per Serving:calories: 239 / fat: 13g / protein: 20g / carbs: 8g / fiber: 1g / sodium: 447mg

Brazilian Tempero Baiano Chicken Drumsticks

Prep time: 30 minutes / Cook time: 20 minutes / Serves 4
- 1 teaspoon cumin seeds
- 1 teaspoon dried oregano
- 1 teaspoon dried parsley
- 1 teaspoon ground turmeric
- ½ teaspoon coriander seeds
- 1 teaspoon kosher salt
- ½ teaspoon black peppercorns
- ½ teaspoon cayenne pepper
- ¼ cup fresh lime juice
- 2 tablespoons olive oil
- 1½ pounds (680 g) chicken drumsticks

1. In a clean coffee grinder or spice mill, combine the cumin, oregano, parsley, turmeric, coriander seeds, salt, peppercorns, and cayenne. Process until finely ground.
2. In a small bowl, combine the ground spices with the lime juice and oil. Place the chicken in a resealable plastic bag. Add the marinade, seal, and massage until the chicken is well coated. Marinate at room temperature for 30 minutes or in the refrigerator for up

to 24 hours.

3. When you are ready to cook, place the drumsticks skin side up in the air fryer basket. Set the air fryer to 400ºF (204ºC) for 20 to 25 minutes, turning the legs halfway through the cooking time. Use a meat thermometer to ensure that the chicken has reached an internal temperature of 165ºF (74ºC).

4. Serve with plenty of napkins.

Per Serving:calories: 267 / fat: 13g / protein: 33g / carbs: 2g / fiber: 1g / sodium: 777mg

Turkey Breast in Yogurt Sauce

Prep time: 10 minutes / Cook time: 16 minutes / Serves 6

- 1 cup plain low-fat yogurt
- 1 teaspoon ground turmeric
- 1 teaspoon ground cumin
- 1 teaspoon yellow mustard seeds
- ¼ teaspoon salt
- ½ teaspoon ground black pepper
- 1 pound (454 g) boneless turkey breast, cut into bite-sized pieces
- 1 tablespoon olive oil
- 1 (1-pound / 454-g) bag frozen baby peas and pearl onions, thawed

1. In a large bowl, mix together yogurt, turmeric, cumin, mustard seeds, salt, and pepper. Stir in in turkey. Cover and refrigerate for 4 hours.

2. Press the Sauté button on the Instant Pot® and heat oil. Add turkey and yogurt mixture. Press the Cancel button, close lid, set steam release to Sealing, press the Manual button, and set time to 8 minutes. When the timer beeps, quick-release the pressure and open lid.

3. Stir in peas and onions. Press the Cancel button, then press the Sauté button and simmer until sauce is thickened, about 8 minutes. Serve hot.

Per Serving:calories: 146 / fat: 6g / protein: 17g / carbs: 7g / fiber: 1g / sodium: 554mg

Grilled Rosemary-Lemon Turkey Cutlets

Prep time: 10 minutes / Cook time: 30 minutes / Serves 4

- 2 tablespoons olive oil
- 2 tablespoons fresh lemon juice
- 1 teaspoon finely chopped fresh rosemary
- 1 clove garlic, minced
- 4 turkey cutlets (6 ounces / 170 g each), pounded to ¼' thickness
- Kosher salt and ground black pepper, to taste
- 2 ripe tomatoes, diced
- ½ red onion, diced
- 1 tablespoon balsamic vinegar
- 2 cups (2 ounces / 57 g) baby arugula

1. In a large bowl, combine the oil, lemon juice, rosemary, and garlic. Add the turkey cutlets and let marinate at room temperature while you prepare the grill, about 20 minutes.

2. Coat a grill rack or grill pan with olive oil and prepare the grill to medium-high heat.

3. Season the turkey with the salt and pepper. Grill the cutlets until grill marks form and the turkey is cooked through, about 4 minutes per side.

4. Meanwhile, in a medium bowl, combine the tomatoes, onion, and vinegar and season to taste with the salt and pepper.

5. Top each cutlet with ½ cup baby arugula and a quarter of the tomato mixture.

Per Serving:calories: 269 / fat: 8g / protein: 43g / carbs: 6g / fiber: 1g / sodium: 398mg

South Indian Pepper Chicken

Prep time: 30 minutes / Cook time: 15 minutes / Serves 4

- Spice Mix:
- 1 dried red chile, or ½ teaspoon dried red pepper flakes
- 1-inch piece cinnamon or cassia bark
- 1½ teaspoons coriander seeds
- 1 teaspoon fennel seeds
- 1 teaspoon cumin seeds
- 1 teaspoon black peppercorns
- ½ teaspoon cardamom seeds
- ¼ teaspoon ground turmeric
- 1 teaspoon kosher salt
- Chicken:
- 1 pound (454 g) boneless, skinless chicken thighs, cut crosswise into thirds
- 2 medium onions, cut into ½-inch-thick slices
- ¼ cup olive oil
- Cauliflower rice, steamed rice, or naan bread, for serving

1. For the spice mix: Combine the dried chile, cinnamon, coriander, fennel, cumin, peppercorns, and cardamom in a clean coffee or spice grinder. Grind, shaking the grinder lightly so all the seeds and bits get into the blades, until the mixture is broken down to a fine powder. Stir in the turmeric and salt.

2. For the chicken: Place the chicken and onions in resealable plastic bag. Add the oil and 1½ tablespoons of the spice mix. Seal the bag and massage until the chicken is well coated. Marinate at room temperature for 30 minutes or in the refrigerator for up to 24 hours.

3. Place the chicken and onions in the air fryer basket. Set the air fryer to 350ºF (177ºC) for 10 minutes, stirring once halfway through the cooking time. Increase the temperature to 400ºF (204ºC) for 5 minutes. Use a meat thermometer to ensure the chicken has reached an internal temperature of 165ºF (74ºC).

4. Serve with steamed rice, cauliflower rice, or naan.

Per Serving:calories: 295 / fat: 19g / protein: 24g / carbs: 9g / fiber: 3g / sodium: 694mg

Kale and Orzo Chicken

Prep time: 10 minutes / Cook time: 16 minutes / Serves 4

- 3 tablespoons light olive oil
- 1 pound (454 g) boneless, skinless chicken breasts
- ½ teaspoon salt
- ½ teaspoon ground black pepper
- ½ medium yellow onion, peeled and chopped
- 4 cups chopped kale
- ¼ teaspoon crushed red pepper flakes
- 2 cups low-sodium chicken broth
- 1½ cups orzo
- ½ cup crumbled feta cheese

1. Press the Sauté button on the Instant Pot® and heat oil. Season chicken with salt and pepper and add to the pot. Brown well on both sides, about 4 minutes per side. Transfer chicken to a plate and set aside.
2. Add onion and cook until just tender, about 2 minutes. Add kale and crushed red pepper flakes, and cook until kale is just wilted, about 2 minutes. Press the Cancel button.
3. Add broth and orzo to the Instant Pot® and stir well. Top with chicken breasts. Close lid, set steam release to Sealing, press the Manual button, and set time to 4 minutes. When the timer beeps, quick-release the pressure until the float valve drops. Press the Cancel button and open lid. Transfer chicken to a cutting board and cut into ½" slices. Arrange slices on a platter along with orzo and kale. Top with feta and serve hot.

Per Serving:calories: 690 / fat: 19g / protein: 56g / carbs: 72g / fiber: 7g / sodium: 835mg

Garlic-Lemon Chicken and Potatoes

Prep time: 10 minutes / Cook time: 45 minutes / Serves 4 to 6

- 1 cup garlic, minced
- 1½ cups lemon juice
- 1 cup plus 2 tablespoons extra-virgin olive oil, divided
- 1½ teaspoons salt, divided
- 1 teaspoon freshly ground black pepper
- 1 whole chicken, cut into 8 pieces
- 1 pound (454 g) fingerling or red potatoes

1. Preheat the oven to 400°F(205°C).
2. In a large bowl, whisk together the garlic, lemon juice, 1 cup of olive oil, 1 teaspoon of salt, and pepper.
3. Put the chicken in a large baking dish and pour half of the lemon sauce over the chicken. Cover the baking dish with foil, and cook for 20 minutes.
4. Cut the potatoes in half, and toss to coat with 2 tablespoons olive oil and 1 teaspoon of salt. Put them on a baking sheet and bake for 20 minutes in the same oven as the chicken.
5. Take both the chicken and potatoes out of the oven. Using a spatula, transfer the potatoes to the baking dish with the chicken. Pour the remaining sauce over the potatoes and chicken. Bake for another 25 minutes.
6. Transfer the chicken and potatoes to a serving dish and spoon the garlic-lemon sauce from the pan on top.

Per Serving:calories: 748 / fat: 59g / protein: 32g / carbs: 24g / fiber: 2g / sodium: 707mg

Harissa-Rubbed Cornish Game Hens

Prep time: 30 minutes / Cook time: 21 minutes / Serves 4

- Harissa:
- ½ cup olive oil
- 6 cloves garlic, minced
- 2 tablespoons smoked paprika
- 1 tablespoon ground coriander
- 1 tablespoon ground cumin
- 1 teaspoon ground caraway
- 1 teaspoon kosher salt
- ½ to 1 teaspoon cayenne pepper
- Hens:
- ½ cup yogurt
- 2 Cornish game hens, any giblets removed, split in half lengthwise

1. For the harissa: In a medium microwave-safe bowl, combine the oil, garlic, paprika, coriander, cumin, caraway, salt, and cayenne. Microwave on high for 1 minute, stirring halfway through the cooking time. (You can also heat this on the stovetop until the oil is hot and bubbling. Or, if you must use your air fryer for everything, cook it in the air fryer at 350°F (177°C) for 5 to 6 minutes, or until the paste is heated through.)
2. For the hens: In a small bowl, combine 1 to 2 tablespoons harissa and the yogurt. Whisk until well combined. Place the hen halves in a resealable plastic bag and pour the marinade over. Seal the bag and massage until all of the pieces are thoroughly coated. Marinate at room temperature for 30 minutes or in the refrigerator for up to 24 hours.
3. Arrange the hen halves in a single layer in the air fryer basket. (If you have a smaller air fryer, you may have to cook this in two batches.) Set the air fryer to 400°F (204°C) for 20 minutes. Use a meat thermometer to ensure the game hens have reached an internal temperature of 165°F (74°C).

Per Serving:calories: 421 / fat: 33g / protein: 26g / carbs: 6g / fiber: 2g / sodium: 683mg

Marinated Chicken

Prep time: 5 minutes / Cook time: 16 minutes / Serves 4

- ½ cup olive oil
- 2 tablespoon fresh rosemary
- 1 teaspoon minced garlic
- Juice and zest of 1 lemon
- ¼ cup chopped flat-leaf parsley
- Sea salt and freshly ground pepper, to taste
- 4 boneless, skinless chicken breasts

1. Mix all ingredients except the chicken together in a

plastic bag or bowl.

2. Place the chicken in the container and shake/stir so the marinade thoroughly coats the chicken.
3. Refrigerate up to 24 hours.
4. Heat a grill to medium heat and cook the chicken for 6–8 minutes a side. Turn only once during the cooking process.
5. Serve with a Greek salad and brown rice.

Per Serving:calories: 571 / fat: 34g / protein: 61g / carbs: 1g / fiber: 0g / sodium: 126mg

Italian Herb Grilled Chicken

Prep time: 20 minutes / Cook time: 10 minutes / Serves 4

- ½ cup lemon juice
- ½ cup extra-virgin olive oil
- 3 tablespoons garlic, minced
- 2 teaspoons dried oregano
- 1 teaspoon red pepper flakes
- 1 teaspoon salt
- 2 pounds (907 g) boneless and skinless chicken breasts

1. In a large bowl, mix together the lemon juice, olive oil, garlic, oregano, red pepper flakes, and salt.
2. Fillet the chicken breast in half horizontally to get 2 thin pieces, repeating with all of the breasts.
3. Put the chicken in the bowl with the marinade and let sit for at least 10 minutes before cooking.
4. Preheat a grill, grill pan, or lightly oiled skillet to high heat. Once hot, cook the chicken for 4 minutes on each side. Serve warm.

Per Serving:calories: 529 / fat: 33g / protein: 52g / carbs: 5g / fiber: 1g / sodium: 583mg

Fiesta Chicken Plate

Prep time: 15 minutes / Cook time: 12 to 15 minutes / Serves 4

- 1 pound (454 g) boneless, skinless chicken breasts (2 large breasts)
- 2 tablespoons lime juice
- 1 teaspoon cumin
- ½ teaspoon salt
- ½ cup grated Pepper Jack cheese
- 1 (16-ounce / 454-g) can refried beans
- ½ cup salsa
- 2 cups shredded lettuce
- 1 medium tomato, chopped
- 2 avocados, peeled and sliced
- 1 small onion, sliced into thin rings
- Sour cream
- Tortilla chips (optional)

1. Split each chicken breast in half lengthwise.
2. Mix lime juice, cumin, and salt together and brush on all surfaces of chicken breasts.
3. Place in air fryer basket and air fry at 390ºF (199ºC) for 12 to 15 minutes, until well done.

4. Divide the cheese evenly over chicken breasts and cook for an additional minute to melt cheese.
5. While chicken is cooking, heat refried beans on stovetop or in microwave.
6. When ready to serve, divide beans among 4 plates. Place chicken breasts on top of beans and spoon salsa over. Arrange the lettuce, tomatoes, and avocados artfully on each plate and scatter with the onion rings.
7. Pass sour cream at the table and serve with tortilla chips if desired.

Per Serving:calories: 497 / fat: 27g / protein: 38g / carbs: 26g / fiber: 12g / sodium: 722mg

Crispy Mediterranean Chicken Thighs

Prep time: 5 minutes / Cook time: 30 to 35 minutes / Serves 6

- 2 tablespoons extra-virgin olive oil
- 2 teaspoons dried rosemary
- 1½ teaspoons ground cumin
- 1½ teaspoons ground coriander
- ¾ teaspoon dried oregano
- ⅛ teaspoon salt
- 6 bone-in, skin-on chicken thighs (about 3 pounds / 1.4 kg)

1. Preheat the oven to 450ºF (235ºC). Line a baking sheet with parchment paper.
2. Place the olive oil and spices into a large bowl and mix together, making a paste. Add the chicken and mix together until evenly coated. Place on the prepared baking sheet.
3. Bake for 30 to 35 minutes, or until golden brown and the chicken registers an internal temperature of 165ºF (74ºC).

Per Serving:calories: 440 / fat: 34g / protein: 30g / carbs: 1g / fiber: 0g / sodium: 180mg

Buffalo Chicken Cheese Sticks

Prep time: 5 minutes / Cook time: 8 minutes / Serves 2

- 1 cup shredded cooked chicken
- ¼ cup buffalo sauce
- 1 cup shredded Mozzarella cheese
- 1 large egg
- ¼ cup crumbled feta

1. In a large bowl, mix all ingredients except the feta. Cut a piece of parchment to fit your air fryer basket and press the mixture into a ½-inch-thick circle.
2. Sprinkle the mixture with feta and place into the air fryer basket.
3. Adjust the temperature to 400ºF (204ºC) and air fry for 8 minutes.
4. After 5 minutes, flip over the cheese mixture.
5. Allow to cool 5 minutes before cutting into sticks. Serve warm.

Per Serving:calories: 413 / fat: 25g / protein: 43g / carbs: 3g / fiber: 0g / sodium: 453mg

Braised Chicken with Mushrooms and Tomatoes

Prep time: 20 minutes / Cook time: 25 minutes / Serves 4
- 1 tablespoon extra-virgin olive oil
- 1 pound (454 g) portobello mushroom caps, gills removed, caps halved and sliced ½ inch thick
- 1 onion, chopped fine
- ¾ teaspoon salt, divided
- 4 garlic cloves, minced
- 1 tablespoon tomato paste
- 1 tablespoon all-purpose flour
- 2 teaspoons minced fresh sage
- ½ cup dry red wine
- 1 (14½ ounces / 411 g) can diced tomatoes, drained
- 4 (5 to 7 ounces / 142 to 198 g) bone-in chicken thighs, skin removed, trimmed
- ¼ teaspoon pepper
- 2 tablespoons chopped fresh parsley
- Shaved Parmesan cheese

1. Using highest sauté function, heat oil in Instant Pot until shimmering. Add mushrooms, onion, and ¼ teaspoon salt. Partially cover and cook until mushrooms are softened and have released their liquid, about 5 minutes. Stir in garlic, tomato paste, flour, and sage and cook until fragrant, about 1 minute. Stir in wine, scraping up any browned bits, then stir in tomatoes.
2. Sprinkle chicken with remaining ½ teaspoon salt and pepper. Nestle chicken skinned side up into pot and spoon some of sauce on top. Lock lid in place and close pressure release valve. Select high pressure cook function and cook for 15 minutes.
3. Turn off Instant Pot and quick-release pressure. Carefully remove lid, allowing steam to escape away from you. Transfer chicken to serving dish, tent with aluminum foil, and let rest while finishing sauce.
4. Using highest sauté function, bring sauce to simmer and cook until thickened slightly, about 5 minutes. Season sauce with salt and pepper to taste. Spoon sauce over chicken and sprinkle with parsley and Parmesan. Serve.

Per Serving:calories: 230 / fat: 7g / protein: 21g / carbs: 15g / fiber:2g / sodium: 730mg

Lemon-Rosemary Spatchcock Chicken

Prep time: 20 minutes / Cook time: 45 minutes / Serves 6 to 8
- ½ cup extra-virgin olive oil, divided
- 1 (3- to 4-pound/ 1.4- to 1.8-kg) roasting chicken
- 8 garlic cloves, roughly chopped
- 2 to 4 tablespoons chopped fresh rosemary
- 2 teaspoons salt, divided
- 1 teaspoon freshly ground black pepper, divided
- 2 lemons, thinly sliced

1. Preheat the oven to 425°F(220ºC).
2. Pour 2 tablespoons olive oil in the bottom of a 9-by-13-inch baking dish or rimmed baking sheet and swirl to coat the bottom.
3. To spatchcock the bird, place the whole chicken breast-side down on a large work surface. Using a very sharp knife, cut along the backbone, starting at the tail end and working your way up to the neck. Pull apart the two sides, opening up the chicken. Flip it over, breast-side up, pressing down with your hands to flatten the bird. Transfer to the prepared baking dish.
4. Loosen the skin over the breasts and thighs by cutting a small incision and sticking one or two fingers inside to pull the skin away from the meat without removing it.
5. To prepare the filling, in a small bowl, combine ¼ cup olive oil, garlic, rosemary, 1 teaspoon salt, and ½ teaspoon pepper and whisk together.
6. Rub the garlic-herb oil evenly under the skin of each breast and each thigh. Add the lemon slices evenly to the same areas.
7. Whisk together the remaining 2 tablespoons olive oil, 1 teaspoon salt, and ½ teaspoon pepper and rub over the outside of the chicken.
8. Place in the oven, uncovered, and roast for 45 minutes, or until cooked through and golden brown. Allow to rest 5 minutes before carving to serve.

Per Serving:calories: 317 / fat: 18g / protein: 35g / carbs: 2g / fiber: 1g / sodium: 710mg

Chicken Breasts Stuffed with Feta and Spinach

Prep time: 10 minutes / Cook time: 14 minutes / Serves 4
- 1 cup chopped frozen spinach, thawed and drained well
- ½ cup crumbled feta cheese
- 4 (6-ounce / 170-g) boneless, skinless chicken breasts
- ¼ teaspoon salt
- ¼ teaspoon ground black pepper
- 2 tablespoons light olive oil, divided
- 1 cup water

1. In a small bowl, combine spinach and feta. Slice a pocket into each chicken breast along one side. Stuff one-quarter of the spinach and feta mixture into the pocket of each breast. Season chicken on all sides with salt and pepper. Set aside.
2. Press the Sauté button on the Instant Pot® and add 1 tablespoon oil. Add two chicken breasts and brown on both sides, about 3 minutes per side. Transfer to a plate and repeat with remaining 1 tablespoon oil and chicken.
3. Add water to pot and place rack inside. Place chicken breasts on rack. Close lid, set steam release to Sealing, press the Manual button, and set time to 8 minutes.
4. When the timer beeps, quick-release the pressure until the float valve drops. Press the Cancel button and open lid. Transfer chicken to a serving platter. Serve hot.

Per Serving:calories: 304 / fat: 17g / protein: 40g / carbs: 2g / fiber: 1g / sodium: 772mg

Apricot-Glazed Turkey Tenderloin

Prep time: 20 minutes / Cook time: 30 minutes / Serves 4

- Olive oil
- ¼ cup sugar-free apricot preserves
- ½ tablespoon spicy brown mustard
- 1½ pounds (680 g) turkey breast tenderloin
- Salt and freshly ground black pepper, to taste

1. Spray the air fryer basket lightly with olive oil.
2. In a small bowl, combine the apricot preserves and mustard to make a paste.
3. Season the turkey with salt and pepper. Spread the apricot paste all over the turkey.
4. Place the turkey in the air fryer basket and lightly spray with olive oil.
5. Air fry at 370ºF (188ºC) for 15 minutes. Flip the turkey over and lightly spray with olive oil. Air fry until the internal temperature reaches at least 170ºF (77ºC), an additional 10 to 15 minutes.
6. Let the turkey rest for 10 minutes before slicing and serving.

Per Serving:calories: 204 / fat: 3g / protein: 40g / carbs: 3g / fiber: 0g / sodium: 214mg

Pesto-Glazed Chicken Breasts

Prep time: 5 minutes / Cook time: 20 minutes / Serves 4

- ¼ cup plus 1 tablespoon extra-virgin olive oil, divided
- 4 boneless, skinless chicken breasts
- ½ teaspoon salt
- ¼ teaspoon freshly ground black pepper
- 1 packed cup fresh basil leaves
- 1 garlic clove, minced
- ¼ cup grated Parmesan cheese
- ¼ cup pine nuts

1. In a large, heavy skillet, heat 1 tablespoon of the olive oil over medium-high heat.
2. Season the chicken breasts on both sides with salt and pepper and place in the skillet. Cook for 10 minutes on the first side, then turn and cook for 5 minutes.
3. Meanwhile, in a blender or food processor, combine the basil, garlic, Parmesan cheese, and pine nuts, and blend on high. Gradually pour in the remaining ¼ cup olive oil and blend until smooth.
4. Spread 1 tablespoon pesto on each chicken breast, cover the skillet, and cook for 5 minutes. Serve the chicken pesto side up.

Per Serving:calories: 531 / fat: 28g / protein: 64g / carbs: 2g / fiber: 0g / sodium: 572mg

Turkey Thighs in Fig Sauce

Prep time: 15 minutes / Cook time: 14 minutes / Serves 4

- 4 (¾-pound / 340-g) bone-in turkey thighs, skin removed
- 1 large onion, peeled and quartered
- 2 large carrots, peeled and sliced
- ½ stalk celery, finely diced
- ½ cup balsamic vinegar
- 2 tablespoons tomato paste
- 1 cup low-sodium chicken broth
- ½ teaspoon salt
- ¾ teaspoon ground black pepper
- 12 dried figs, cut in half

1. Add the turkey, onion, carrots, and celery to the Instant Pot®. Whisk vinegar, tomato paste, broth, salt, and pepper in a small bowl. Pour into pot. Add figs. Close lid, set steam release to Sealing, press the Manual button, and set time to 14 minutes. When the timer beeps, let pressure release naturally, about 25 minutes.
2. Open the lid. Transfer thighs, carrots, and figs to a serving platter. Tent loosely with aluminum foil and keep warm while you finish the sauce.
3. Strain pan juices. Discard onion and celery. Skim and discard fat. Pour strained sauce over the thighs. Serve immediately.

Per Serving:calories: 565 / fat: 17g / protein: 68g / carbs: 26g / fiber: 5g / sodium: 685mg

Bruschetta Chicken Burgers

Prep time: 15 minutes / Cook time: 15 minutes / Serves 2

- 1 tablespoon olive oil
- 3 tablespoons finely minced onion
- 2 garlic cloves, minced
- 1 teaspoon dried basil
- ¼ teaspoon salt
- 3 tablespoons minced sun-dried tomatoes packed in olive oil
- 8 ounces (227 g) ground chicken breast
- 3 pieces small mozzarella balls (ciliegine), minced

1. Heat the grill to high heat (about 400°F/ 205ºC) and oil the grill grates. Alternatively, you can cook these in a nonstick skillet.
2. Heat the olive oil in a small skillet over medium-high heat. Add the onion and garlic and sauté for 5 minutes, until softened. Stir in the basil. Remove from the heat and place in a medium bowl.
3. Add the salt, sun-dried tomatoes, and ground chicken and stir to combine. Mix in the mozzarella balls.
4. Divide the chicken mixture in half and form into two burgers, each about ¾-inch thick.
5. Place the burgers on the grill and cook for five minutes, or until golden on the bottom. Flip the burgers over and grill for another five minutes, or until they reach an internal temperature of 165°F(74ºC).
6. If cooking the burgers in a skillet on the stovetop, heat a nonstick skillet over medium-high heat and add the burgers. Cook them for 5 to 6 minutes on the first side, or until golden brown on the bottom. Flip the burgers and cook for an additional 5 minutes, or until they reach an internal temperature of 165°F(74ºC).

Per Serving:calories: 301 / fat: 17g / protein: 32g / carbs:

6g / fiber: 1g / sodium: 725mg

Cajun-Breaded Chicken Bites

Prep time: 10 minutes / Cook time: 12 minutes / Serves 4

- 1 pound (454 g) boneless, skinless chicken breasts, cut into 1-inch cubes
- ½ cup heavy whipping cream
- ½ teaspoon salt
- ¼ teaspoon ground black pepper
- 1 ounce (28 g) plain pork rinds, finely crushed
- ¼ cup unflavored whey protein powder
- ½ teaspoon Cajun seasoning

1. Place chicken in a medium bowl and pour in cream. Stir to coat. Sprinkle with salt and pepper.
2. In a separate large bowl, combine pork rinds, protein powder, and Cajun seasoning. Remove chicken from cream, shaking off any excess, and toss in dry mix until fully coated.
3. Place bites into ungreased air fryer basket. Adjust the temperature to 400ºF (204ºC) and air fry for 12 minutes, shaking the basket twice during cooking. Bites will be done when golden brown and have an internal temperature of at least 165ºF (74ºC). Serve warm.

Per Serving:calories: 272 / fat: 13g / protein: 35g / carbs: 2g / fiber: 1g / sodium: 513mg

Chicken with Lentils and Butternut Squash

Prep time: 15 minutes / Cook time: 28 minutes / Serves 4

- 2 large shallots, halved and sliced thin, divided
- 5 teaspoons extra-virgin olive oil, divided
- ½ teaspoon grated lemon zest plus 2 teaspoons juice
- 1 teaspoon table salt, divided
- 4 (5 to 7 ounces / 142 to 198 g) bone-in chicken thighs, trimmed
- ¼ teaspoon pepper
- 2 garlic cloves, minced
- 1½ teaspoons caraway seeds
- 1 teaspoon ground coriander
- 1 teaspoon ground cumin
- ½ teaspoon paprika
- ⅛ teaspoon cayenne pepper
- 2 cups chicken broth
- 1 cup French green lentils, picked over and rinsed
- 2 pounds (907 g) butternut squash, peeled, seeded, and cut into 1½-inch pieces
- 1 cup fresh parsley or cilantro leaves

1. Combine half of shallots, 1 tablespoon oil, lemon zest and juice, and ¼ teaspoon salt in bowl; set aside. Pat chicken dry with paper towels and sprinkle with ½ teaspoon salt and pepper. Using highest sauté function, heat remaining 2 teaspoons oil in Instant Pot for 5 minutes (or until just smoking). Place chicken skin side down in pot and cook until well browned on first side, about 5 minutes; transfer to plate.
2. Add remaining shallot and remaining ¼ teaspoon salt

to fat left in pot and cook, using highest sauté function, until shallot is softened, about 2 minutes. Stir in garlic, caraway, coriander, cumin, paprika, and cayenne and cook until fragrant, about 30 seconds. Stir in broth, scraping up any browned bits, then stir in lentils.
3. Nestle chicken skin side up into lentils and add any accumulated juices. Arrange squash on top. Lock lid in place and close pressure release valve. Select high pressure cook function and cook for 15 minutes.
4. Turn off Instant Pot and quick-release pressure. Carefully remove lid, allowing steam to escape away from you. Transfer chicken to plate and discard skin, if desired. Season lentil mixture with salt and pepper to taste. Add parsley to shallot mixture and toss to combine. Serve chicken with lentil mixture, topping individual portions with shallot-parsley salad.

Per Serving:calories: 513 / fat: 14g / protein: 42g / carbs: 60g / fiber: 17g / sodium: 773mg

Lemon Chicken with Artichokes and Crispy Kale

Prep time: 15 minutes / Cook time: 35 minutes / Serves 4

- 3 tablespoons extra-virgin olive oil, divided
- 2 tablespoons lemon juice
- Zest of 1 lemon
- 2 garlic cloves, minced
- 2 teaspoons dried rosemary
- ½ teaspoon kosher salt
- ¼ teaspoon freshly ground black pepper
- 1½ pounds (680 g) boneless, skinless chicken breast
- 2 (14-ounce / 397-g) cans artichoke hearts, drained
- 1 bunch (about 6 ounces / 170 g) lacinato kale, stemmed and torn or chopped into pieces

1. In a large bowl or zip-top bag, combine 2 tablespoons of the olive oil, the lemon juice, lemon zest, garlic, rosemary, salt, and black pepper. Mix well and then add the chicken and artichokes. Marinate for at least 30 minutes, and up to 4 hours in the refrigerator.
2. Preheat the oven to 350ºF (180ºC). Line a baking sheet with parchment paper or foil. Remove the chicken and artichokes from the marinade and spread them in a single layer on the baking sheet. Roast for 15 minutes, turn the chicken over, and roast another 15 minutes. Remove the baking sheet and put the chicken, artichokes, and juices on a platter or large plate. Tent with foil to keep warm.
3. Change the oven temperature to broil. In a large bowl, combine the kale with the remaining 1 tablespoon of the olive oil. Arrange the kale on the baking sheet and broil until golden brown in spots and as crispy as you like, about 3 to 5 minutes. Place the kale on top of the chicken and artichokes.

Per Serving:calories: 430 / fat: 16g / protein: 46g / carbs: 29g / fiber: 19g / sodium: 350mg

Pecan Turkey Cutlets

Prep time: 10 minutes / Cook time: 10 to 12 minutes per batch / Serves 4

- ¾ cup panko bread crumbs
- ¼ teaspoon salt
- ¼ teaspoon pepper
- ¼ teaspoon dry mustard
- ¼ teaspoon poultry seasoning
- ½ cup pecans
- ¼ cup cornstarch
- 1 egg, beaten
- 1 pound (454 g) turkey cutlets, ½-inch thick
- Salt and pepper, to taste
- Oil for misting or cooking spray

1. Place the panko crumbs, ¼ teaspoon salt, ¼ teaspoon pepper, mustard, and poultry seasoning in food processor. Process until crumbs are finely crushed. Add pecans and process in short pulses just until nuts are finely chopped. Go easy so you don't overdo it!
2. Preheat the air fryer to 360ºF (182ºC).
3. Place cornstarch in one shallow dish and beaten egg in another. Transfer coating mixture from food processor into a third shallow dish.
4. Sprinkle turkey cutlets with salt and pepper to taste.
5. Dip cutlets in cornstarch and shake off excess. Then dip in beaten egg and roll in crumbs, pressing to coat well. Spray both sides with oil or cooking spray.
6. Place 2 cutlets in air fryer basket in a single layer and cook for 10 to 12 minutes or until juices run clear.
7. Repeat step 6 to cook remaining cutlets.

Per Serving:calories: 340 / fat: 13g / protein: 31g / carbs: 24g / fiber: 4g / sodium: 447mg

Mediterranean White Wine Chicken

Serves: 4/Prep time: 35 minutes / Cook time: 15 minutes

- 3 garlic cloves, minced
- ½ cup diced onion
- 3 cups tomatoes, chopped
- 2 tsp olive oil
- 4 skinless, boneless chicken breast halves
- ½ cup plus 2 tbsp white wine
- 1 tbsp basil, chopped
- ¼ cup parsley, chopped
- 2 tsp thyme, chopped
- Ground black pepper and salt to taste

1. Over medium stove flame, heat the oil and 2 tbsp white wine in a skillet or saucepan (preferably of medium size).
2. Add the chicken and fry until evenly brown. Set it aside.
3. Add the garlic and sauté for 30 seconds. Add the onion and sauté for 2–3 minutes.
4. Mix in the tomatoes and bring the mixture to a simmer.
5. Reduce the heat and mix in ½ cup white wine; simmer the mix for 10 minutes and add the basil and thyme.

Cook for another 5 minutes.

6. Add the chicken; combine and cook over low heat for 7–10 minutes. Add the parsley on top. Season with black pepper and salt.
7. Serve warm.

Per Serving:Calories: 293 / Fat: 8 g / Carbs: 14 g / Fiber: 3 g /Protein: 36 g

Arugula Fig Chicken

Serves: 2/Prep time: 15 minutes / Cook time: 30 minutes

- 2 tsp cornstarch
- 2 garlic cloves, crushed
- ¾ cup Mission figs, chopped
- ¼ cup black or green olives, chopped
- 1 bag baby arugula
- ½ cup chicken broth
- 8 skinless chicken thighs
- 2 tsp olive oil
- 2 tsp brown sugar
- ½ cup red wine vinegar
- Ground black pepper and salt, to taste

1. Over medium stove flame, heat the oil in a skillet or saucepan (preferably of medium size).
2. Add the chicken, sprinkle with some salt and cook until evenly brown. Set it aside.
3. Add and sauté the garlic.
4. In a mixing bowl, combine the vinegar, broth, cornstarch and sugar. Add the mixture into the pan and simmer until the sauce thickens.
5. Add the figs and olives; simmer for a few minutes. Serve warm with chopped arugula on top.

Per Serving:Calories: 364 / Fat: 14 g / Carbs: 29 g / Fiber: 5 g /Protein: 31 g

Chicken Loaf

Serves: 2/Prep time: 10 minutes / Cook time: 40 minutes

- 2 cups ground chicken
- 1 egg, beaten
- 1 tbsp fresh dill, chopped
- 1 garlic clove, chopped
- ½ tsp salt
- 1 tsp chili flakes
- 1 onion, minced

1. In the mixing bowl, combine all Ingredients and mix up until you get a smooth mass.
2. Then line the loaf dish with baking paper and put the ground chicken mixture inside.
3. Flatten the surface well.
4. Bake the chicken loaf for 40 minutes at 355°F.
5. Then chill the chicken loaf to room temperature and remove it from the loaf dish.
6. Slice it.

Per Serving:Calories: 167 / Fat: 6.2 g / Fiber: 0.8 g / Carbs: 3.4 g / Protein: 32.2 g

Chapter 4 Beef, Pork, and Lamb

Ground Lamb with Lentils and Pomegranate Seeds

Prep time: 15 minutes / Cook time: 15 minutes / Serves 4

- 1 tablespoon extra-virgin olive oil
- ½ pound (227 g) ground lamb
- 1 teaspoon red pepper flakes
- ½ teaspoon ground cumin
- ½ teaspoon kosher salt
- ¼ teaspoon freshly ground black pepper
- 2 garlic cloves, minced
- 2 cups cooked, drained lentils
- 1 hothouse or English cucumber, diced
- ⅓ cup fresh mint, chopped
- ⅓ cup fresh parsley, chopped
- Zest of 1 lemon
- 1 cup plain Greek yogurt
- ½ cup pomegranate seeds

1. Heat the olive oil in a large skillet or sauté pan over medium-high heat. Add the lamb and season with the red pepper flakes, cumin, salt, and black pepper. Cook the lamb without stirring until the bottom is brown and crispy, about 5 minutes. Stir and cook for another 5 minutes. Using a spatula, break up the lamb into smaller pieces. Add the garlic and cook, stirring occasionally, for 1 minute. Transfer the lamb mixture to a medium bowl.
2. Add the lentils to the skillet and cook, stirring occasionally, until brown and crisp, about 5 minutes. Return the lamb to the skillet, mix, and warm through, about 3 minutes. Transfer to the large bowl. Add the cucumber, mint, parsley, and lemon zest, mixing together gently.
3. Spoon the yogurt into 4 bowls and top each with some of the lamb mixture. Garnish with the pomegranate seeds.

Per Serving:calories: 370 / fat: 18g / protein: 24g / carbs: 30g / fiber: 10g / sodium: 197mg

Smoky Pork Tenderloin

Prep time: 5 minutes / Cook time: 19 to 22 minutes / Serves 6

- 1½ pounds (680 g) pork tenderloin
- 1 tablespoon avocado oil
- 1 teaspoon chili powder
- 1 teaspoon smoked paprika
- 1 teaspoon garlic powder
- 1 teaspoon sea salt
- 1 teaspoon freshly ground black pepper

1. Pierce the tenderloin all over with a fork and rub the oil all over the meat.
2. In a small dish, stir together the chili powder, smoked paprika, garlic powder, salt, and pepper.
3. Rub the spice mixture all over the tenderloin.

4. Set the air fryer to 400ºF (204ºC). Place the pork in the air fryer basket and air fry for 10 minutes. Flip the tenderloin and cook for 9 to 12 minutes more, until an instant-read thermometer reads at least 145ºF (63ºC).
5. Allow the tenderloin to rest for 5 minutes, then slice and serve.

Per Serving:calories: 149 / fat: 5g / protein: 24g / carbs: 1g / fiber: 0g / sodium: 461mg

Lamb with Olives and Potatoes

Prep time: 20 minutes / Cook time: 4 hours / Serves 4

- 1¼ pounds (567 g) small potatoes, halved
- 4 large shallots, cut into ½-inch wedges
- 3 cloves garlic, minced
- 1 tablespoon lemon zest
- 3 sprigs fresh rosemary
- Coarse sea salt
- Black pepper
- 4 tablespoons all-purpose flour
- ¾ cup chicken stock
- 3½ pounds (1.6 kg) lamb shanks, cut crosswise into 1½-inch pieces and fat trimmed
- 2 tablespoons extra-virgin olive oil
- ½ cup dry white wine
- 1 cup pitted green olives, halved
- 2 tablespoons lemon juice

1. Combine the potatoes, shallots, garlic, lemon zest, and rosemary sprigs in the slow cooker. Season with salt and pepper.
2. In a small bowl, whisk together 1 tablespoon of the flour and the stock. Add to the slow cooker.
3. Place the remaining 3 tablespoons flour on a plate. Season the lamb with salt and pepper; then coat in the flour, shaking off any excess.
4. In a large skillet over medium-high, heat the olive oil. In batches, cook the lamb until browned on all sides, about 10 minutes. Transfer to the slow cooker.
5. Add the wine to the skillet and cook, stiring with a wooden spoon and scraping up the flavorful browned bits from the bottom of the pan, until reduced by half, about 2 minutes. Then add to the slow cooker.
6. Cover and cook until the lamb is tender, on high for about 3½ hours, or on low for 7 hours.
7. Stir in olive halves, then cover, and cook 20 additional minutes.
8. To serve, transfer the lamb and vegetables to warm plates.
9. Skim the fat from the cooking liquid, then stir in the lemon juice, and season the sauce with salt and pepper.
10. Serve the sauce with the lamb and vegetables.

Per Serving:calories: 765 / fat: 26g / protein: 93g / carbs: 38g / fiber: 5g / sodium: 596mg

Short Ribs with Chimichurri

Prep time: 30 minutes / Cook time: 13 minutes / Serves 4

- 1 pound (454 g) boneless short ribs
- 1½ teaspoons sea salt, divided
- ½ teaspoon freshly ground black pepper, divided
- ½ cup fresh parsley leaves
- ½ cup fresh cilantro leaves
- 1 teaspoon minced garlic
- 1 tablespoon freshly squeezed lemon juice
- ½ teaspoon ground cumin
- ¼ teaspoon red pepper flakes
- 2 tablespoons extra-virgin olive oil
- Avocado oil spray

1. Pat the short ribs dry with paper towels. Sprinkle the ribs all over with 1 teaspoon salt and ¼ teaspoon black pepper. Let sit at room temperature for 45 minutes.
2. Meanwhile, place the parsley, cilantro, garlic, lemon juice, cumin, red pepper flakes, the remaining ½ teaspoon salt, and the remaining ¼ teaspoon black pepper in a blender or food processor. With the blender running, slowly drizzle in the olive oil. Blend for about 1 minute, until the mixture is smooth and well combined.
3. Set the air fryer to 400ºF (204ºC). Spray both sides of the ribs with oil. Place in the basket and air fry for 8 minutes. Flip and cook for another 5 minutes, until an instant-read thermometer reads 125ºF (52ºC) for medium-rare (or to your desired doneness).
4. Allow the meat to rest for 5 to 10 minutes, then slice. Serve warm with the chimichurri sauce.

Per Serving:calories: 251 / fat: 17g / protein: 25g / carbs: 1g / fiber: 1g / sodium: 651mg

Lamb Shanks and Potatoes

Prep time: 10 minutes / Cook time: 8 hours / Serves 6

- 1(15-ounce/ 425-g) can crushed tomatoes in purée
- 3 tablespoons tomato paste
- 2 tablespoons apricot jam
- 6 cloves garlic, thinly sliced
- 3 strips orange zest
- ¾ teaspoon crushed dried rosemary
- ½ teaspoon ground ginger
- ½ teaspoon ground cinnamon
- Coarse sea salt
- Black pepper
- 3½ pounds (1.6 kg) lamb shanks, trimmed of excess fat and cut into 1½-inch slices
- 1¼ pounds (567 g) small new potatoes, halved (or quartered, if large)

1. Stir together the tomatoes and purée, tomato paste, jam, garlic, orange zest, rosemary, ginger, and cinnamon in the slow cooker. Season with salt and pepper.
2. Add the lamb and potatoes, and spoon the tomato mixture over the lamb to coat.
3. Cover and cook until the lamb and potatoes are tender,

on low for 8 hours or on high for 5 hours. Season again with salt and pepper, if desired.
4. Serve hot.

Per Serving:calories: 438 / fat: 10g / protein: 62g / carbs: 26g / fiber: 4g / sodium: 248mg

Mustard Lamb Chops

Prep time: 5 minutes / Cook time: 14 minutes / Serves 4

- Oil, for spraying
- 1 tablespoon Dijon mustard
- 2 teaspoons lemon juice
- ½ teaspoon dried tarragon
- ¼ teaspoon salt
- ¼ teaspoon freshly ground black pepper
- 4 (1¼-inch-thick) loin lamb chops

1. Preheat the air fryer to 390ºF (199ºC). Line the air fryer basket with parchment and spray lightly with oil.
2. In a small bowl, mix together the mustard, lemon juice, tarragon, salt, and black pepper.
3. Pat dry the lamb chops with a paper towel. Brush the chops on both sides with the mustard mixture.
4. Place the chops in the prepared basket. You may need to work in batches, depending on the size of your air fryer.
5. Cook for 8 minutes, flip, and cook for another 6 minutes, or until the internal temperature reaches 125ºF (52ºC) for rare, 145ºF (63ºC) for medium-rare, or 155ºF (68ºC) for medium.

Per Serving:calories: 96 / fat: 4g / protein: 14g / carbs: 0g / fiber: 0g / sodium: 233mg

Braised Pork Loin with Port and Dried Plums

Prep time: 20 minutes / Cook time: 6 hours 25 minutes / Serves 10

- 1 (3¼-pound / 1.5-kg)boneless pork loin roast, trimmed
- 1½ teaspoons black pepper
- 1 teaspoon sea salt
- 1 teaspoon dry mustard
- 1 teaspoon dried sage
- ½ teaspoon dried thyme
- 1 tablespoon olive oil
- 2 large yellow onions, sliced
- 1 cup finely chopped leek, white and light green parts, rinsed
- 1 large carrot, finely chopped
- ½ cup port or other sweet red wine
- ⅔ cup chicken stock
- 1 cup pitted dried plums (about 20)
- 2 bay leaves
- 2 tablespoons cornstarch
- 2 tablespoons water

1. Cut the pork roast in half crosswise.
2. Combine the pepper, salt, dry mustard, sage, and thyme in a small bowl. Rub the seasoning mixture over the

surface of the roast halves.

3. Heat a Dutch oven over medium-high heat. Add the olive oil to pan and swirl to coat. Add the pork and brown on all sides, about 4 minutes. Place the pork in the slow cooker.

4. Add the onions, leek, and carrot to the Dutch oven, and sauté for 5 minutes or until vegetables are golden.

5. Stir in the wine and stock, and cook for about 1 minute, scraping the bottom of the pan with a wooden spoon to loosen up the flavorful browned bits.

6. Pour the wine-vegetable mixture over the pork in slow cooker. Add the plums and bay leaves.

7. Cover and cook on high for 1 hour. Reduce the heat to low, and cook for 5 to 6 hours, or until the pork is tender.

8. Remove the pork from the slow cooker, set aside on a platter, and keep warm. Increase the heat to high.

9. Combine the cornstarch and 2 tablespoons water in a small bowl. Whisk to combine, and then whisk into the cooking liquid in the slow cooker.

10. Cook, uncovered, for 15 minutes or until the sauce is thick, stirring frequently.

11. Discard the bay leaves. Slice the pork, and serve hot with the sauce.

Per Serving:calories: 269 / fat: 8g / protein: 37g / carbs: 9g / fiber: 1g / sodium: 329mg

Indian Mint and Chile Kebabs

Prep time: 30 minutes / Cook time: 15 minutes / Serves 4
- 1 pound (454 g) ground lamb
- ½ cup finely minced onion
- ¼ cup chopped fresh mint
- ¼ cup chopped fresh cilantro
- 1 tablespoon minced garlic
- ½ teaspoon ground turmeric
- ½ teaspoon cayenne pepper
- ¼ teaspoon ground cardamom
- ¼ teaspoon ground cinnamon
- 1 teaspoon kosher salt

1. In the bowl of a stand mixer fitted with the paddle attachment, combine the lamb, onion, mint, cilantro, garlic, turmeric, cayenne, cardamom, cinnamon, and salt. Mix on low speed until you have a sticky mess of spiced meat. If you have time, let the mixture stand at room temperature for 30 minutes (or cover and refrigerate for up to a day or two, until you're ready to make the kebabs).

2. Divide the meat into eight equal portions. Form each into a long sausage shape. Place the kebabs in a single layer in the air fryer basket. Set the air fryer to 350°F (177°C) for 10 minutes. Increase the air fryer temperature to 400°F (204°C) and cook for 3 to 4 minutes more to brown the kebabs. Use a meat thermometer to ensure the kebabs have reached an internal temperature of 160°F / 71°C (medium).

Per Serving:calories: 231 / fat: 14g / protein: 23g / carbs: 3g / fiber: 1g / sodium: 648mg

Lebanese Ground Meat with Rice

Prep time: 10 minutes / Cook time: 35 minutes / Serves 6
- 3 tablespoons olive oil, divided
- 4 ounces (113 g) cremini (baby bella) mushrooms, sliced
- ½ red onion, finely chopped
- 2 garlic cloves, minced
- 1 pound (454 g) lean ground beef
- ¾ teaspoon ground cinnamon
- ¼ teaspoon ground cloves
- ¼ teaspoon ground nutmeg
- Sea salt
- Freshly ground black pepper
- 1½ cups basmati rice
- 2¾ cups chicken broth
- ½ cup pine nuts
- ½ cup coarsely chopped fresh Italian parsley

1. In a sauté pan, heat 2 tablespoons of olive oil over medium-high heat. Add the mushrooms, onion, and garlic and sauté until the mushrooms release their liquid and the onion becomes translucent, about 5 minutes. Add the ground beef, cinnamon, cloves, and nutmeg and season with salt and pepper. Reduce the heat to medium and cook, stirring often, for 5 to 7 minutes, until the meat is cooked through. Remove the beef mixture from the pan with a slotted spoon and set aside in a medium bowl.

2. In the same pan, heat the remaining 1 tablespoon of olive oil over medium-high heat. Add the rice and fry for about 5 minutes. Return the meat mixture to the pan and mix well to combine with the rice. Add the broth and bring to a boil, then reduce the heat to low, cover, and simmer for 15 minutes, or until you can fluff the rice with a fork.

3. Add the pine nuts and mix well. Garnish with the parsley and serve.

Per Serving:calories: 422 / fat: 19g / protein: 22g / carbs: 43g / fiber: 2g / sodium: 81mg

Greek-Style Ground Beef Pita Sandwiches

Prep Time: 15 minutes / Cook Time: 10 minutes / Serves 2
- For the beef
- 1 tablespoon olive oil
- ½ medium onion, minced
- 2 garlic cloves, minced
- 6 ounces (170 g) lean ground beef
- 1 teaspoon dried oregano
- For the yogurt sauce
- ⅓ cup plain Greek yogurt
- 1 ounce (28 g) crumbled feta cheese (about 3 tablespoons)
- 1 tablespoon minced fresh parsley
- 1 tablespoon minced scallion
- 1 tablespoon freshly squeezed lemon juice
- Pinch salt
- For the sandwiches
- 2 large Greek-style pitas
- ½ cup cherry tomatoes, halved

- 1 cup diced cucumber
- Salt
- Freshly ground black pepper

1. Make the beef Heat the olive oil in a sauté pan over medium high-heat. Add the onion, garlic, and ground beef and sauté for 7 minutes, breaking up the meat well. When the meat is no longer pink, drain off any fat and stir in the oregano. Turn off the heat. Make the yogurt sauce In a small bowl, combine the yogurt, feta, parsley, scallion, lemon juice, and salt. To assemble the sandwiches 1. Warm the pitas in the microwave for 20 seconds each.
2. To serve, spread some of the yogurt sauce over each warm pita. Top with the ground beef, cherry tomatoes, and diced cucumber. Season with salt and pepper. Add additional yogurt sauce if desired.

Per Serving:calories: 541 / fat: 21g / protein: 29g / carbs: 57g / fiber: 4g / sodium: 694mg

Pork Stew with Leeks

Prep time: 15 minutes / Cook time: 55 minutes / Serves 4
- 2 tablespoons olive oil
- 2 leeks, white parts only, chopped and rinsed well
- 1 onion, chopped
- 2 garlic cloves, minced
- 1 carrot, chopped
- 1 celery stalk, chopped
- 2 pounds (907 g) boneless pork loin chops, cut into 2-inch pieces
- 4 cups beef broth
- 2 cups water
- 3 potatoes, peeled and chopped
- 1 tablespoon tomato paste
- Sea salt
- Freshly ground black pepper

1. In a large skillet, heat the olive oil over medium-high heat. Add the leeks, onion, and garlic and sauté for 5 minutes, or until softened. Add the carrot and celery and cook for 3 minutes. Add the pork, broth, water, potatoes, and tomato paste and bring to a boil.
2. Reduce the heat to low, cover, and simmer for 45 minutes, or until the pork is cooked through. Season to taste with salt and pepper and serve.

Per Serving:calories: 623 / fat: 16g / protein: 57g / carbs: 60g / fiber: 8g / sodium: 193mg

Herb-Crusted Lamb Chops

Prep time: 10 minutes / Cook time: 5 minutes / Serves 2
- 1 large egg
- 2 cloves garlic, minced
- ¼ cup pork dust
- ¼ cup powdered Parmesan cheese
- 1 tablespoon chopped fresh oregano leaves
- 1 tablespoon chopped fresh rosemary leaves
- 1 teaspoon chopped fresh thyme leaves

- ½ teaspoon ground black pepper
- 4 (1-inch-thick) lamb chops
- For Garnish/Serving (Optional):
- Sprigs of fresh oregano
- Sprigs of fresh rosemary
- Sprigs of fresh thyme
- Lavender flowers
- Lemon slices

1. Spray the air fryer basket with avocado oil. Preheat the air fryer to 400ºF (204ºC).
2. Beat the egg in a shallow bowl, add the garlic, and stir well to combine. In another shallow bowl, mix together the pork dust, Parmesan, herbs, and pepper.
3. One at a time, dip the lamb chops into the egg mixture, shake off the excess egg, and then dredge them in the Parmesan mixture. Use your hands to coat the chops well in the Parmesan mixture and form a nice crust on all sides; if necessary, dip the chops again in both the egg and the Parmesan mixture.
4. Place the lamb chops in the air fryer basket, leaving space between them, and air fry for 5 minutes, or until the internal temperature reaches 145ºF (63ºC) for medium doneness. Allow to rest for 10 minutes before serving.
5. Garnish with sprigs of oregano, rosemary, and thyme, and lavender flowers, if desired. Serve with lemon slices, if desired.
6. Best served fresh. Store leftovers in an airtight container in the fridge for up to 4 days. Serve chilled over a salad, or reheat in a 350ºF (177ºC) air fryer for 3 minutes, or until heated through.

Per Serving:calories: 510 / fat: 42g / protein: 30g / carbs: 3g / fiber: 1g / sodium: 380mg

Rosemary Roast Beef

Prep time: 30 minutes / Cook time: 30 to 35 minutes / Serves 8
- 1 (2-pound / 907-g) top round beef roast, tied with kitchen string
- Sea salt and freshly ground black pepper, to taste
- 2 teaspoons minced garlic
- 2 tablespoons finely chopped fresh rosemary
- ¼ cup avocado oil

1. Season the roast generously with salt and pepper.
2. In a small bowl, whisk together the garlic, rosemary, and avocado oil. Rub this all over the roast. Cover loosely with aluminum foil or plastic wrap and refrigerate for at least 12 hours or up to 2 days.
3. Remove the roast from the refrigerator and allow to sit at room temperature for about 1 hour.
4. Set the air fryer to 325ºF (163ºC). Place the roast in the air fryer basket and roast for 15 minutes. Flip the roast and cook for 15 to 20 minutes more, until the meat is browned and an instant-read thermometer reads 120ºF (49ºC) at the thickest part (for medium-rare).

5. Transfer the meat to a cutting board, and let it rest for 15 minutes before thinly slicing and serving.

Per Serving:calories: 208 / fat: 12g / protein: 25g / carbs: 0g / fiber: 0g / sodium: 68mg

Beef Meatballs in Garlic Cream Sauce

Prep time: 15 minutes / Cook time: 6 to 8 hours / Serves 4

- For the Sauce:
- 1 cup low-sodium vegetable broth or low-sodium chicken broth
- 1 tablespoon extra-virgin olive oil
- 2 garlic cloves, minced
- 1 tablespoon dried onion flakes
- 1 teaspoon dried rosemary
- 2 tablespoons freshly squeezed lemon juice
- Pinch sea salt
- Pinch freshly ground black pepper
- For the Meatballs:
- 1 pound (454 g) raw ground beef
- 1 large egg
- 2 tablespoons bread crumbs
- 1 teaspoon ground cumin
- 1 teaspoon salt
- ½ teaspoon freshly ground black pepper
- To Finish
- 2 cups plain Greek yogurt
- 2 tablespoons chopped fresh parsley

1. Make the Sauce: 1. In a medium bowl, whisk together the vegetable broth, olive oil, garlic, onion flakes, rosemary, lemon juice, salt, and pepper until combined. Make the Meatballs:
2. In a large bowl, mix together the ground beef, egg, bread crumbs, cumin, salt, and pepper until combined. Shape the meat mixture into 10 to 12 (2½-inch) meatballs.
3. Pour the sauce into the slow cooker.
4. Add the meatballs to the slow cooker.
5. Cover the cooker and cook for 6 to 8 hours on Low heat.
6. Stir in the yogurt. Replace the cover on the cooker and cook for 15 to 30 minutes on Low heat, or until the sauce has thickened.
7. Garnish with fresh parsley for serving.

Per Serving:calories: 345 / fat: 20g / protein: 29g / carbs: 13g / fiber: 1g / sodium: 842mg

Mediterranean Pork Chops

Prep time: 20 minutes / Cook time: 10 minutes / Serves 4

- ¼ cup extra-virgin olive oil
- 1 teaspoon smoked paprika
- 2 tablespoons fresh thyme leaves
- 1 teaspoon salt
- 4 pork loin chops, ½-inch-thick

1. In a small bowl, mix together the olive oil, paprika, thyme, and salt.
2. Put the pork chops in a plastic zip-top bag or a bowl and coat them with the spice mix. Let them marinate for 15 minutes.
3. Preheat a grill, grill pan, or lightly oiled skillet to high heat. Cook the pork chops for 4 minutes on each side. Serve with a Greek salad.

Per Serving:calories: 282 / fat: 23g / protein: 21g / carbs: 1g / fiber: 0g / sodium: 832mg

Tenderloin with Crispy Shallots

Prep time: 30 minutes / Cook time: 18 to 20 minutes / Serves 6

- 1½ pounds (680 g) beef tenderloin steaks
- Sea salt and freshly ground black pepper, to taste
- 4 medium shallots
- 1 teaspoon olive oil or avocado oil

1. Season both sides of the steaks with salt and pepper, and let them sit at room temperature for 45 minutes.
2. Set the air fryer to 400ºF (204ºC) and let it preheat for 5 minutes.
3. Working in batches if necessary, place the steaks in the air fryer basket in a single layer and air fry for 5 minutes. Flip and cook for 5 minutes longer, until an instant-read thermometer inserted in the center of the steaks registers 120ºF (49ºC) for medium-rare (or as desired). Remove the steaks and tent with aluminum foil to rest.
4. Set the air fryer to 300ºF (149ºC). In a medium bowl, toss the shallots with the oil. Place the shallots in the basket and air fry for 5 minutes, then give them a toss and cook for 3 to 5 minutes more, until crispy and golden brown.
5. Place the steaks on serving plates and arrange the shallots on top.

Per Serving:calories: 166 / fat: 8g / protein: 24g / carbs: 1g / fiber: 0g / sodium: 72mg

Garlic-Marinated Flank Steak

Prep time: 30 minutes / Cook time: 8 to 10 minutes / Serves 6

- ½ cup avocado oil
- ¼ cup coconut aminos
- 1 shallot, minced
- 1 tablespoon minced garlic
- 2 tablespoons chopped fresh oregano, or 2 teaspoons dried
- 1½ teaspoons sea salt
- 1 teaspoon freshly ground black pepper
- ¼ teaspoon red pepper flakes
- 2 pounds (907 g) flank steak

1. In a blender, combine the avocado oil, coconut aminos, shallot, garlic, oregano, salt, black pepper, and red pepper flakes. Process until smooth.
2. Place the steak in a zip-top plastic bag or shallow dish with the marinade. Seal the bag or cover the dish and marinate in the refrigerator for at least 2 hours or overnight.
3. Remove the steak from the bag and discard the marinade.
4. Set the air fryer to 400ºF (204ºC). Place the steak in the air fryer basket (if needed, cut into sections and work

in batches). Air fry for 4 to 6 minutes, flip the steak, and cook for another 4 minutes or until the internal temperature reaches 120ºF (49ºC) in the thickest part for medium-rare (or as desired).

Per Serving:calories: 373 / fat: 26g / protein: 33g / carbs: 1g / fiber: 0g / sodium: 672mg

Garlic Balsamic London Broil

Prep time: 30 minutes / Cook time: 8 to 10 minutes / Serves 8

- 2 pounds (907 g) London broil
- 3 large garlic cloves, minced
- 3 tablespoons balsamic vinegar
- 3 tablespoons whole-grain mustard
- 2 tablespoons olive oil
- Sea salt and ground black pepper, to taste
- ½ teaspoon dried hot red pepper flakes

1. Score both sides of the cleaned London broil.
2. Thoroughly combine the remaining ingredients; massage this mixture into the meat to coat it on all sides. Let it marinate for at least 3 hours.
3. Set the air fryer to 400ºF (204ºC); Then cook the London broil for 15 minutes. Flip it over and cook another 10 to 12 minutes. Bon appétit!

Per Serving:calories: 240 / fat: 15g / protein: 23g / carbs: 2g / fiber: 0g / sodium: 141mg

Italian Steak Rolls

Prep time: 30 minutes / Cook time: 9 minutes / Serves 4

- 1 tablespoon vegetable oil
- 2 cloves garlic, minced
- 2 teaspoons dried Italian seasoning
- 1 teaspoon kosher salt
- 1 teaspoon black pepper
- 1 pound (454 g) flank or skirt steak, ¼ to ½ inch thick
- 1 (10-ounce / 283-g) package frozen spinach, thawed and squeezed dry
- ½ cup diced jarred roasted red pepper
- 1 cup shredded Mozzarella cheese

1. In a large bowl, combine the oil, garlic, Italian seasoning, salt, and pepper. Whisk to combine. Add the steak to the bowl, turning to ensure the entire steak is covered with the seasonings. Cover and marinate at room temperature for 30 minutes or in the refrigerator for up to 24 hours.
2. Lay the steak on a flat surface. Spread the spinach evenly over the steak, leaving a ¼-inch border at the edge. Evenly top each steak with the red pepper and cheese.
3. Starting at a long end, roll up the steak as tightly as possible, ending seam side down. Use 2 or 3 wooden toothpicks to hold the roll together. Using a sharp knife, cut the roll in half so that it better fits in the air fryer basket.
4. Place the steak roll, seam side down, in the air fryer basket. Set the air fryer to 400ºF (204ºC) for 9 minutes. Use a meat thermometer to ensure the steak has reached

an internal temperature of 145ºF (63ºC). (It is critical to not overcook flank steak, so as to not toughen the meat.)
5. Let the steak rest for 10 minutes before cutting into slices to serve.

Per Serving:calories: 311 / fat: 15g / protein: 36g / carbs: 7g / fiber: 3g / sodium: 803mg

Spicy Lamb Burgers with Harissa Mayo

Prep Time: 15 minutes / Cook Time: 10 minutes / Serves 2

- ½ small onion, minced
- 1 garlic clove, minced
- 2 teaspoons minced fresh parsley
- 2 teaspoons minced fresh mint
- ¼ teaspoon salt
- Pinch freshly ground black pepper
- 1 teaspoon cumin
- 1 teaspoon smoked paprika
- ¼ teaspoon coriander
- 8 ounces (227 g) lean ground lamb
- 2 tablespoons olive oil mayonnaise
- ½ teaspoon harissa paste (more or less to taste)
- 2 hamburger buns or pitas, fresh greens, tomato slices (optional, for serving)

1. Preheat the grill to medium-high and oil the grill grate. Alternatively, you can cook these in a heavy pan (cast iron is best) on the stovetop.
2. In a large bowl, combine the onion, garlic, parsley, mint, salt, pepper, cumin, paprika, and coriander. Add the lamb and, using your hands, combine the meat with the spices so they are evenly distributed. Form meat mixture into 2 patties.
3. Grill the burgers for 4 minutes per side, or until the internal temperature registers 160ºF (71ºC) for medium.
4. If cooking on the stovetop, heat the pan to medium-high and oil the pan. Cook the burgers for 5 to 6 minutes per side, or until the internal temperature registers 160ºF(71ºC).
5. While the burgers are cooking, combine the mayonnaise and harissa in a small bowl.
6. Serve the burgers with the harissa mayonnaise and slices of tomato and fresh greens on a bun or pita—or skip the bun altogether.

Per Serving:calories: 381 / fat: 20g / protein: 22g / carbs: 27g / fiber: 2g / sodium: 653mg

Cube Steak Roll-Ups

Prep time: 30 minutes / Cook time: 8 to 10 minutes / Serves 4

- 4 cube steaks (6 ounces / 170 g each)
- 1 (16-ounce / 454-g) bottle Italian dressing
- 1 teaspoon salt
- ½ teaspoon freshly ground black pepper
- ½ cup finely chopped yellow onion
- ½ cup finely chopped green bell pepper
- ½ cup finely chopped mushrooms

- 1 to 2 tablespoons oil
1. In a large resealable bag or airtight storage container, combine the steaks and Italian dressing. Seal the bag and refrigerate to marinate for 2 hours.
2. Remove the steaks from the marinade and place them on a cutting board. Discard the marinade. Evenly season the steaks with salt and pepper.
3. In a small bowl, stir together the onion, bell pepper, and mushrooms. Sprinkle the onion mixture evenly over the steaks. Roll up the steaks, jelly roll-style, and secure with toothpicks.
4. Preheat the air fryer to 400ºF (204ºC).
5. Place the steaks in the air fryer basket.
6. Cook for 4 minutes. Flip the steaks and spritz them with oil. Cook for 4 to 6 minutes more until the internal temperature reaches 145ºF (63ºC). Let rest for 5 minutes before serving.

Per Serving:calories: 364 / fat: 20g / protein: 37g / carbs: 7g / fiber: 1g / sodium: 715mg

Bone-in Pork Chops

Prep time: 5 minutes / Cook time: 10 to 12 minutes / Serves 2

- 1 pound (454 g) bone-in pork chops
- 1 tablespoon avocado oil
- 1 teaspoon smoked paprika
- ½ teaspoon onion powder
- ¼ teaspoon cayenne pepper
- Sea salt and freshly ground black pepper, to taste

1. Brush the pork chops with the avocado oil. In a small dish, mix together the smoked paprika, onion powder, cayenne pepper, and salt and black pepper to taste. Sprinkle the seasonings over both sides of the pork chops.
2. Set the air fryer to 400ºF (204ºC). Place the chops in the air fryer basket in a single layer, working in batches if necessary. Air fry for 10 to 12 minutes, until an instant-read thermometer reads 145ºF (63ºC) at the chops' thickest point.
3. Remove the chops from the air fryer and allow them to rest for 5 minutes before serving.

Per Serving:calories: 356 / fat: 16g / protein: 50g / carbs: 1g / fiber: 1g / sodium: 133mg

Kheema Meatloaf

Prep time: 10 minutes / Cook time: 15 minutes / Serves 4

- 1 pound (454 g) 85% lean ground beef
- 2 large eggs, lightly beaten
- 1 cup diced yellow onion
- ¼ cup chopped fresh cilantro
- 1 tablespoon minced fresh ginger
- 1 tablespoon minced garlic
- 2 teaspoons garam masala
- 1 teaspoon kosher salt
- 1 teaspoon ground turmeric
- 1 teaspoon cayenne pepper

- ½ teaspoon ground cinnamon
- ⅛ teaspoon ground cardamom

1. In a large bowl, gently mix the ground beef, eggs, onion, cilantro, ginger, garlic, garam masala, salt, turmeric, cayenne, cinnamon, and cardamom until thoroughly combined.
2. Place the seasoned meat in a baking pan. Place the pan in the air fryer basket. Set the air fryer to 350ºF (177ºC) for 15 minutes. Use a meat thermometer to ensure the meat loaf has reached an internal temperature of 160ºF / 71ºC (medium).
3. Drain the fat and liquid from the pan and let stand for 5 minutes before slicing.
4. Slice and serve hot.

Per Serving:calories: 205 / fat: 8g / protein: 28g / carbs: 5g / fiber: 1g / sodium: 696mg

Hearty Stewed Beef in Tomato Sauce

Prep time: 20 minutes / Cook time: 1 hour 45 minutes / Serves 5

- 3 tablespoons extra virgin olive oil
- 2 pounds (907 g) boneless beef chuck, cut into 2-inch (5cm) chunks
- 1 medium onion (any variety), diced
- 4 garlic cloves, minced
- ⅓ cup white wine
- 2 tablespoons tomato paste
- 1 cinnamon stick
- 4 cloves
- 4 allspice berries
- 1 bay leaf
- ¼ teaspoon freshly ground black pepper
- 15 ounces (425 g) canned crushed tomatoes or chopped fresh tomatoes
- 1 cup hot water
- ½ teaspoon fine sea salt

1. Add the olive oil to a deep pan over medium heat. When the oil starts to shimmer, place half the beef in the pan. Brown the meat until a crust develops, about 3–4 minutes per side, then transfer the meat to a plate, and set aside. Repeat with the remaining pieces.
2. Add the onions to the pan and sauté for 3 minutes or until soft, using a wooden spatula to scrape the browned bits from the bottom of the pan. Add the garlic and sauté for 1 minute, then add the wine and deglaze the pan for 1 more minute, again using the wooden spatula to scrape any browned bits from the bottom of the pan.
3. Add the tomato paste to the pan while stirring rapidly, then add the cinnamon stick, cloves, allspice berries, bay leaf, black pepper, crushed tomatoes, and hot water. Mix well.
4. Add the beef back to the pan. Stir, then cover and reduce the heat to low. Simmer for 1 hour 30 minutes or until the beef is cooked through and tender, and the sauce has thickened. (If the sauce becomes too dry, add more hot water as needed.)

5. About 10 minutes before the cooking time is complete, add the sea salt and stir. When ready to serve, remove the cinnamon stick, bay leaf, allspice berries, and cloves. Store in the refrigerator for up to 3 days.

Per Serving:calories: 357 / fat: 19g / protein: 39g / carbs: 8g / fiber: 2g / sodium: 403mg

Pork Tenderloin with Brussels Sprouts and Pearl Onions

Prep time: 5 minutes / Cook time: 40 minutes / Serves 4

- 1 pork tenderloin (about 1 pound / 454 g), trimmed
- 2 tablespoons olive oil, divided
- ½ teaspoon kosher salt
- ¼ teaspoon ground black pepper
- 2 cups frozen and thawed peeled pearl onions
- 2 cups Brussels sprouts, halved
- 2 or 3 sprigs fresh rosemary
- 1 cup red wine or low-sodium chicken broth

1. Preheat the oven to 400°F(205°C).
2. Pat the tenderloin dry, rub with 1 tablespoon of the oil, and sprinkle with the salt and pepper. In a large ovenproof skillet over medium heat, sear the tenderloin on all sides until browned, about 3 minutes per side. Remove from the heat and set aside.
3. Toss the onions, Brussels sprouts, and rosemary with the remaining 1 tablespoon oil in the skillet. Place the tenderloin on top of the vegetables and herbs and roast until a thermometer placed in the thickest part reaches 145°F(63°C), about 15 minutes. Remove the skillet from the oven and transfer the tenderloin and vegetables to a serving plate to rest while you make the sauce.
4. On the stove top, add the wine or broth to the skillet and bring to a boil, scraping up any browned bits on the bottom of the skillet. Cook until reduced and slightly thickened, 10 to 15 minutes. Remove the rosemary sprigs. Slice the tenderloin and serve with the vegetables and sauce.

Per Serving:calories: 310 / fat: 9g / protein: 27g / carbs: 20g / fiber: 2g / sodium: 380mg

Pork Tenderloin with Chermoula Sauce

Prep Time: 15 minutes / Cook Time: 20 minutes / Serves 2

- ½ cup fresh parsley
- ½ cup fresh cilantro
- 6 small garlic cloves
- 3 tablespoons olive oil, divided
- 3 tablespoons freshly squeezed lemon juice
- 1 teaspoon smoked paprika
- 2 teaspoons cumin
- ½ teaspoon salt, divided
- Pinch freshly ground black pepper
- 1 (8-ounce / 227-g) pork tenderloin

1. Preheat the oven to 425°F (220°C) and set the rack to the middle position.

2. In the bowl of a food processor, combine the parsley, cilantro, garlic, 2 tablespoons of olive oil, the lemon juice, paprika, cumin, and ¼ teaspoon of salt. Pulse 15 to 20 times, or until the mixture is fairly smooth. Scrape the sides down as needed to incorporate all of the ingredients. Transfer the sauce to a small bowl and set aside.
3. Season the pork tenderloin on all sides with the remaining ¼ teaspoon of salt and a generous pinch of pepper.
4. Heat the remaining 1 tablespoon of olive oil in a sauté pan. Add the pork and sear for 3 minutes, turning often, until it's golden on all sides.
5. Transfer the pork to an oven-safe baking dish and roast for 15 minutes, or until the internal temperature registers 145°F (63°C).

Per Serving:calories: 168 / fat: 13g / protein: 11g / carbs: 3g / fiber: 1g / sodium: 333mg

Smoky Herb Lamb Chops and Lemon-Rosemary Dressing

Prep time: 1 hour 35 minutes / Cook time: 10 minutes / Serves 6

- 4 large cloves garlic
- 1 cup lemon juice
- ⅓ cup fresh rosemary
- 1 cup extra-virgin olive oil
- 1½ teaspoons salt
- 1 teaspoon freshly ground black pepper
- 6 (1-inch-thick) lamb chops

1. In a food processor or blender, blend the garlic, lemon juice, rosemary, olive oil, salt, and black pepper for 15 seconds. Set aside.
2. Put the lamb chops in a large plastic zip-top bag or container. Cover the lamb with two-thirds of the rosemary dressing, making sure that all of the lamb chops are coated with the dressing. Let the lamb marinate in the fridge for 1 hour.
3. When you are almost ready to eat, take the lamb chops out of the fridge and let them sit on the counter-top for 20 minutes. Preheat a grill, grill pan, or lightly oiled skillet to high heat.
4. Cook the lamb chops for 3 minutes on each side. To serve, drizzle the lamb with the remaining dressing.

Per Serving:calories: 484 / fat: 42g / protein: 24g / carbs: 5g / fiber: 1g / sodium: 655mg

Parmesan-Crusted Pork Chops

Prep time: 5 minutes / Cook time: 12 minutes / Serves 4

- 1 large egg
- ½ cup grated Parmesan cheese
- 4 (4-ounce / 113-g) boneless pork chops
- ½ teaspoon salt
- ¼ teaspoon ground black pepper

1. Whisk egg in a medium bowl and place Parmesan in a separate medium bowl.

2. Sprinkle pork chops on both sides with salt and pepper. Dip each pork chop into egg, then press both sides into Parmesan.

3. Place pork chops into ungreased air fryer basket. Adjust the temperature to 400ºF (204ºC) and air fry for 12 minutes, turning chops halfway through cooking. Pork chops will be golden and have an internal temperature of at least 145ºF (63ºC) when done. Serve warm.

Per Serving: calories: 218 / fat: 9g / protein: 32g / carbs: 1g / fiber: 0g / sodium: 372mg

Pork with Orzo

Prep time: 10 minutes / Cook time: 30 minutes / Serves 4

- 2 tablespoons olive oil
- 2 yellow squash, diced
- 2 carrots, chopped
- ½ red onion, chopped
- 2 garlic cloves, minced
- 1 pound (454 g) boneless pork loin chops, cut into 2-inch pieces
- 1 teaspoon Italian seasoning
- 2 cups chicken broth
- 1 cup dried orzo
- 2 cups arugula
- Sea salt
- Freshly ground black pepper
- Grated Parmesan cheese (optional)

1. In a Dutch oven, heat the olive oil over medium-high heat. Add the squash, carrots, onion, and garlic and sauté for 5 minutes, or until softened. Add the pork and Italian seasoning and sauté, stirring occasionally, for 3 to 5 minutes, until browned.

2. Increase the heat to high, add the broth, and bring to a boil. Add the orzo, reduce the heat to medium-low, and simmer, stirring occasionally, for 8 minutes. Add the arugula and stir until wilted. Turn off the heat, cover, and let sit for 5 minutes.

3. Season with salt and pepper and serve topped with Parmesan, if desired.

Per Serving: calories: 423 / fat: 11g / protein: 31g / carbs: 48g / fiber: 4g / sodium: 127mg

Wedding Soup

Prep time: 15 minutes / Cook time: 17 minutes / Serves 6

- 3 (1-ounce/ 28-g) slices Italian bread, toasted
- ¾ pound (340 g) 90% lean ground beef
- 1 large egg, beaten
- 1 medium onion, peeled and chopped
- 3 cloves garlic, peeled and minced
- ¼ cup chopped fresh parsley
- 1 tablespoon minced fresh oregano
- 1 tablespoon minced fresh basil
- 1 teaspoon salt
- ½ teaspoon ground black pepper
- ½ cup grated Parmesan cheese, divided

- 2 tablespoons olive oil
- 8 cups low-sodium chicken broth
- 5 ounces (142 g) baby spinach

1. Wet toasted bread with water and then squeeze out all the liquid. Place soaked bread in a large bowl. Add ground beef, egg, onion, garlic, parsley, oregano, basil, salt, pepper, and ¼ cup cheese. Mix well. Form the mixture into 1" balls.

2. Press the Sauté button on the Instant Pot® and heat oil. Brown meatballs in batches on all sides, about 3 minutes per side. Transfer meatballs to a plate. Press the Cancel button.

3. Add broth to pot, stirring well to release any browned bits. Add meatballs and stir well. Close lid, set steam release to Sealing, press the Manual button, and set time to 10 minutes. When the timer beeps, quick-release the pressure until the float valve drops. Open lid.

4. Add spinach and stir until wilted, about 1 minute. Ladle the soup into bowls and sprinkle with remaining ¼ cup cheese.

Per Serving: calories: 270 / fat: 16g / protein: 24g / carbs: 10g / fiber: 1g / sodium: 590mg

Zesty Grilled Flank Steak

Prep time: 10 minutes / Cook time: 18 minutes / Serves 6

- ¼ cup olive oil
- 3 tablespoons red wine vinegar
- 1 teaspoon dried rosemary
- 1 teaspoon dried marjoram
- 1 teaspoon dried oregano
- 1 teaspoon paprika
- 2 cloves garlic, minced
- 1 teaspoon freshly ground pepper
- 2 pounds (907 g) flank steak

1. Combine the olive oil, vinegar, herbs, and seasonings in a small bowl. Place the flank steak in a shallow dish, and rub the marinade into the meat. Cover and refrigerate for up to 24 hours.

2. Heat a charcoal or gas grill to medium heat (375ºF / 190ºC).

3. Grill the steak for 18–21 minutes, turning once halfway through the cooking time.

4. An internal meat thermometer should read 140ºF (60ºC) when the meat is done.

5. Transfer the meat to a cutting board, and cover with aluminum foil. Let steak rest for at least 10 minutes.

6. Slice against the grain very thinly and serve.

Per Serving: calories: 292 / fat: 17g / protein: 33g / carbs: 1g / fiber: 0g / sodium: 81mg

Baby Back Ribs

Prep time: 5 minutes / Cook time: 25 minutes / Serves 4

- 2 pounds (907 g) baby back ribs
- 2 teaspoons chili powder
- 1 teaspoon paprika
- ½ teaspoon onion powder
- ½ teaspoon garlic powder

- ¼ teaspoon ground cayenne pepper
- ½ cup low-carb, sugar-free barbecue sauce
1. Rub ribs with all ingredients except barbecue sauce. Place into the air fryer basket.
2. Adjust the temperature to 400ºF (204ºC) and roast for 25 minutes.
3. When done, ribs will be dark and charred with an internal temperature of at least 185ºF (85ºC). Brush ribs with barbecue sauce and serve warm.

Per Serving:calories: 571 / fat: 36g / protein: 45g / carbs: 17g / fiber: 1g / sodium: 541mg

Zesty London Broil

Prep time: 30 minutes / Cook time: 20 to 28 minutes / Serves 4 to 6

- ⅔ cup ketchup
- ¼ cup honey
- ¼ cup olive oil
- 2 tablespoons apple cider vinegar
- 2 tablespoons Worcestershire sauce
- 2 tablespoons minced onion
- ½ teaspoon paprika
- 1 teaspoon salt
- 1 teaspoon freshly ground black pepper
- 2 pounds (907 g) London broil, top round or flank steak (about 1-inch thick)
1. Combine the ketchup, honey, olive oil, apple cider vinegar, Worcestershire sauce, minced onion, paprika, salt and pepper in a small bowl and whisk together.
2. Generously pierce both sides of the meat with a fork or meat tenderizer and place it in a shallow dish. Pour the marinade mixture over the steak, making sure all sides of the meat get coated with the marinade. Cover and refrigerate overnight.
3. Preheat the air fryer to 400ºF (204ºC).
4. Transfer the London broil to the air fryer basket and air fry for 20 to 28 minutes, depending on how rare or well done you like your steak. Flip the steak over halfway through the cooking time.
5. Remove the London broil from the air fryer and let it rest for five minutes on a cutting board. To serve, thinly slice the meat against the grain and transfer to a serving platter.

Per Serving:calories: 411 / fat: 21g / protein: 34g / carbs: 21g / fiber: 0g / sodium: 536mg

Beef Whirls

Prep time: 30 minutes / Cook time: 18 minutes / Serves 6
- 3 cube steaks (6 ounces / 170 g each)
- 1 (16-ounce / 454-g) bottle Italian dressing
- 1 cup Italian-style bread crumbs
- ½ cup grated Parmesan cheese
- 1 teaspoon dried basil
- 1 teaspoon dried oregano
- 1 teaspoon dried parsley
- ¼ cup beef broth

- 1 to 2 tablespoons oil
1. In a large resealable bag, combine the steaks and Italian dressing. Seal the bag and refrigerate to marinate for 2 hours.
2. In a medium bowl, whisk the bread crumbs, cheese, basil, oregano, and parsley until blended. Stir in the beef broth.
3. Place the steaks on a cutting board and cut each in half so you have 6 equal pieces. Sprinkle with the bread crumb mixture. Roll up the steaks, jelly roll-style, and secure with toothpicks.
4. Preheat the air fryer to 400ºF (204ºC).
5. Place 3 roll-ups in the air fryer basket.
6. Cook for 5 minutes. Flip the roll-ups and spritz with oil. Cook for 4 minutes more until the internal temperature reaches 145ºF (63ºC). Repeat with the remaining roll-ups. Let rest for 5 to 10 minutes before serving.

Per Serving:calories: 307 / fat: 15g / protein: 24g / carbs: 17g / fiber: 1g / sodium: 236mg

Pork Tenderloin with Vegetable Ragu

Prep time: 25 minutes / Cook time: 18 minutes / Serves 6
- 2 tablespoons light olive oil, divided
- 1 (1½-pound / 680-g) pork tenderloin
- ¼ teaspoon salt
- ¼ teaspoon ground black pepper
- 1 medium zucchini, trimmed and sliced
- 1 medium yellow squash, sliced
- 1 medium onion, peeled and chopped
- 1 medium carrot, peeled and grated
- 1 (14½-ounce / 411-g) can diced tomatoes, drained
- 2 cloves garlic, peeled and minced
- ¼ teaspoon crushed red pepper flakes
- 1 tablespoon chopped fresh basil
- 1 tablespoon chopped fresh oregano
- 1 sprig fresh thyme
- ½ cup red wine
1. Press the Sauté button on the Instant Pot® and heat 1 tablespoon oil. Season pork with salt and black pepper. Brown pork lightly on all sides, about 2 minutes per side. Transfer pork to a plate and set aside.
2. Add remaining 1 tablespoon oil to the pot. Add zucchini and squash, and cook until tender, about 5 minutes. Add onion and carrot, and cook until just softened, about 5 minutes. Add tomatoes, garlic, crushed red pepper flakes, basil, oregano, thyme, and red wine to pot, and stir well. Press the Cancel button.
3. Top vegetable mixture with browned pork. Close lid, set steam release to Sealing, press the Manual button, and set time to 3 minutes. When the timer beeps, quick-release the pressure until the float valve drops and open lid. Transfer pork to a cutting board and cut into 1" slices. Pour sauce on a serving platter and arrange pork slices on top. Serve immediately.

Per Serving:calories: 190 / fat: 7g / protein: 23g / carbs: 9g / fiber: 2g / sodium: 606mg

Chapter 5 Fish and Seafood

Mediterranean Cod

Prep time: 15 minutes / Cook time: 6 minutes / Serves 2
- 1 cup water
- 2 (5-ounce / 142-g) cod fillets
- 2 teaspoons olive oil
- ½ teaspoon salt
- 10 Kalamata olives, pitted and halved
- 1 small Roma tomato, diced
- 3 tablespoons chopped fresh basil leaves, divided

1. Add water to the Instant Pot® and place the rack inside.
2. Place each piece of cod on a 10" × 10" square of aluminum foil. Drizzle each fillet with 1 teaspoon oil and sprinkle with ¼ teaspoon salt. Add 5 olives, half of the tomatoes, and 1 tablespoon basil on top of each fillet. Bring up the sides of the foil and crimp at the top to create a foil pocket.
3. Place both fish packets on rack. Close lid, set steam release to Sealing, press the Manual button, and set time to 6 minutes. When the timer beeps, quick-release the pressure until the float valve drops and open lid.
4. Remove foil packets and transfer fish and toppings to two plates. Garnish each serving with half of the remaining 1 tablespoon basil.

Per Serving:calories: 181 / fat: 8g / protein: 26g / carbs: 2g / fiber: 1g / sodium: 662mg

Fried Fresh Sardines

Prep time: 5 minutes / Cook time: 5 minutes / Serves 4
- Avocado oil
- 1½ pounds (680 g) whole fresh sardines, scales removed
- 1 teaspoon salt
- 1 teaspoon freshly ground black pepper
- 2 cups flour

1. Preheat a deep skillet over medium heat. Pour in enough oil so there is about 1 inch of it in the pan.
2. Season the fish with the salt and pepper.
3. Dredge the fish in the flour so it is completely covered.
4. Slowly drop in 1 fish at a time, making sure not to overcrowd the pan.
5. Cook for about 3 minutes on each side or just until the fish begins to brown on all sides. Serve warm.

Per Serving:calories: 581 / fat: 20g / protein: 48g / carbs: 48g / fiber: 2g / sodium: 583mg

Mediterranean Cod Stew

Prep time: 10 minutes / Cook time: 20 minutes / Serves: 6
- 2 tablespoons extra-virgin olive oil
- 2 cups chopped onion (about 1 medium onion)
- 2 garlic cloves, minced (about 1 teaspoon)
- ¾ teaspoon smoked paprika
- 1 (14½-ounce / 411-g) can diced tomatoes, undrained
- 1 (12-ounce / 340-g) jar roasted red peppers, drained and chopped
- 1 cup sliced olives, green or black
- ⅓ cup dry red wine
- ¼ teaspoon freshly ground black pepper
- ¼ teaspoon kosher or sea salt
- 1½ pounds (680 g) cod fillets, cut into 1-inch pieces
- 3 cups sliced mushrooms (about 8 ounces / 227 g)

1. In a large stockpot over medium heat, heat the oil. Add the onion and cook for 4 minutes, stirring occasionally. Add the garlic and smoked paprika and cook for 1 minute, stirring often.
2. Mix in the tomatoes with their juices, roasted peppers, olives, wine, pepper, and salt, and turn the heat up to medium-high. Bring to a boil. Add the cod and mushrooms, and reduce the heat to medium.
3. Cover and cook for about 10 minutes, stirring a few times, until the cod is cooked through and flakes easily, and serve.

Per Serving:calories: 209 / fat: 8g / protein: 23g / carbs: 12g / fiber: 4g / sodium: 334mg

Steamed Clams

Prep time: 10 minutes / Cook time: 8 minutes / Serves 4
- 2 pounds (907 g) fresh clams, rinsed
- 1 tablespoon olive oil
- 1 small white onion, peeled and diced
- 1 clove garlic, peeled and quartered
- ½ cup Chardonnay
- ½ cup water

1. Place clams in the Instant Pot® steamer basket. Set aside.
2. Press the Sauté button and heat oil. Add onion and cook until tender, about 3 minutes. Add garlic and cook about 30 seconds. Pour in Chardonnay and water. Insert steamer basket with clams. Press the Cancel button.
3. Close lid, set steam release to Sealing, press the Manual button, and set time to 4 minutes. When the timer beeps, quick-release the pressure until the float valve drops. Open lid.
4. Transfer clams to four bowls and top with a generous scoop of cooking liquid.

Per Serving:calories: 205 / fat: 6g / protein: 30g / carbs: 7g / fiber: 0g / sodium: 135mg

Pan-Roasted Wild Cod with Tomatoes, Olives, and Artichokes

Prep time: 10 minutes / Cook time: 20 minutes / Serves 2

- 1 tablespoon olive oil
- ½ medium onion, minced
- 2 garlic cloves, minced
- 1 teaspoon oregano
- 1 (15-ounce / 425-g) can diced tomatoes with basil
- 1 (15-ounce / 425-g) can artichoke hearts in water, drained and halved
- ¼ cup pitted Greek olives, drained
- 10 ounces (283 g) wild cod (2 smaller pieces may fit better in the pan)
- Salt
- Freshly ground black pepper

1. Heat olive oil in a sauté pan over medium-high heat. Add the onion and sauté for about 10 minutes, or until golden. Add the garlic and oregano and cook for another 30 seconds.
2. Mix in the tomatoes, artichoke hearts, and olives.
3. Place the cod on top of the vegetables. Cover the pan and cook for 10 minutes, or until the fish is opaque and flakes apart easily. Season with salt and pepper.

Per Serving:calories: 346 / fat: 10g / protein: 34g / carbs: 35g / fiber: 17g / sodium: 423mg

Shrimp with Arugula Pesto and Zucchini Noodles

Prep time: 20 minutes / Cook time: 5 minutes / Serves 2
- 3 cups lightly packed arugula
- ½ cup lightly packed basil leaves
- 3 medium garlic cloves
- ¼ cup walnuts
- 3 tablespoons olive oil
- 2 tablespoons grated Parmesan cheese
- 1 tablespoon freshly squeezed lemon juice
- Salt
- Freshly ground black pepper
- 1 (10-ounce / 283-g) package zucchini noodles
- 8 ounces (227 g) cooked, shelled shrimp
- 2 Roma tomatoes, diced

1. Combine the arugula, basil, garlic, walnuts, olive oil, Parmesan cheese, and lemon juice in a food processor fitted with the chopping blade. Process until smooth, scraping down the sides as needed. Season with salt and pepper.
2. Heat a sauté pan over medium heat. Add the pesto, zucchini noodles, and shrimp. Toss to combine the sauce over the noodles and shrimp, and cook until warmed through. Don't overcook or the zucchini will become limp.
3. Taste and add additional salt and pepper if needed. Top with the diced tomatoes.

Per Serving:calories: 434 / fat: 30g / protein: 33g / carbs: 15g / fiber: 5g / sodium: 412mg

Sage-Stuffed Whole Trout with Roasted Vegetables

Prep time: 10 minutes / Cook time: 35 minutes / Serves 4
- 2 red bell peppers, seeded and cut into 1-inch-wide strips
- 1 (15-ounce / 425-g) can artichoke hearts, drained and cut into quarters
- 1 large red onion, halved through the stem and cut into 1-inch-wide wedges
- 4 cloves garlic, halved
- 3 tablespoons olive oil, divided
- 1½ teaspoons salt, divided
- ¾ teaspoon freshly ground black pepper, divided
- 2 whole rainbow trout, cleaned with head on
- 3 cups sage leaves
- Juice of ½ lemon

1. Preheat the oven to 475ºF (245ºC).
2. In a large baking dish, toss the bell peppers, artichoke hearts, onion, and garlic with 2 tablespoons of the olive oil. Sprinkle with 1 teaspoon of salt and ½ teaspoon of pepper. Roast the vegetables in the preheated oven for 20 minutes. Reduce the heat to 375°F(190ºC).
3. While the vegetables are roasting, prepare the fish. Brush the fish inside and out with the remaining 1 tablespoon of olive oil and season with the remaining ½ teaspoon of salt and ¼ teaspoon of pepper. Stuff each fish with half of the sage leaves.
4. Remove the vegetables from the oven and place the fish on top. Put back in the oven and bake at 375°F (190ºC) for about 15 minutes more, until the fish is cooked through. Remove from the oven, squeeze the lemon juice over the fish, and let rest for 5 minutes.
5. To serve, halve the fish. Spoon roasted vegetables onto 4 serving plates and serve half a fish alongside each, topped with some of the sage leaves.

Per Serving:calories: 349 / fat: 16g / protein: 24g / carbs: 34g / fiber: 17g / sodium: 879mg

Salmon with Provolone Cheese

Prep time: 5 minutes / Cook time: 15 minutes / Serves 4
- 1 pound (454 g) salmon fillet, chopped
- 2 ounces (57 g) Provolone, grated
- 1 teaspoon avocado oil
- ¼ teaspoon ground paprika

1. Sprinkle the salmon fillets with avocado oil and put in the air fryer.
2. Then sprinkle the fish with ground paprika and top with Provolone cheese.
3. Cook the fish at 360ºF (182ºC) for 15 minutes.

Per Serving:calories: 204 / fat: 10g / protein: 27g / carbs: 0g / fiber: 0g / sodium: 209mg

Paprika Crab Burgers

Prep time: 30 minutes / Cook time: 14 minutes / Serves 3

- 2 eggs, beaten
- 1 shallot, chopped
- 2 garlic cloves, crushed
- 1 tablespoon olive oil
- 1 teaspoon yellow mustard
- 1 teaspoon fresh cilantro, chopped
- 10 ounces (283 g) crab meat
- 1 teaspoon smoked paprika
- ½ teaspoon ground black pepper
- Sea salt, to taste
- ¾ cup Parmesan cheese

1. In a mixing bowl, thoroughly combine the eggs, shallot, garlic, olive oil, mustard, cilantro, crab meat, paprika, black pepper, and salt. Mix until well combined.
2. Shape the mixture into 6 patties. Roll the crab patties over grated Parmesan cheese, coating well on all sides. Place in your refrigerator for 2 hours.
3. Spritz the crab patties with cooking oil on both sides. Cook in the preheated air fryer at 360ºF (182ºC) for 14 minutes. Serve on dinner rolls if desired. Bon appétit!

Per Serving:calories: 288 / fat: 16g / protein: 32g / carbs: 4g / fiber: 1g / sodium: 355mg

Cod with Tomatoes and Garlic

Prep time: 10 minutes / Cook time: 20 minutes / Serves 4

- 1 pound (454 g) cod or your favorite white-fleshed fish
- Sea salt
- Freshly ground black pepper
- 2 tablespoons olive oil
- 2 garlic cloves, minced
- 1 (15-ounce / 425-g) can diced tomatoes, with their juices
- ¼ cup white wine
- ¼ cup chopped fresh Italian parsley

1. Pat the fish dry with paper towels and season with salt and pepper.
2. In a large skillet, heat the olive oil over medium heat. Add the cod and cook for 3 to 5 minutes on each side, or until cooked through. Transfer the fish to a plate, cover loosely with aluminum foil, and set aside.
3. Add the garlic to the skillet and sauté until fragrant, about 3 minutes. Add the tomatoes and wine and increase the heat to medium-high. Cook the tomato mixture for about 4 minutes. Season with salt and pepper.
4. Return the fish to the skillet and spoon the tomato mixture over it. Serve garnished with the parsley.

Per Serving:calories: 170 / fat: 7g / protein: 18g / carbs: 5g / fiber: 2g / sodium: 507mg

Baked Halibut with Cherry Tomatoes

Prep time: 5 minutes / Cook time: 15 minutes / Serves 4

- 4 (5-ounce / 142-g) pieces of boneless halibut, skin on
- 1 pint (2 cups) cherry tomatoes
- 3 tablespoons garlic, minced
- ½ cup lemon juice
- ¼ cup extra-virgin olive oil
- 1 teaspoon salt

1. Preheat the oven to 425ºF(220ºC).
2. Put the halibut in a large baking dish; place the tomatoes around the halibut.
3. In a small bowl, combine the garlic, lemon juice, olive oil, and salt.
4. Pour the sauce over the halibut and tomatoes. Put the baking dish in the oven and bake for 15 minutes. Serve immediately.

Per Serving:calories: 350 / fat: 18g / protein: 39g / carbs: 8g / fiber: 1g / sodium: 687mg

Ahi Tuna Steaks

Prep time: 5 minutes / Cook time: 14 minutes / Serves 2

- 2 (6 ounces / 170 g) ahi tuna steaks
- 2 tablespoons olive oil
- 3 tablespoons everything bagel seasoning

1. Drizzle both sides of each steak with olive oil. Place seasoning on a medium plate and press each side of tuna steaks into seasoning to form a thick layer.
2. Place steaks into ungreased air fryer basket. Adjust the temperature to 400ºF (204ºC) and air fry for 14 minutes, turning steaks halfway through cooking. Steaks will be done when internal temperature is at least 145ºF (63ºC) for well-done. Serve warm.

Per Serving:calories: 305 / fat: 14g / protein: 42g / carbs: 0g / fiber: 0g / sodium: 377mg

Balsamic-Glazed Black Pepper Salmon

Prep time: 5 minutes / Cook time: 8 minutes / Serves 4

- ½ cup balsamic vinegar
- 1 tablespoon honey
- 4 (8-ounce / 227-g) salmon fillets
- Sea salt and freshly ground pepper, to taste
- 1 tablespoon olive oil

1. Heat a cast-iron skillet over medium-high heat. Mix the vinegar and honey in a small bowl.
2. Season the salmon fillets with the sea salt and freshly ground pepper; brush with the honey-balsamic glaze.
3. Add olive oil to the skillet, and sear the salmon fillets, cooking for 3–4 minutes on each side until lightly browned and medium rare in the center.
4. Let sit for 5 minutes before serving.

Per Serving:calories: 478 / fat: 17g / protein: 65g / carbs: 10g / fiber: 0g / sodium: 246mg

Braised Monkfish with Sherry and Almonds

Prep time: 10 minutes / Cook time: 25 minutes / Serves 4

- 2 tablespoons olive oil
- 1 medium onion, diced

- 2 red bell peppers, diced
- 1½ teaspoons salt
- ½ teaspoon freshly ground black pepper
- 3 cloves garlic, minced
- ⅓ cup dry sherry
- 1 cup bottled clam juice
- ¼ cup blanched slivered almonds
- 4 monkfish fillets, about 6 ounces (170 g) each
- 2 tablespoons chopped flat-leaf parsley

1. Heat the olive oil in a large saucepan over medium heat. Add the onion, peppers, salt, and pepper and cook, stirring frequently, for about 5 minutes, until the vegetables are softened. Add the garlic and sherry and cook for 1 more minute. Stir in the clam juice and bring to a simmer. Reduce the heat to low, cover, and simmer for 10 minutes.
2. Transfer the onion mixture to a food processor or blender and process to a smooth purée. Add the almonds and pulse until they are finely ground. Pour the sauce back into the saucepan and return to a simmer over medium heat.
3. Add the fish to the sauce, cover the pan, and simmer for 10 to 12 minutes, until the fish is just cooked through. Slice the fish into ¼-inch thick slices and serve immediately, garnished with parsley.

Per Serving:calories: 291 / fat: 13g / protein: 28g / carbs: 15g / fiber: 3g / sodium: 877mg

Roasted Red Snapper

Prep time: 5 minutes / Cook time: 45 minutes / Serves 4
- 1 (2 to 2½ pounds / 907 g to 1.1 kg) whole red snapper, cleaned and scaled
- 2 lemons, sliced (about 10 slices)
- 3 cloves garlic, sliced
- 4 or 5 sprigs of thyme
- 3 tablespoons cold salted butter, cut into small cubes, divided

1. Preheat the oven to 350°F(180°C).
2. Cut a piece of foil to about the size of your baking sheet; put the foil on the baking sheet.
3. Make a horizontal slice through the belly of the fish to create a pocket.
4. Place 3 slices of lemon on the foil and the fish on top of the lemons.
5. Stuff the fish with the garlic, thyme, 3 lemon slices and butter. Reserve 3 pieces of butter.
6. Place the reserved 3 pieces of butter on top of the fish, and 3 or 4 slices of lemon on top of the butter. Bring the foil together and seal it to make a pocket around the fish.
7. Put the fish in the oven and bake for 45 minutes. Serve with remaining fresh lemon slices.

Per Serving:calories: 345 / fat: 13g / protein: 54g / carbs: 12g / fiber: 3g / sodium: 170mg

Shrimp Foil Packets

Prep time: 15 minutes / Cook time: 4 to 6 hours / Serves 4
- 1½ pounds (680 g) whole raw medium shrimp, peeled, deveined, and divided into 4 (6-ounce / 170-g) portions
- Sea salt
- Freshly ground black pepper
- 2 teaspoons extra-virgin olive oil, divided
- 4 teaspoons balsamic vinegar, divided
- 4 garlic cloves, minced
- 1 red onion, cut into chunks
- 1 large zucchini, sliced
- 4 Roma tomatoes, chopped
- 4 teaspoons dried oregano, divided
- Juice of 1 lemon

1. Place a large sheet of aluminum foil on a work surface. Lay one-quarter of the shrimp in the center of the foil and season it with salt and pepper. Drizzle with ½ teaspoon of olive oil and 1 teaspoon of vinegar.
2. Top the shrimp with one-quarter each of the garlic, onion, and zucchini, plus 1 tomato and 1 teaspoon of oregano. Place a second sheet of foil on top of the ingredients. Fold the corners over to seal the packet.
3. Repeat to make 3 more foil packets. Place the packets in a slow cooker in a single layer, or stack them if needed.
4. Cover the cooker and cook for 4 to 6 hours on Low heat.
5. Be careful when serving: Very hot steam will release when you open the foil packets. Drizzle each opened packet with lemon juice for serving.

Per Serving:calories: 210 / fat: 5g / protein: 30g / carbs: 17g / fiber: 3g / sodium: 187mg

Salmon with Wild Rice and Orange Salad

Prep time: 20 minutes / Cook time: 18 minutes / Serves 4
- 1 cup wild rice, picked over and rinsed
- 3 tablespoons extra-virgin olive oil, divided
- 1½ teaspoon table salt, for cooking rice
- 2 oranges, plus ⅛ teaspoon grated orange zest
- 4 (6-ounce / 170-g) skinless salmon fillets, 1½ inches thick
- 1 teaspoon ground dried Aleppo pepper
- ½ teaspoon table salt
- 1 small shallot, minced
- 1 tablespoon red wine vinegar
- 2 teaspoons Dijon mustard
- 1 teaspoon honey
- 2 carrots, peeled and shredded
- ¼ cup chopped fresh mint

1. Combine 6 cups water, rice, 1 tablespoon oil, and 1½ teaspoons salt in Instant Pot. Lock lid in place and close pressure release valve. Select high pressure cook function and cook for 15 minutes. Turn off Instant Pot and let pressure release naturally for 15 minutes. Quick-

release any remaining pressure, then carefully remove lid, allowing steam to escape away from you. Drain rice and set aside to cool slightly. Wipe pot clean with paper towels.

2. Add ½ cup water to now-empty Instant Pot. Fold sheet of aluminum foil into 16 by 6-inch sling. Slice 1 orange ¼ inch thick and shingle widthwise in 3 rows across center of sling. Sprinkle flesh side of salmon with Aleppo pepper and ½ teaspoon salt, then arrange skinned side down on top of orange slices. Using sling, lower salmon into Instant Pot; allow narrow edges of sling to rest along sides of insert. Lock lid in place and close pressure release valve. Select high pressure cook function and cook for 3 minutes.

3. Meanwhile, cut away peel and pith from remaining 1 orange. Quarter orange, then slice crosswise into ¼-inch pieces. Whisk remaining 2 tablespoons oil, shallot, vinegar, mustard, honey, and orange zest together in large bowl. Add rice, orange pieces, carrots, and mint, and gently toss to combine. Season with salt and pepper to taste.

4. Turn off Instant Pot and quick-release pressure. Carefully remove lid, allowing steam to escape away from you. Using sling, transfer salmon to large plate. Gently lift and tilt fillets with spatula to remove orange slices. Serve salmon with salad.

Per Serving:calories: 690 / fat: 34g / protein: 43g / carbs: 51g / fiber: 5g / sodium: 770mg

Poached Salmon

Prep time: 10 minutes / Cook time: 5 minutes / Serves 4
- 1 lemon, sliced ¼ inch thick
- 4 (6-ounce / 170-g) skinless salmon fillets, 1½ inches thick
- ½ teaspoon table salt
- ¼ teaspoon pepper

1. Add ½ cup water to Instant Pot. Fold sheet of aluminum foil into 16 by 6-inch sling. Arrange lemon slices widthwise in 2 rows across center of sling. Sprinkle flesh side of salmon with salt and pepper, then arrange skinned side down on top of lemon slices.

2. Using sling, lower salmon into Instant Pot; allow narrow edges of sling to rest along sides of insert. Lock lid in place and close pressure release valve. Select high pressure cook function and cook for 3 minutes.

3. Turn off Instant Pot and quick-release pressure. Carefully remove lid, allowing steam to escape away from you. Using sling, transfer salmon to large plate. Gently lift and tilt fillets with spatula to remove lemon slices. Serve.

Per Serving:calories: 350 / fat: 23g / protein: 35g / carbs: 0g / fiber: 0g / sodium: 390mg

Lemon Pepper Shrimp

Prep time: 15 minutes / Cook time: 8 minutes / Serves 2

- Oil, for spraying
- 12 ounces (340 g) medium raw shrimp, peeled and deveined
- 3 tablespoons lemon juice
- 1 tablespoon olive oil
- 1 teaspoon lemon pepper
- ¼ teaspoon paprika
- ¼ teaspoon granulated garlic

1. Preheat the air fryer to 400ºF (204ºC). Line the air fryer basket with parchment and spray lightly with oil.

2. In a medium bowl, toss together the shrimp, lemon juice, olive oil, lemon pepper, paprika, and garlic until evenly coated.

3. Place the shrimp in the prepared basket.

4. Cook for 6 to 8 minutes, or until pink and firm. Serve immediately.

Per Serving:calories: 211 / fat: 8g / protein: 34g / carbs: 2g / fiber: 0g / sodium: 203mg

Herbed Tuna Steaks

Prep time: 10 minutes / Cook time: 4 to 6 hours / Serves 4
- Nonstick cooking spray
- 4 (1-inch-thick) fresh tuna steaks (about 2 pounds / 907 g total)
- 1 teaspoon sea salt
- ¼ teaspoon freshly ground black pepper
- 2 teaspoons extra-virgin olive oil
- 2 teaspoons dried thyme
- 2 teaspoons dried rosemary

1. Coat a slow-cooker insert with cooking spray, or line the bottom and sides with parchment paper or aluminum foil.

2. Season the tuna steaks all over with salt and pepper and place them in the prepared slow cooker in a single layer. Drizzle with the olive oil and sprinkle with the thyme and rosemary.

3. Cover the cooker and cook for 4 to 6 hours on Low heat.

Per Serving:calories: 339 / fat: 5g / protein: 68g / carbs: 1g / fiber: 1g / sodium: 689mg

Pistachio-Crusted Whitefish

Prep time: 10 minutes / Cook time: 20 minutes / Serves 2
- ¼ cup shelled pistachios
- 1 tablespoon fresh parsley
- 1 tablespoon grated Parmesan cheese
- 1 tablespoon panko bread crumbs
- 2 tablespoons olive oil
- ¼ teaspoon salt
- 10 ounces (283 g) skinless whitefish (1 large piece or 2 smaller ones)

1. Preheat the oven to 350°F(180ºC) and set the rack to the middle position. Line a sheet pan with foil or parchment paper.

2. Combine all of the ingredients except the fish in a mini food processor, and pulse until the nuts are finely ground. Alternatively, you can mince the nuts with a chef's knife and combine the ingredients by hand in a small bowl.
3. Place the fish on the sheet pan. Spread the nut mixture evenly over the fish and pat it down lightly.
4. Bake the fish for 20 to 30 minutes, depending on the thickness, until it flakes easily with a fork.

Per Serving:calories: 267 / fat: 18g / protein: 28g / carbs: 1g / fiber: 0g / sodium: 85mg

Tilapia with Pecans

Prep time: 20 minutes / Cook time: 16 minutes / Serves 5
- 2 tablespoons ground flaxseeds
- 1 teaspoon paprika
- Sea salt and white pepper, to taste
- 1 teaspoon garlic paste
- 2 tablespoons extra-virgin olive oil
- ½ cup pecans, ground
- 5 tilapia fillets, sliced into halves

1. Combine the ground flaxseeds, paprika, salt, white pepper, garlic paste, olive oil, and ground pecans in a Ziploc bag. Add the fish fillets and shake to coat well.
2. Spritz the air fryer basket with cooking spray. Cook in the preheated air fryer at 400ºF (204ºC) for 10 minutes; turn them over and cook for 6 minutes more. Work in batches.
3. Serve with lemon wedges, if desired. Enjoy!

Per Serving:calories: 252 / fat: 17g / protein: 25g / carbs: 3g / fiber: 2g / sodium: 65mg

Cod and Cauliflower Chowder

Prep time: 15 minutes / Cook time: 40 minutes / Serves 4
- 2 tablespoons extra-virgin olive oil
- 1 leek, white and light green parts only, cut in half lengthwise and sliced thinly
- 4 garlic cloves, sliced
- 1 medium head cauliflower, coarsely chopped
- 1 teaspoon kosher salt
- ¼ teaspoon freshly ground black pepper
- 2 pints cherry tomatoes
- 2 cups no-salt-added vegetable stock
- ¼ cup green olives, pitted and chopped
- 1 to 1½ pounds (454 to 680 g) cod
- ¼ cup fresh parsley, minced

1. Heat the olive oil in a Dutch oven or large pot over medium heat. Add the leek and sauté until lightly golden brown, about 5 minutes. Add the garlic and sauté for 30 seconds. Add the cauliflower, salt, and black pepper and sauté 2 to 3 minutes.
2. Add the tomatoes and vegetable stock, increase the heat to high and bring to a boil, then turn the heat to low and simmer for 10 minutes.

3. Add the olives and mix together. Add the fish, cover, and simmer 20 minutes, or until fish is opaque and flakes easily. Gently mix in the parsley.

Per Serving:calories: 270 / fat: 9g / protein: 30g / carbs: 19g / fiber: 5g / sodium: 545mg

Roasted Sea Bass

Prep time: 5 minutes / Cook time: 15 minutes / Serves 6
- ¼ cup olive oil
- Whole sea bass or fillets
- Sea salt and freshly ground pepper, to taste
- ¼ cup dry white wine
- 3 teaspoons fresh dill
- 2 teaspoons fresh thyme
- 1 garlic clove, minced

1. Preheat the oven to 425ºF (220ºC).
2. Brush the bottom of a roasting pan with olive oil. Place the fish in the pan and brush the fish with oil.
3. Season fish with sea salt and freshly ground pepper. Combine the remaining ingredients and pour over the fish. Bake for 10–15 minutes, depending on the size of the fish. Sea bass is done when the flesh is firm and opaque.

Per Serving:calories: 217 / fat: 12g / protein: 24g / carbs: 1g / fiber: 0g / sodium: 88mg

Citrus Mediterranean Salmon with Lemon Caper Sauce

Prep time: 15 minutes / Cook time: 22 minutes / Serves 2
- 2 tablespoons fresh lemon juice
- ⅓ cup orange juice
- 1 tablespoon extra virgin olive oil
- ⅛ teaspoon freshly ground black pepper
- 2 (6-ounce / 170-g) salmon fillets
- Lemon Caper Sauce:
- 2 tablespoons extra virgin olive oil
- 1 tablespoon finely chopped red onion
- 1 garlic clove, minced
- 2 tablespoons fresh lemon juice
- 5 ounces (142) dry white wine
- 2 tablespoons capers, rinsed
- ⅛ teaspoon freshly ground black pepper

1. Preheat the oven to 350°F (180°C).
2. In a small bowl, combine the lemon juice, orange juice, olive oil, and black pepper. Whisk until blended, then pour the mixture into a zipper-lock bag. Place the fillets in the bag, shake gently, and transfer the salmon to the refrigerator to marinate for 10 minutes.
3. When the salmon is done marinating, transfer the fillets and marinade to a medium baking dish. Bake for 10–15 minutes or until the salmon is cooked through and the internal temperature reaches 165°F (74°C). Remove the salmon from the oven and cover loosely with foil. Set aside to rest.

4. While the salmon is resting, make the lemon caper sauce by heating the olive oil in a medium pan over medium heat. When the olive oil begins to shimmer, add the onions and sauté for 3 minutes, stirring frequently, then add the garlic and sauté for another 30 seconds.
5. Add the lemon juice and wine. Bring the mixture to a boil and cook until the sauce becomes thick, about 2–3 minutes, then remove the pan from the heat. Add the capers and black pepper, and stir.
6. Transfer the fillets to 2 plates, and spoon 1½ tablespoons of the sauce over each fillet. Store covered in the refrigerator for up to 3 days.

Per Serving:calories: 485 / fat: 28g / protein: 36g / carbs: 11g / fiber: 1g / sodium: 331mg

Poached Octopus

Prep time: 10 minutes / Cook time: 16 minutes / Serves 8

- 2 pounds (907 g) potatoes (about 6 medium)
- 3 teaspoons salt, divided
- 1 (2-pound / 907-g) frozen octopus, thawed, cleaned, and rinsed
- 3 cloves garlic, peeled, divided
- 1 bay leaf
- 2 teaspoons whole peppercorns
- ½ cup olive oil
- ¼ cup white wine vinegar
- ½ teaspoon ground black pepper
- ½ cup chopped fresh parsley

1. Place potatoes in the Instant Pot® with 2 teaspoons salt and enough water to just cover the potatoes halfway. Close lid, set steam release to Sealing, press the Manual button, and set time to 6 minutes. When the timer beeps, quick-release the pressure until the float valve drops and open lid. Press the Cancel button.
2. Remove potatoes with tongs (reserve the cooking water), and peel them as soon as you can handle them. Dice potatoes into bite-sized pieces. Set aside.
3. Add octopus to potato cooking water in the pot and add more water to cover if needed. Add 1 garlic clove, bay leaf, and peppercorns. Close lid, set steam release to Sealing, press the Manual button, and set time to 10 minutes. When the timer beeps, quick-release the pressure until the float valve drops and open lid. Remove and discard bay leaf.
4. Check octopus for tenderness by seeing if a fork will sink easily into the thickest part of the flesh. If not, close the top and bring it to pressure for another minute or two and check again.
5. Remove octopus and drain. Chop head and tentacles into small, bite-sized chunks.
6. Crush remaining 2 garlic cloves and place in a small jar or plastic container. Add olive oil, vinegar, remaining 1 teaspoon salt, and pepper. Close the lid and shake well.

7. In a large serving bowl, mix potatoes with octopus, cover with vinaigrette, and sprinkle with parsley.

Per Serving:calories: 301 / fat: 15g / protein: 15g / carbs: 30g / fiber: 2g / sodium: 883mg

Shrimp with Marinara Sauce

Prep time: 15 minutes / Cook time: 6 to 7 hours / Serves 4

- 1 (15-ounce / 425-g) can diced tomatoes, with the juice
- 1 (6-ounce / 170-g) can tomato paste
- 1 clove garlic, minced
- 2 tablespoons minced fresh flat-leaf parsley
- ½ teaspoon dried basil
- 1 teaspoon dried oregano
- 1 teaspoon garlic powder
- 1½ teaspoons sea salt
- ¼ teaspoon black pepper
- 1 pound (454 g) cooked shrimp, peeled and deveined
- 2 cups hot cooked spaghetti or linguine, for serving
- ½ cup grated parmesan cheese, for serving

1. Combine the tomatoes, tomato paste, and minced garlic in the slow cooker. Sprinkle with the parsley, basil, oregano, garlic powder, salt, and pepper.
2. Cover and cook on low for 6 to 7 hours.
3. Turn up the heat to high, stir in the cooked shrimp, and cover and cook on high for about 15 minutes longer.
4. Serve hot over the cooked pasta. Top with Parmesan cheese.

Per Serving:calories: 313 / fat: 5g / protein: 39g / carbs: 32g / fiber: 7g / sodium: 876mg

Flounder Fillets

Prep time: 10 minutes / Cook time: 5 to 8 minutes / Serves 4

- 1 egg white
- 1 tablespoon water
- 1 cup panko bread crumbs
- 2 tablespoons extra-light virgin olive oil
- 4 (4-ounce / 113-g) flounder fillets
- Salt and pepper, to taste
- Oil for misting or cooking spray

1. Preheat the air fryer to 390ºF (199ºC).
2. Beat together egg white and water in shallow dish.
3. In another shallow dish, mix panko crumbs and oil until well combined and crumbly (best done by hand).
4. Season flounder fillets with salt and pepper to taste. Dip each fillet into egg mixture and then roll in panko crumbs, pressing in crumbs so that fish is nicely coated.
5. Spray the air fryer basket with nonstick cooking spray and add fillets. Air fry at 390ºF (199ºC) for 3 minutes.
6. Spray fish fillets but do not turn. Cook 2 to 5 minutes longer or until golden brown and crispy. Using a spatula, carefully remove fish from basket and serve.

Per Serving:calories: 252 / fat: 10g / protein: 19g / carbs: 19g / fiber: 1g / sodium: 212mg

Italian Halibut with Grapes and Olive Oil

Prep time: 15 minutes / Cook time: 20 minutes / Serves 4

- ¼ cup extra-virgin olive oil
- 4 boneless halibut fillets, 4 ounces (113 g) each
- 4 cloves garlic, roughly chopped
- 1 small red chile pepper, finely chopped
- 2 cups seedless green grapes
- A handful of fresh basil leaves, roughly torn
- ½ teaspoon unrefined sea salt or salt
- Freshly ground black pepper

1. Heat the olive oil in a large, heavy-bottomed skillet over medium-high heat. Add the halibut, followed by the garlic, chile pepper, grapes, basil, and the salt and pepper. Pour in 1¾ cups of water, turn the heat down to medium-low, cover, and cook the fish until opaque, or for 7 minutes on each side.
2. Remove the fish from the pan and place on a large serving dish. Raise the heat, cook the sauce for 30 seconds to concentrate the flavors slightly. Taste and adjust salt and pepper. Pour sauce over the fish.

Per Serving:calories: 389 / fat: 29g / protein: 17g / carbs: 15g / fiber: 1g / sodium: 384mg

Olive Oil–Poached Fish over Citrus Salad

Prep time: 10 minutes / Cook time: 25 minutes / Serves 4

- Fish
- 4 skinless white fish fillets (1¼ to 1½ pounds / 567 to 680 g total), such as halibut, sole, or cod, ¾'–1' thick
- ¼ teaspoon kosher salt
- ¼ teaspoon ground black pepper
- 5–7 cups olive oil
- 1 lemon, thinly sliced
- Salad
- ¼ cup white wine vinegar
- 1 Earl Grey tea bag
- 2 blood oranges or tangerines
- 1 ruby red grapefruit or pomelo
- 6 kumquats, thinly sliced, or 2 clementines, peeled and sectioned
- 4 cups baby arugula
- ½ cup pomegranate seeds
- ¼ cup extra-virgin olive oil
- 2 teaspoons minced shallot
- ½ teaspoon kosher salt
- ¼ teaspoon ground black pepper
- ¼ cup mint leaves, coarsely chopped

1. Make the fish: Season the fish with the salt and pepper and set aside for 30 minutes.
2. Preheat the oven to 225°F.
3. In a large high-sided ovenproof skillet or roasting pan over medium heat, warm 1' to 1½' of the oil and the lemon slices until the temperature reaches 120°F (use a candy thermometer). Add the fish fillets to the oil,

without overlapping, making sure they're completely submerged.
4. Transfer the skillet or pan to the oven, uncovered. Bake for 25 minutes. Transfer the fish to a rack to drain for 5 minutes.
5. Make the salad: In a small saucepan, heat the vinegar until almost boiling. Add the tea bag and set aside to steep for 10 minutes.
6. Meanwhile, with a paring knife, cut off enough of the top and bottom of 1 of the oranges or tangerines to reveal the flesh. Cut along the inside of the peel, between the pith and the flesh, taking off as much pith as possible. Over a large bowl, hold the orange in 1 hand. With the paring knife, cut along the membranes between each section, allowing the fruit to fall into the bowl. Once all the fruit segments have been released, squeeze the remaining membranes over a small bowl. Repeat with the second orange and the grapefruit or pomelo.
7. In the large bowl with the segmented fruit, add the kumquats or clementines, arugula, and pomegranate seeds. Gently toss to distribute.
8. Remove the tea bag from the vinegar and squeeze out as much liquid as possible. Discard the bag and add the vinegar to the small bowl with the citrus juice. Slowly whisk in the oil, shallot, salt, and pepper. Drizzle 3 to 4 tablespoons over the salad and gently toss. (Store the remaining vinaigrette in the refrigerator for up to 1 week.)
9. Sprinkle the salad with the mint and serve with the fish.

Per Serving:calories: 280 / fat: 7g / protein: 29g / carbs: 25g / fiber: 6g / sodium: 249mg

Spicy Steamed Chili Crab

Prep time: 10 minutes / Cook time: 3 minutes / Serves 2

- 2 tablespoons garlic chili sauce
- 1 tablespoon hoisin sauce
- 1 tablespoon minced fresh ginger
- 1 teaspoon fish sauce
- 2 cloves garlic, peeled and minced
- 2 small bird's eye chilies, minced
- 2 (2-pound / 907-g) Dungeness crabs
- 1 cup water

1. In a medium bowl, combine garlic chili sauce, hoisin sauce, ginger, fish sauce, garlic, and chilies. Mix well. Coat crabs in chili mixture.
2. Add water to the Instant Pot® and insert steamer basket. Add crabs to basket. Close lid, set steam release to Sealing, press the Manual button, and set time to 3 minutes.
3. When the timer beeps, quick-release the pressure until the float valve drops. Press the Cancel button and open lid. Transfer crabs to a serving platter. Serve hot.

Per Serving:calories: 128 / fat: 1g / protein: 25g / carbs: 1g / fiber: 0g / sodium: 619mg

Citrus Swordfish

Prep time: 10 minutes / Cook time: 1½ hours / Serves 2

- Nonstick cooking oil spray
- 1½ pounds (680 g) swordfish fillets
- Sea salt
- Black pepper
- 1 yellow onion, chopped
- 5 tablespoons chopped fresh flat-leaf parsley
- 1 tablespoon olive oil
- 2 teaspoons lemon zest
- 2 teaspoons orange zest
- Orange and lemon slices, for garnish
- Fresh parsley sprigs, for garnish

1. Coat the interior of the slow cooker crock with nonstick cooking oil spray.
2. Season the fish fillets with salt and pepper. Place the fish in the slow cooker.
3. Distribute the onion, parsley, olive oil, lemon zest, and orange zest over fish.
4. Cover and cook on low for 1½ hours.
5. Serve hot, garnished with orange and lemon slices and sprigs of fresh parsley.

Per Serving:calories: 578 / fat: 30g / protein: 68g / carbs: 7g / fiber: 2g / sodium: 283mg

Moroccan Fish

Prep time: 10 minutes / Cook time: 2 to 4 hours / Serves 4

- Ras Al-Hanout:
- ¼ teaspoon ground cumin
- ¼ teaspoon ground ginger
- ¼ teaspoon ground turmeric
- ¼ teaspoon paprika
- ¼ teaspoon garlic powder
- ¼ teaspoon red pepper flakes
- ⅛ teaspoon ground cinnamon
- ⅛ teaspoon ground coriander
- ⅛ teaspoon ground nutmeg
- ⅛ teaspoon ground cloves
- ⅛ teaspoon sea salt
- ⅛ teaspoon freshly ground black pepper
- Fish:
- Nonstick cooking spray
- 2 pounds (907 g) fresh white-fleshed fish fillets of your choice
- 2 garlic cloves, minced

1. Make the Ras Al-Hanout: In a small bowl, stir together the cumin, ginger, turmeric, paprika, garlic powder, red pepper flakes, cinnamon, coriander, nutmeg, cloves, salt, and pepper. Make the Fish: 1. Coat a slow-cooker insert with cooking spray, or line the bottom and sides with parchment paper or aluminum foil.
2. Season the fish all over with the ras al-hanout and garlic. Place the fish in the prepared slow cooker in a single layer, cutting it into pieces to fit if needed.
3. Cover the cooker and cook for 2 to 4 hours on Low heat.

Per Serving:calories: 243 / fat: 2g / protein: 51g / carbs: 1g / fiber: 0g / sodium: 216mg

Tomato-Poached Fish

Prep time: 10 minutes / Cook time: 8 minutes / Serves 4

- 2 tablespoons olive oil
- 1 medium onion, peeled and chopped
- 2 cloves garlic, peeled and minced
- 1 tablespoon chopped fresh oregano
- 1 teaspoon fresh thyme leaves
- ½ teaspoon ground fennel
- ¼ teaspoon ground black pepper
- ¼ teaspoon crushed red pepper flakes
- 1 (14½-ounce / 411-g) can diced tomatoes
- 1 cup vegetable broth
- 1 pound (454 g) halibut fillets
- 2 tablespoons chopped fresh parsley

1. Press the Sauté button on the Instant Pot® and heat oil. Add onion and cook until soft, about 4 minutes. Add garlic, oregano, thyme, and fennel. Cook until fragrant, about 30 seconds, then add black pepper, red pepper flakes, tomatoes, and vegetable broth. Press the Cancel button.
2. Top vegetables with fish, close lid, set steam release to Sealing, press the Manual button, and set time to 3 minutes.
3. When the timer beeps, quick-release the pressure until the float valve drops and open lid. Carefully transfer fillets to a serving platter and spoon sauce over fillets. Sprinkle with parsley and serve hot.

Per Serving:calories: 212 / fat: 8g / protein: 24g / carbs: 10g / fiber: 2g / sodium: 449mg

Basil Cod Kebabs

Prep time: 15 minutes / Cook time: 2 minutes / Serves 4

- 1 cup water
- 4 (4-ounce / 113-g) cod or other white fish fillets, cut into 1" pieces
- ½ medium onion, peeled and cut into 1" pieces
- ½ medium red bell pepper, seeded and cut into 1" pieces
- 2 tablespoons extra-virgin olive oil
- 2 tablespoons chopped fresh basil
- ½ teaspoon salt
- ½ teaspoon ground black pepper
- 1 small lemon, cut into wedges

1. Place rack inside the Instant Pot® and add water.
2. Thread fish, onion, and bell pepper alternately onto four wooden skewers. Brush skewers with olive oil, then top with basil, salt, and black pepper. Place skewers on rack. Close lid, set steam release to Sealing, press Steam, and set time to 2 minutes.

3. When the timer beeps, quick-release the pressure until the float valve drops. Press the Cancel button and open lid. Serve with lemon.

Per Serving:calories: 93 / fat: 7g / protein: 5g / carbs: 2g / fiber: 1g / sodium: 312mg

CRAB STEW

Serves: 2/Prep time: 13 minutes / Cook time: 15 minutes
- ½ lb. lump crab meat
- 2 tbsp heavy cream
- 1 tbsp olive oil
- 2 cups fish stock
- ½ lb. shrimp, shelled and chopped
- 1 celery stalk, chopped
- ½ tsp garlic, chopped
- ¼ onion, chopped
- Pepper
- Salt

1. Add oil to the instant pot's inner pot and select the sauté setting. Add the onion and sauté for 3 to 4 minutes. Stir in garlic, cooking for 30 seconds. Add the remaining ingredients, excluding the heavy cream, and mix thoroughly.
2. Cover and simmer on high for ten minutes. Once complete, release pressure with a rapid release. Remove lid. Add heavy cream, then serve.

Per Serving:Calories 376 / Fat 23.5g / Carbs 5.8g / / Fiber 6.2g /Protein 48g /

FETA TOMATO SEA BASS

Serves: 4/Prep time: 10 minutes / Cook time: 10 minutes
Ingredients:
- 4 sea bass fillets
- 1 ½ cups water
- 1 tbsp olive oil
- 1 tsp garlic, minced
- 1 tsp basil, chopped
- 1 tsp parsley, chopped
- 1/2 cup feta cheese, crumbled
- 1 cup can tomato, diced
- Pepper
- Salt

1. Add pepper and salt to fillets of fish. Pour two cups of water into the instant pot, followed by the steamer rack.

Place fish fillets on the pot's steamer rack. Cook for 5 minutes on high after securing the lid.
2. Once complete, release pressure with a rapid release. Remove lid. Remove the fish fillets from the pot and clean it. Pour oil into the instant pot's inner pot and select the sauté setting. Stir in garlic, cook for one minute.
3. Add the parsley, tomatoes, and basil and simmer for 1 minute, stirring well. Add fish fillets and cheese crumbs, then heat for one minute. Serve up.

Per Serving:Calories 219 /Fat 10.1 g /Carb 4 g/ Fiber 2.8 g/ Protein 27.1 g

PAPRIKA SALMON AND GREEN BEANS

Serves 3/Prep time: 10 minutes / Cook time: 22 minutes
- ¼ cup olive oil
- ½ tablespoon onion powder
- ½ teaspoon bouillon powder
- ½ teaspoon cayenne pepper
- 1 tablespoon smoked paprika
- 1-pound green beans
- 2 teaspoon minced garlic
- 3 tablespoon fresh herbs
- 6 ounces of salmon steak
- Salt and pepper to taste

1. Preheat the oven to 400 degrees Fahrenheit. Grease and put aside a baking sheet. In a skillet heated over medium-low heat, add olive oil. Sauté the garlic, smoked paprika, fresh herbs, cayenne pepper, and onion for 3 minutes.
2. Stir the mixture for one minute, then let it settle for five minutes. Set aside
3. Place the salmon steaks in a container and season them with the salt and paprika mixture. Rub the salmon to coat it.
4. Cook for 18 minutes after placing the fish on the baking sheet.
5. Meanwhile, blanch the green beans in salted boiling water. Complement the fish with the beans.

Per Serving:Calories 945 / Fat 66.6g / Carbs 43g / Fiber 1.5g /Protein 43g

Chapter 6 Snacks and Appetizers

Garlic Edamame

Prep time: 5 minutes / Cook time: 10 minutes / Serves 4

- Olive oil
- 1 (16-ounce / 454-g) bag frozen edamame in pods
- ½ teaspoon salt
- ½ teaspoon garlic salt
- ¼ teaspoon freshly ground black pepper
- ½ teaspoon red pepper flakes (optional)

1. Spray the air fryer basket lightly with olive oil.
2. In a medium bowl, add the frozen edamame and lightly spray with olive oil. Toss to coat.
3. In a small bowl, mix together the salt, garlic salt, black pepper, and red pepper flakes (if using). Add the mixture to the edamame and toss until evenly coated.
4. Place half the edamame in the air fryer basket. Do not overfill the basket.
5. Air fry at 375°F (191°C) for 5 minutes. Shake the basket and cook until the edamame is starting to brown and get crispy, 3 to 5 more minutes.
6. Repeat with the remaining edamame and serve immediately.

Per Serving:calories: 125 / fat: 5g / protein: 12g / carbs: 10g / fiber: 5g / sodium: 443mg

Ranch Oyster Snack Crackers

Prep time: 3 minutes / Cook time: 12 minutes / Serves 6

- Oil, for spraying
- ¼ cup olive oil
- 2 teaspoons dry ranch seasoning
- 1 teaspoon chili powder
- ½ teaspoon dried dill
- ½ teaspoon granulated garlic
- ½ teaspoon salt
- 1 (9 ounces / 255 g) bag oyster crackers

1. Preheat the air fryer to 325°F (163°C). Line the air fryer basket with parchment and spray lightly with oil.
2. In a large bowl, mix together the olive oil, ranch seasoning, chili powder, dill, garlic, and salt. Add the crackers and toss until evenly coated.
3. Place the mixture in the prepared basket.
4. Cook for 10 to 12 minutes, shaking or stirring every 3 to 4 minutes, or until crisp and golden brown.

Per Serving:calories: 261 / fat: 13g / protein: 4g / carbs: 32g / fiber: 1g / sodium: 621mg

Roasted Pepper Bruschetta with Capers and Basil

Prep time: 10 minutes / Cook time: 15 minutes / Serves 6 to 8

- 2 red bell peppers
- 2 yellow bell peppers
- 2 orange bell peppers
- 2 tablespoons olive oil, plus ¼ cup
- ¾ teaspoon salt, divided
- ½ teaspoon freshly ground black pepper, divided
- 3 tablespoons red wine vinegar
- 1 teaspoon Dijon mustard
- 1 clove garlic, minced
- 2 tablespoons capers, drained
- ¼ cup chopped fresh basil leaves, divided
- 1 whole-wheat baguette or other crusty bread, thinly sliced

1. Preheat the broiler to high and line a large baking sheet with aluminum foil.
2. Brush the peppers all over with 2 tablespoons of the olive oil and sprinkle with ½ teaspoon of the salt and ¼ teaspoon of the pepper.
3. Broil the peppers, turning every 3 minutes or so, until the skin is charred on all sides. Place them in a bowl, cover with plastic wrap, and let steam for 10 minutes. Slip the skins off and discard them. Seed and dice the peppers.
4. In a large bowl, whisk together the vinegar, mustard, garlic, the remaining ¼ teaspoon salt, and the remaining ¼ teaspoon of pepper. Still whisking, slowly add the remaining ¼ cup oil in a thin stream until the dressing is emulsified. Stir in the capers, 2 tablespoons of the basil, and the diced peppers.
5. Toast the bread slices and then spoon the pepper mixture over them, drizzling with extra dressing. Garnish with the remaining basil and serve immediately.

Per Serving:calories: 243 / fat: 6g / protein: 8g / carbs: 39g / fiber: 4g / sodium: 755mg

Black Olive and Lentil Pesto

Prep time: 10 minutes / Cook time: 20 minutes / Serves 10 to 12

- ¾ cup green lentils, rinsed
- ¼ teaspoon salt
- ½ cup pitted Kalamata olives
- 2 tablespoons fresh Greek oregano
- 2 garlic cloves, minced
- 2 tablespoons coarsely chopped fresh parsley
- 3 tablespoons fresh lemon juice
- 5 tablespoons olive oil

1. Place the lentils in a large saucepan and add cold water to cover by 1 inch. Bring the water to a boil; cover and simmer for 20 minutes, or until the lentils are soft but not disintegrating. Drain and let cool.
2. Shake the colander a few times to remove any excess water, then transfer the lentils to a blender or food processor. Add the salt, olives, oregano, garlic, and parsley. With the machine running, add the lemon juice,

then the olive oil, and blend until smooth.

3. Serve with pita chips, pita bread, or as a dip for fresh vegetables.

Per Serving:1 cup: calories: 70 / fat: 7g / protein: 1g / carbs: 2g / fiber: 1g / sodium: 99mg

Roasted Chickpeas with Herbs and Spices

Prep time: 5 minutes / Cook time: 22 minutes / Serves 4

- 1 (15-ounce / 425-g) can chickpeas, drained and rinsed
- 1 tablespoon olive oil
- 1 teaspoon za'atar
- ½ teaspoon ground sumac
- 1 teaspoon Aleppo pepper
- 1 teaspoon brown sugar
- ½ teaspoon kosher salt
- 2 tablespoons chopped fresh parsley

1. Preheat the oven to 350ºF (180ºC).
2. Spread the chickpeas in an even layer on an ungreased rimmed baking sheet and bake for 10 minutes, or until they are dried. Remove from the oven; keep the oven on.
3. Meanwhile, in a medium bowl, whisk together the olive oil, za'atar, sumac, Aleppo pepper, brown sugar, and salt until well combined.
4. Add the warm chickpeas to the oil-spice mixture and stir until they are completely coated. Return the chickpeas to the baking sheet and spread them into an even layer. Bake for 10 to 12 minutes more, until fragrant.
5. Transfer the chickpeas to a serving bowl, toss with the parsley, and serve.

Per Serving:1 cup: calories: 122 / fat: 5g / protein: 5g / carbs: 16g / fiber: 4g / sodium: 427mg

Tuna Croquettes

Prep time: 40 minutes / Cook time: 25 minutes / Makes 36 croquettes

- 6 tablespoons extra-virgin olive oil, plus 1 to 2 cups
- 5 tablespoons almond flour, plus 1 cup, divided
- 1¼ cups heavy cream
- 1 (4 ounces / 113 g) can olive oil-packed yellowfin tuna
- 1 tablespoon chopped red onion
- 2 teaspoons minced capers
- ½ teaspoon dried dill
- ¼ teaspoon freshly ground black pepper
- 2 large eggs
- 1 cup panko breadcrumbs (or a gluten-free version)

1. In a large skillet, heat 6 tablespoons olive oil over medium-low heat. Add 5 tablespoons almond flour and cook, stirring constantly, until a smooth paste forms and the flour browns slightly, 2 to 3 minutes.
2. Increase the heat to medium-high and gradually add the heavy cream, whisking constantly until completely smooth and thickened, another 4 to 5 minutes.
3. Remove from the heat and stir in the tuna, red onion, capers, dill, and pepper.
4. Transfer the mixture to an 8-inch square baking dish that is well coated with olive oil and allow to cool to room temperature. Cover and refrigerate until chilled, at least 4 hours or up to overnight.
5. To form the croquettes, set out three bowls. In one, beat together the eggs. In another, add the remaining almond flour. In the third, add the panko. Line a baking sheet with parchment paper.
6. Using a spoon, place about a tablespoon of cold prepared dough into the flour mixture and roll to coat. Shake off excess and, using your hands, roll into an oval.
7. Dip the croquette into the beaten egg, then lightly coat in panko. Set on lined baking sheet and repeat with the remaining dough.
8. In a small saucepan, heat the remaining 1 to 2 cups of olive oil, so that the oil is about 1 inch deep, over medium-high heat. The smaller the pan, the less oil you will need, but you will need more for each batch.
9. Test if the oil is ready by throwing a pinch of panko into pot. If it sizzles, the oil is ready for frying. If it sinks, it's not quite ready. Once the oil is heated, fry the croquettes 3 or 4 at a time, depending on the size of your pan, removing with a slotted spoon when golden brown. You will need to adjust the temperature of the oil occasionally to prevent burning. If the croquettes get dark brown very quickly, lower the temperature.

Per Serving:2 croquettes: calories: 271 / fat: 26g / protein: 5g / carbs: 6g / fiber: 1g / sodium: 89mg
calories: 94 / fat: 8g / protein: 3g / carbs: 2g / net carbs: 1g / fiber: 1g

Fried Baby Artichokes with Lemon-Garlic Aioli

Prep time: 5 minutes / Cook time: 50 minutes / Serves 10

- Artichokes:
- 15 baby artichokes
- ½ lemon
- 3 cups olive oil
- Kosher salt, to taste
- Aioli:
- 1 egg
- 2 cloves garlic, chopped
- 1 tablespoon fresh lemon juice
- ½ teaspoon Dijon mustard
- ½ cup olive oil
- Kosher salt and ground black pepper, to taste

1. Make the Artichokes: Wash and drain the artichokes. With a paring knife, strip off the coarse outer leaves around the base and stalk, leaving the softer leaves on. Carefully peel the stalks and trim off all but 2' below the base. Slice off the top ½' of the artichokes. Cut each artichoke in half. Rub the cut surfaces with a lemon half to keep from browning.
2. In a medium saucepan fitted with a deep-fry thermometer over medium heat, warm the oil to about 280°F(138ºC). Working in batches, cook the artichokes

in the hot oil until tender, about 15 minutes. Using a slotted spoon, remove and drain on a paper towel–lined plate. Repeat with all the artichoke halves.

3. Increase the heat of the oil to 375°F(190ºC). In batches, cook the precooked baby artichokes until browned at the edges and crisp, about 1 minute. Transfer to a paper towel–lined plate. Season with the salt to taste. Repeat with the remaining artichokes.

4. Make the aioli: In a blender, pulse together the egg, garlic, lemon juice, and mustard until combined. With the blender running, slowly drizzle in the oil a few drops at a time until the mixture thickens like mayonnaise, about 2 minutes. Transfer to a bowl and season to taste with the salt and pepper.

5. Serve the warm artichokes with the aioli on the side.

Per Serving:calories: 236 / fat: 17g / protein: 6g / carbs: 21g / fiber: 10g / sodium: 283mg

Turmeric-Spiced Crunchy Chickpeas

Prep time: 15 minutes / Cook time: 30 minutes / Serves 4

- 2 (15-ounce / 425-g) cans organic chickpeas, drained and rinsed
- 3 tablespoons extra-virgin olive oil
- 2 teaspoons Turkish or smoked paprika
- 2 teaspoons turmeric
- ½ teaspoon dried oregano
- ½ teaspoon salt
- ¼ teaspoon ground ginger
- ⅛ teaspoon ground white pepper (optional)

1. Preheat the oven to 400°F(205ºC). Line a baking sheet with parchment paper and set aside.

2. Completely dry the chickpeas. Lay the chickpeas out on a baking sheet, roll them around with paper towels, and allow them to air-dry. I usually let them dry for at least 2½ hours, but can also be left to dry overnight.

3. In a medium bowl, combine the olive oil, paprika, turmeric, oregano, salt, ginger, and white pepper (if using).

4. Add the dry chickpeas to the bowl and toss to combine.

5. Put the chickpeas on the prepared baking sheet and cook for 30 minutes, or until the chickpeas turn golden brown. At 15 minutes, move the chickpeas around on the baking sheet to avoid burning. Check every 10 minutes in case the chickpeas begin to crisp up before the full cooking time has elapsed.

6. Remove from the oven and set them aside to cool.

Per Serving:½ cup: calories: 308 / fat: 13g / protein: 11g / carbs: 40g / fiber: 11g / sodium: 292mg

Lemon-Pepper Chicken Drumsticks

Prep time: 30 minutes / Cook time: 30 minutes / Serves 2

- 2 teaspoons freshly ground coarse black pepper
- 1 teaspoon baking powder
- ½ teaspoon garlic powder
- 4 chicken drumsticks (4 ounces / 113 g each)

- Kosher salt, to taste
- 1 lemon

1. In a small bowl, stir together the pepper, baking powder, and garlic powder. Place the drumsticks on a plate and sprinkle evenly with the baking powder mixture, turning the drumsticks so they're well coated. Let the drumsticks stand in the refrigerator for at least 1 hour or up to overnight.

2. Sprinkle the drumsticks with salt, then transfer them to the air fryer, standing them bone-end up and leaning against the wall of the air fryer basket. Air fry at 375°F (191ºC) until cooked through and crisp on the outside, about 30 minutes.

3. Transfer the drumsticks to a serving platter and finely grate the zest of the lemon over them while they're hot. Cut the lemon into wedges and serve with the warm drumsticks.

Per Serving:calories: 438 / fat: 24g / protein: 48g / carbs: 6g / fiber: 2g / sodium: 279mg

Quick Garlic Mushrooms

Prep time: 10 minutes / Cook time: 10 minutes / Serves 4 to 6

- 2 pounds (907 g) cremini mushrooms, cleaned
- 3 tablespoons unsalted butter
- 2 tablespoons garlic, minced
- ½ teaspoon salt
- ½ teaspoon freshly ground black pepper

1. Cut each mushroom in half, stem to top, and put them into a bowl.

2. Preheat a large sauté pan or skillet over medium heat.

3. Cook the butter and garlic in the pan for 2 minutes, stirring occasionally.

4. Add the mushrooms and salt to the pan and toss together with the garlic butter mixture. Cook for 7 to 8 minutes, stirring every 2 minutes.

5. Remove the mushrooms from the pan and pour into a serving dish. Top with black pepper.

Per Serving:calories: 183 / fat: 9g / protein: 9g / carbs: 10g / fiber: 3g / sodium: 334mg

Cheese-Stuffed Dates

Prep time: 10 minutes / Cook time: 10 minutes / Serves 4

- 2 ounces (57 g) low-fat cream cheese, at room temperature
- 2 tablespoons sweet pickle relish
- 1 tablespoon low-fat plain Greek yogurt
- 1 teaspoon finely chopped fresh chives
- ¼ teaspoon kosher salt
- ⅛ teaspoon ground black pepper
- Dash of hot sauce
- 2 tablespoons pistachios, chopped
- 8 Medjool dates, pitted and halved

1. In a small bowl, stir together the cream cheese, relish, yogurt, chives, salt, pepper, and hot sauce.

2. Put the pistachios on a clean plate. Put the cream cheese mixture into a resealable plastic bag, and snip off 1 corner of the bag. Pipe the cream cheese mixture into the date halves and press the tops into the pistachios to coat.

Per Serving:calories: 196 / fat: 4g / protein: 3g / carbs: 41g / fiber: 4g / sodium: 294mg

Greens Chips with Curried Yogurt Sauce

Prep time: 10 minutes / Cook time: 5 to 6 minutes / Serves 4

- 1 cup low-fat Greek yogurt
- 1 tablespoon freshly squeezed lemon juice
- 1 tablespoon curry powder
- ½ bunch curly kale, stemmed, ribs removed and discarded, leaves cut into 2- to 3-inch pieces
- ½ bunch chard, stemmed, ribs removed and discarded, leaves cut into 2- to 3-inch pieces
- 1½ teaspoons olive oil

1. In a small bowl, stir together the yogurt, lemon juice, and curry powder. Set aside.
2. In a large bowl, toss the kale and chard with the olive oil, working the oil into the leaves with your hands. This helps break up the fibers in the leaves so the chips are tender.
3. Air fry the greens in batches at 390ºF (199ºC) for 5 to 6 minutes, until crisp, shaking the basket once during cooking. Serve with the yogurt sauce.

Per Serving:calories: 98 / fat: 4g / protein: 7g / carbs: 13g / fiber: 4g / sodium: 186mg

Mixed-Vegetable Caponata

Prep time: 15 minutes / Cook time: 40 minutes / Serves 8

- 1 eggplant, chopped
- 1 zucchini, chopped
- 1 red bell pepper, seeded and chopped
- 1 small red onion, chopped
- 2 tablespoons extra-virgin olive oil, divided
- 1 cup canned tomato sauce
- 3 tablespoons red wine vinegar
- 1 tablespoon honey
- ¼ teaspoon red-pepper flakes
- ¼ teaspoon kosher salt
- ½ cup pitted, chopped green olives
- 2 tablespoons drained capers
- 2 tablespoons raisins
- 2 tablespoons chopped fresh flat-leaf parsley

1. Preheat the oven to 400°F(205ºC).
2. On a large rimmed baking sheet, toss the eggplant, zucchini, bell pepper, and onion with 1 tablespoon of the oil. Roast until the vegetables are tender, about 30 minutes.
3. In a medium saucepan over medium heat, warm the remaining 1 tablespoon oil. Add the tomato sauce, vinegar, honey, pepper flakes, and salt and stir to combine. Add the roasted vegetables, olives, capers, raisins, and parsley and cook until bubbly and

thickened, 10 minutes.
4. Remove from the heat and cool to room temperature. Serve immediately or store in an airtight container in the refrigerator for up to 1 week.

Per Serving:calories: 100 / fat: 5g / protein: 2g / carbs: 13g / fiber: 4g / sodium: 464mg

Mediterranean-Style Stuffed Mushrooms

Prep time: 10 minutes / Cook time: 20 minutes / Serves 4

- 2 ounces (57 g) feta
- 1 tablespoon cream cheese
- 2 teaspoons dried oregano
- 1 tablespoon finely chopped fresh parsley
- 2 tablespoons finely chopped fresh basil
- 2 tablespoons finely chopped fresh mint
- ¼ teaspoon freshly ground black pepper
- 3 tablespoons unseasoned breadcrumbs, divided
- 2 tablespoons extra virgin olive oil, divided
- 20 medium button mushrooms, washed, dried, and stems removed

1. Preheat the oven to 400°F (205ºC). Line a large baking pan with foil.
2. In a medium bowl, combine the feta, cream cheese, oregano, parsley, basil, mint, black pepper, 2 tablespoons of the breadcrumbs, and 1 tablespoon of the olive oil. Use a fork to mash the ingredients until they're combined and somewhat creamy.
3. Stuff the mushrooms with the filling and then place them in the prepared pan.
4. Sprinkle the remaining 1 tablespoon of breadcrumbs over the mushrooms and then drizzle the remaining olive oil over the top.
5. Bake for 15–20 minutes or until the tops are golden brown. Serve promptly.

Per Serving:calories: 151 / fat: 12g / protein: 6g / carbs: 8g / fiber: 1g / sodium: 186mg

Mexican Potato Skins

Prep time: 10 minutes / Cook time: 55 minutes / Serves 6

- Olive oil
- 6 medium russet potatoes, scrubbed
- Salt and freshly ground black pepper, to taste
- 1 cup fat-free refried black beans
- 1 tablespoon taco seasoning
- ½ cup salsa
- ¾ cup reduced-fat shredded Cheddar cheese

1. Spray the air fryer basket lightly with olive oil.
2. Spray the potatoes lightly with oil and season with salt and pepper. Pierce each potato a few times with a fork.
3. Place the potatoes in the air fryer basket. Air fry at 400ºF (204ºC) until fork-tender, 30 to 40 minutes. The cooking time will depend on the size of the potatoes. You can cook the potatoes in the microwave or a standard oven, but they won't get the same lovely crispy

skin they will get in the air fryer.

4. While the potatoes are cooking, in a small bowl, mix together the beans and taco seasoning. Set aside until the potatoes are cool enough to handle.

5. Cut each potato in half lengthwise. Scoop out most of the insides, leaving about ¼ inch in the skins so the potato skins hold their shape.

6. Season the insides of the potato skins with salt and black pepper. Lightly spray the insides of the potato skins with oil. You may need to cook them in batches.

7. Place them into the air fryer basket, skin-side down, and air fry until crisp and golden, 8 to 10 minutes.

8. Transfer the skins to a work surface and spoon ½ tablespoon of seasoned refried black beans into each one. Top each with 2 teaspoons salsa and 1 tablespoon shredded Cheddar cheese.

9. Place filled potato skins in the air fryer basket in a single layer. Lightly spray with oil.

10. Air fry until the cheese is melted and bubbly, 2 to 3 minutes.

Per Serving:calories: 239 / fat: 2g / protein: 10g / carbs: 46g / fiber: 5g / sodium: 492mg

Spanish Home Fries with Spicy Tomato Sauce

Prep time: 5 minutes / Cook time: 1 hour / Serves 6

- 4 russet potatoes, peeled, cut into large dice
- ¼ cup olive oil plus 1 tablespoon, divided
- ½ cup crushed tomatoes
- 1½ teaspoons red wine
- 1 teaspoon hot smoked paprika
- 1 serrano chile, seeded and chopped
- ½ teaspoon salt
- ¼ teaspoon freshly ground black pepper

1. Preheat the oven to 425°F(220ºC).

2. Toss the potatoes with ¼ cup of olive oil and spread on a large baking sheet. Season with salt and pepper and roast in the preheated oven for about 50 to 60 minutes, turning once in the middle, until the potatoes are golden brown and crisp.

3. Meanwhile, make the sauce by combining the tomatoes, the remaining 1 tablespoon olive oil, wine, paprika, chile, salt, and pepper in a food processor or blender and process until smooth.

4. Serve the potatoes hot with the sauce on the side for dipping or spooned over the top.

Per Serving:calories: 201 / fat: 11g / protein: 3g / carbs: 25g / fiber: 4g / sodium: 243mg

Manchego Crackers

Prep time: 15 minutes / Cook time: 15 minutes / Makes 40 crackers

- 4 tablespoons butter, at room temperature
- 1 cup finely shredded Manchego cheese
- 1 cup almond flour
- 1 teaspoon salt, divided
- ¼ teaspoon freshly ground black pepper
- 1 large egg

1. Using an electric mixer, cream together the butter and shredded cheese until well combined and smooth.

2. In a small bowl, combine the almond flour with ½ teaspoon salt and pepper. Slowly add the almond flour mixture to the cheese, mixing constantly until the dough just comes together to form a ball.

3. Transfer to a piece of parchment or plastic wrap and roll into a cylinder log about 1½ inches thick. Wrap tightly and refrigerate for at least 1 hour.

4. Preheat the oven to 350°F(180ºC). Line two baking sheets with parchment paper or silicone baking mats.

5. To make the egg wash, in a small bowl, whisk together the egg and remaining ½ teaspoon salt.

6. Slice the refrigerated dough into small rounds, about ¼ inch thick, and place on the lined baking sheets.

7. Brush the tops of the crackers with egg wash and bake until the crackers are golden and crispy, 12 to 15 minutes. Remove from the oven and allow to cool on a wire rack.

8. Serve warm or, once fully cooled, store in an airtight container in the refrigerator for up to 1 week.

Per Serving:2 crackers: calories: 73 / fat: 7g / protein: 3g / carbs: 1g / fiber: 1g / sodium: 154mg

Flatbread with Ricotta and Orange-Raisin Relish

Prep time: 5 minutes / Cook time: 8 minutes / Serves 4 to 6

- ¾ cup golden raisins, roughly chopped
- 1 shallot, finely diced
- 1 tablespoon olive oil
- 1 tablespoon red wine vinegar
- 1 tablespoon honey
- 1 tablespoon chopped flat-leaf parsley
- 1 tablespoon fresh orange zest strips
- Pinch of salt
- 1 oval prebaked whole-wheat flatbread, such as naan or pocketless pita
- 8 ounces (227 g) whole-milk ricotta cheese
- ½ cup baby arugula

1. Preheat the oven to 450°F(235ºC).

2. In a small bowl, stir together the raisins, shallot, olive oil, vinegar, honey, parsley, orange zest, and salt.

3. Place the flatbread on a large baking sheet and toast in the preheated oven until the edges are lightly browned, about 8 minutes.

4. Spoon the ricotta cheese onto the flatbread, spreading with the back of the spoon. Scatter the arugula over the cheese. Cut the flatbread into triangles and top each piece with a dollop of the relish. Serve immediately.

Per Serving:calories: 195 / fat: 9g / protein: 6g / carbs: 25g / fiber: 1g / sodium: 135mg

Savory Mackerel & Goat'S Cheese "Paradox" Balls

Prep time: 10 minutes / Cook time: 0 minutes / Makes 10 fat bombs

- 2 smoked or cooked mackerel fillets, boneless, skin removed
- 4.4 ounces (125 g) soft goat's cheese
- 1 tablespoon fresh lemon juice
- 1 teaspoon Dijon or yellow mustard
- 1 small red onion, finely diced
- 2 tablespoons chopped fresh chives or herbs of choice
- ¾ cup pecans, crushed
- 10 leaves baby gem lettuce

1. In a food processor, combine the mackerel, goat's cheese, lemon juice, and mustard. Pulse until smooth. Transfer to a bowl, add the onion and herbs, and mix with a spoon. Refrigerate for 20 to 30 minutes, or until set.
2. Using a large spoon or an ice cream scoop, divide the mixture into 10 balls, about 40 g/1.4 ounces each. Roll each ball in the crushed pecans. Place each ball on a small lettuce leaf and serve. Keep the fat bombs refrigerated in a sealed container for up to 5 days.

Per Serving: 1 fat bomb: calories: 165 / fat: 12g / protein: 12g / carbs: 2g / fiber: 1g / sodium: 102mg

Sea Salt Potato Chips

Prep time: 30 minutes / Cook time: 27 minutes / Serves 4

- Oil, for spraying
- 4 medium yellow potatoes
- 1 tablespoon oil
- ⅛ to ¼ teaspoon fine sea salt

1. Line the air fryer basket with parchment and spray lightly with oil.
2. Using a mandoline or a very sharp knife, cut the potatoes into very thin slices.
3. Place the slices in a bowl of cold water and let soak for about 20 minutes.
4. Drain the potatoes, transfer them to a plate lined with paper towels, and pat dry.
5. Drizzle the oil over the potatoes, sprinkle with the salt, and toss to combine. Transfer to the prepared basket.
6. Air fry at 200°F (93°C) for 20 minutes. Toss the chips, increase the heat to 400°F (204°C), and cook for another 5 to 7 minutes, until crispy.

Per Serving: calories: 194 / fat: 4g / protein: 4g / carbs: 37g / fiber: 5g / sodium: 90mg

Burrata Caprese Stack

Prep time: 5 minutes / Cook time: 0 minutes / Serves 4

- 1 large organic tomato, preferably heirloom
- ½ teaspoon salt
- ¼ teaspoon freshly ground black pepper
- 1 (4 ounces / 113 g) ball burrata cheese
- 8 fresh basil leaves, thinly sliced
- 2 tablespoons extra-virgin olive oil
- 1 tablespoon red wine or balsamic vinegar

1. Slice the tomato into 4 thick slices, removing any tough center core and sprinkle with salt and pepper. Place the tomatoes, seasoned-side up, on a plate.
2. On a separate rimmed plate, slice the burrata into 4 thick slices and place one slice on top of each tomato slice. Top each with one-quarter of the basil and pour any reserved burrata cream from the rimmed plate over top.
3. Drizzle with olive oil and vinegar and serve with a fork and knife.

Per Serving: calories: 109 / fat: 7g / protein: 9g / carbs: 3g / fiber: 1g / sodium: 504mg

Buffalo Bites

Prep time: 15 minutes / Cook time: 11 to 12 minutes per batch / Makes 16 meatballs

- 1½ cups cooked jasmine or sushi rice
- ¼ teaspoon salt
- 1 pound (454 g) ground chicken
- 8 tablespoons buffalo wing sauce
- 2 ounces (57 g) Gruyère cheese, cut into 16 cubes
- 1 tablespoon maple syrup

1. Mix 4 tablespoons buffalo wing sauce into all the ground chicken.
2. Shape chicken into a log and divide into 16 equal portions.
3. With slightly damp hands, mold each chicken portion around a cube of cheese and shape into a firm ball. When you have shaped 8 meatballs, place them in air fryer basket.
4. Air fry at 390°F (199°C) for approximately 5 minutes. Shake basket, reduce temperature to 360°F (182°C), and cook for 5 to 6 minutes longer.
5. While the first batch is cooking, shape remaining chicken and cheese into 8 more meatballs.
6. Repeat step 4 to cook second batch of meatballs.
7. In a medium bowl, mix the remaining 4 tablespoons of buffalo wing sauce with the maple syrup. Add all the cooked meatballs and toss to coat.
8. Place meatballs back into air fryer basket and air fry at 390°F (199°C) for 2 to 3 minutes to set the glaze. Skewer each with a toothpick and serve.

Per Serving: calories: 85 / fat: 4g / protein: 7g / carbs: 6g / fiber: 0g / sodium: 236mg

Goat Cheese–Mackerel Pâté

Prep time: 10 minutes / Cook time: 0 minutes / Serves 4

- 4 ounces (113 g) olive oil-packed wild-caught mackerel
- 2 ounces (57 g) goat cheese
- Zest and juice of 1 lemon
- 2 tablespoons chopped fresh parsley
- 2 tablespoons chopped fresh arugula
- 1 tablespoon extra-virgin olive oil
- 2 teaspoons chopped capers
- 1 to 2 teaspoons fresh horseradish (optional)

- Crackers, cucumber rounds, endive spears, or celery, for serving (optional)
1. In a food processor, blender, or large bowl with immersion blender, combine the mackerel, goat cheese, lemon zest and juice, parsley, arugula, olive oil, capers, and horseradish (if using). Process or blend until smooth and creamy.
2. Serve with crackers, cucumber rounds, endive spears, or celery.
3. Store covered in the refrigerator for up to 1 week.

Per Serving:calories: 142 / fat: 10g / protein: 11g / carbs: 1g / fiber: 0g / sodium: 203mg

Mini Lettuce Wraps

Prep time: 10 minutes / Cook time: 0 minutes / Makes about 1 dozen wraps

- 1 tomato, diced
- 1 cucumber, diced
- 1 red onion, sliced
- 1 ounce (28 g) low-fat feta cheese, crumbled
- Juice of 1 lemon
- 1 tablespoon olive oil
- Sea salt and freshly ground pepper, to taste
- 12 small, intact iceberg lettuce leaves

1. Combine the tomato, cucumber, onion, and feta in a bowl with the lemon juice and olive oil.
2. Season with sea salt and freshly ground pepper.
3. Without tearing the leaves, gently fill each leaf with a tablespoon of the veggie mixture.
4. Roll them as tightly as you can, and lay them seam-side-down on a serving platter.

Per Serving:1 wrap: calories: 26 / fat: 2g / protein: 1g / carbs: 2g / fiber: 1g / sodium: 20mg

Marinated Olives

Prep time: 5 minutes / Cook time: 5 minutes / Serves 8 to 10

- 3 tablespoons olive oil
- Zest and juice of 1 lemon
- ½ teaspoon Aleppo pepper or red pepper flakes
- ¼ teaspoon ground sumac
- 1 cup pitted Kalamata olives
- 1 cup pitted green olives, such as Castelvetrano
- 2 tablespoons finely chopped fresh parsley

1. In a medium skillet, heat the olive oil over medium heat. Add the lemon zest, Aleppo pepper, and sumac and cook for 1 to 2 minutes, occasionally stirring, until fragrant. Remove from the heat and stir in the olives, lemon juice, and parsley.
2. Transfer the olives to a bowl and serve immediately, or let cool, then transfer to an airtight container and store in the refrigerator for up to 1 week. The flavor will continue to develop and is best after 8 to 12 hours.

Per Serving:1 cup: calories: 59 / fat: 6g / protein: 0g / carbs: 1g / fiber: 1g / sodium: 115mg

Taste of the Mediterranean Fat Bombs

Prep time: 15 minutes / Makes 6 fat bombs

- 1 cup crumbled goat cheese
- 4 tablespoons jarred pesto
- 12 pitted Kalamata olives, finely chopped
- ½ cup finely chopped walnuts
- 1 tablespoon chopped fresh rosemary

1. In a medium bowl, combine the goat cheese, pesto, and olives and mix well using a fork. Place in the refrigerator for at least 4 hours to harden.
2. Using your hands, form the mixture into 6 balls, about ¾-inch diameter. The mixture will be sticky.
3. In a small bowl, place the walnuts and rosemary and roll the goat cheese balls in the nut mixture to coat.
4. Store the fat bombs in the refrigerator for up to 1 week or in the freezer for up to 1 month.

Per Serving:1 fat bomb: calories: 235 / fat: 22g / protein: 10g / carbs: 2g / fiber: 1g / sodium: 365mg

Grilled Halloumi with Watermelon, Cherry Tomatoes, Olives, and Herb Oil

Prep time: 5 minutes / Cook time: 5 minutes / Serves 4

- ½ cup coarsely chopped fresh basil
- 3 tablespoons coarsely chopped fresh mint leaves, plus thinly sliced mint for garnish
- 1 clove garlic, coarsely chopped
- ½ cup olive oil, plus more for brushing
- ½ teaspoon salt, plus a pinch
- ½ teaspoon freshly ground black pepper, plus a pinch
- ¾ pound (340 g) cherry tomatoes
- 8 ounces (227 g) Halloumi cheese, cut crosswise into 8 slices
- 2 cups thinly sliced watermelon, rind removed
- ¼ cup sliced, pitted Kalamata olives

1. Heat a grill or grill pan to high.
2. In a food processor or blender, combine the basil, chopped mint, and garlic and pulse to chop. While the machine is running, add the olive oil in a thin stream. Strain the oil through a fine-meshed sieve and discard the solids. Stir in ½ teaspoon of salt and ½ teaspoon of pepper.
3. Brush the grill rack with olive oil. Drizzle 2 tablespoons of the herb oil over the tomatoes and cheese and season them with pinches of salt and pepper. Place the tomatoes on the grill and cook, turning occasionally, until their skins become blistered and begin to burst, about 4 minutes. Place the cheese on the grill and cook until grill marks appear and the cheese begins to get melty, about 1 minute per side.
4. Arrange the watermelon on a serving platter. Arrange the grilled cheese and tomatoes on top of the melon. Drizzle the herb oil over the top and garnish with the olives and sliced mint. Serve immediately.

Per Serving:calories: 535 / fat: 50g / protein: 14g / carbs: 12g / fiber: 2g / sodium: 663mg

Chapter 7 Vegetables and Sides

Potato Vegetable Hash

Prep time: 20 minutes / Cook time: 5 to 7 hours / Serves 4
- 1½ pounds (680 g) red potatoes, diced
- 8 ounces (227 g) green beans, trimmed and cut into ½-inch pieces
- 4 ounces (113 g) mushrooms, chopped
- 1 large tomato, chopped
- 1 large zucchini, diced
- 1 small onion, diced
- 1 red bell pepper, seeded and chopped
- ⅓ cup low-sodium vegetable broth
- 1 teaspoon sea salt
- ½ teaspoon garlic powder
- ½ teaspoon freshly ground black pepper
- ¼ teaspoon red pepper flakes
- ¼ cup shredded cheese of your choice (optional)

1. In a slow cooker, combine the potatoes, green beans, mushrooms, tomato, zucchini, onion, bell pepper, vegetable broth, salt, garlic powder, black pepper, and red pepper flakes. Stir to mix well.
2. Cover the cooker and cook for 5 to 7 hours on Low heat.
3. Garnish with cheese for serving (if using).

Per Serving:calories: 183 / fat: 1g / protein: 7g / carbs: 41g / fiber: 8g / sodium: 642mg

Chermoula-Roasted Beets

Prep time: 15 minutes / Cook time: 25 minutes / Serves 4
- Chermoula:
- 1 cup packed fresh cilantro leaves
- ½ cup packed fresh parsley leaves
- 6 cloves garlic, peeled
- 2 teaspoons smoked paprika
- 2 teaspoons ground cumin
- 1 teaspoon ground coriander
- ½ to 1 teaspoon cayenne pepper
- Pinch crushed saffron (optional)
- ½ cup extra-virgin olive oil
- Kosher salt, to taste
- Beets:
- 3 medium beets, trimmed, peeled, and cut into 1-inch chunks
- 2 tablespoons chopped fresh cilantro
- 2 tablespoons chopped fresh parsley

1. For the chermoula: In a food processor, combine the cilantro, parsley, garlic, paprika, cumin, coriander, and cayenne. Pulse until coarsely chopped. Add the saffron, if using, and process until combined. With the food processor running, slowly add the olive oil in a steady stream; process until the sauce is uniform. Season to taste with salt.
2. For the beets: In a large bowl, drizzle the beets with ½ cup of the chermoula, or enough to coat. Arrange the beets in the air fryer basket. Set the air fryer to 375ºF (191ºC) for 25 to minutes, or until the beets are tender.
3. Transfer the beets to a serving platter. Sprinkle with chopped cilantro and parsley and serve.

Per Serving:calories: 61 / fat: 2g / protein: 2g / carbs: 9g / fiber: 3g / sodium: 59mg

Garlicky Broccoli Rabe with Artichokes

Prep time: 5 minutes / Cook time: 10 minutes / Serves 4
- 2 pounds (907 g) fresh broccoli rabe
- ½ cup extra-virgin olive oil, divided
- 3 garlic cloves, finely minced
- 1 teaspoon salt
- 1 teaspoon red pepper flakes
- 1 (13¾-ounce / 390-g) can artichoke hearts, drained and quartered
- 1 tablespoon water
- 2 tablespoons red wine vinegar
- Freshly ground black pepper

1. Trim away any thick lower stems and yellow leaves from the broccoli rabe and discard. Cut into individual florets with a couple inches of thin stem attached.
2. In a large skillet, heat ¼ cup olive oil over medium-high heat. Add the trimmed broccoli, garlic, salt, and red pepper flakes and sauté for 5 minutes, until the broccoli begins to soften. Add the artichoke hearts and sauté for another 2 minutes.
3. Add the water and reduce the heat to low. Cover and simmer until the broccoli stems are tender, 3 to 5 minutes.
4. In a small bowl, whisk together remaining ¼ cup olive oil and the vinegar. Drizzle over the broccoli and artichokes. Season with ground black pepper, if desired.

Per Serving:calories: 341 / fat: 28g / protein: 11g / carbs: 18g / fiber: 12g / sodium: 750mg

Roasted Asparagus and Fingerling Potatoes with Thyme

Prep time: 5 minutes / Cook time: 20 minutes / Serves 4
- 1 pound (454 g) asparagus, trimmed
- 1 pound (454 g) fingerling potatoes, cut into thin rounds
- 2 scallions, thinly sliced
- 3 tablespoons olive oil
- ¾ teaspoon salt

- ¼ teaspoon freshly ground black pepper
- 1 tablespoon fresh thyme leaves
1. Preheat the oven to 450°F (235°C).
2. In a large baking dish, combine the asparagus, potatoes, and scallions and toss to mix. Add the olive oil, salt, and pepper and toss again to coat all of the vegetables in the oil. Spread the vegetables out in as thin a layer as possible and roast in the preheated oven, stirring once, until the vegetables are tender and nicely browned, about 20 minutes. Just before serving, sprinkle with the thyme leaves. Serve hot.

Per Serving: calories: 197 / fat: 11g / protein: 5g / carbs: 24g / fiber: 5g / sodium: 449mg

Mashed Sweet Potato Tots

Prep time: 10 minutes / Cook time: 12 to 13 minutes per batch / Makes 18 to 24 tots
- 1 cup cooked mashed sweet potatoes
- 1 egg white, beaten
- ⅛ teaspoon ground cinnamon
- 1 dash nutmeg
- 2 tablespoons chopped pecans
- 1½ teaspoons honey
- Salt, to taste
- ½ cup panko bread crumbs
- Oil for misting or cooking spray
1. Preheat the air fryer to 390°F (199°C).
2. In a large bowl, mix together the potatoes, egg white, cinnamon, nutmeg, pecans, honey, and salt to taste.
3. Place panko crumbs on a sheet of wax paper.
4. For each tot, use about 2 teaspoons of sweet potato mixture. To shape, drop the measure of potato mixture onto panko crumbs and push crumbs up and around potatoes to coat edges. Then turn tot over to coat other side with crumbs.
5. Mist tots with oil or cooking spray and place in air fryer basket in single layer.
6. Air fry at 390°F (199°C) for 12 to 13 minutes, until browned and crispy.
7. Repeat steps 5 and 6 to cook remaining tots.

Per Serving: calories: 51 / fat: 1g / protein: 1g / carbs: 9g / fiber: 1g / sodium: 45mg

Honey and Spice Glazed Carrots

Prep time: 5 minutes / Cook time: 5 minutes / Serves 4
- 4 large carrots, peeled and sliced on the diagonal into ½-inch-thick rounds
- 1 teaspoon ground cinnamon
- 1 teaspoon ground ginger
- 3 tablespoons olive oil
- ½ cup honey
- 1 tablespoon red wine vinegar
- 1 tablespoon chopped flat-leaf parsley
- 1 tablespoon chopped cilantro

- 2 tablespoons toasted pine nuts
1. Bring a large saucepan of lightly salted water to a boil and add the carrots. Cover and cook for about 5 minutes, until the carrots are just tender. Drain in a colander, then transfer to a medium bowl.
2. Add the cinnamon, ginger, olive oil, honey, and vinegar and toss to combine well. Add the parsley and cilantro and toss again to incorporate. Garnish with the pine nuts. Serve immediately or let cool to room temperature.

Per Serving: calories: 281 / fat: 14g / protein: 1g / carbs: 43g / fiber: 2g / sodium: 48mg

Roasted Cauliflower with Lemon Tahini Sauce

Prep time: 10 minutes / Cook time: 20 minutes / Serves 2
- ½ large head cauliflower, stemmed and broken into florets (about 3 cups)
- 1 tablespoon olive oil
- 2 tablespoons tahini
- 2 tablespoons freshly squeezed lemon juice
- 1 teaspoon harissa paste
- Pinch salt
1. Preheat the oven to 400°F (205°C) and set the rack to the lowest position. Line a sheet pan with parchment paper or foil.
2. Toss the cauliflower florets with the olive oil in a large bowl and transfer to the sheet pan. Reserve the bowl to make the tahini sauce.
3. Roast the cauliflower for 15 minutes, turning it once or twice, until it starts to turn golden.
4. In the same bowl, combine the tahini, lemon juice, harissa, and salt.
5. When the cauliflower is tender, remove it from the oven and toss it with the tahini sauce. Return to the sheet pan and roast for 5 minutes more.

Per Serving: calories: 205 / fat: 15g / protein: 7g / carbs: 15g / fiber: 7g / sodium: 161mg

Cucumbers with Feta, Mint, and Sumac

Prep time: 15 minutes / Cook time: 0 minutes / Serves 4
- 1 tablespoon extra-virgin olive oil
- 1 tablespoon lemon juice
- 2 teaspoons ground sumac
- ½ teaspoon kosher salt
- 2 hothouse or English cucumbers, diced
- ¼ cup crumbled feta cheese
- 1 tablespoon fresh mint, chopped
- 1 tablespoon fresh parsley, chopped
- ⅛ teaspoon red pepper flakes
1. In a large bowl, whisk together the olive oil, lemon juice, sumac, and salt. Add the cucumber and feta cheese and toss well.
2. Transfer to a serving dish and sprinkle with the mint,

parsley, and red pepper flakes.
Per Serving:calories: 85 / fat: 6g / protein: 3g / carbs: 8g / fiber: 1g / sodium: 230mg

Roasted Vegetables with Lemon Tahini

Prep time: 15 minutes / Cook time: 25 minutes / Serves 4
- For the Dressing:
- ½ cup tahini
- ½ cup water, as needed
- 3 tablespoons freshly squeezed lemon juice
- Sea salt
- For the Vegetables:
- 8 ounces (227 g) baby potatoes, halved
- 8 ounces (227 g) baby carrots
- 1 head cauliflower, cored and cut into large chunks
- 2 red bell peppers, quartered
- 1 zucchini, cut into 1-inch pieces
- ¼ cup olive oil
- 1½ teaspoons garlic powder
- ¼ teaspoon dried oregano
- ¼ teaspoon dried thyme
- Sea salt
- Freshly ground black pepper
- Red pepper flakes (optional)
1. Make the Dressing: 1. In a small bowl, stir together the tahini, water, and lemon juice until well blended.
2. Taste, season with salt, and set aside. Make the Vegetables:
3. Preheat the oven to 425°F(220ºC). Line a baking sheet with parchment paper.
4. Place the potatoes in a microwave-safe bowl with 3 tablespoons water, cover with a paper plate, and microwave on high for 4 minutes. Drain any excess water.
5. Transfer the potatoes to a large bowl and add the carrots, cauliflower, bell peppers, zucchini, olive oil, garlic powder, oregano, and thyme. Season with salt and black pepper.
6. Spread the vegetables in a single layer on the prepared baking sheet and roast until fork-tender and a little charred, about 25 minutes.
7. Transfer the vegetables to a large bowl and add the dressing and red pepper flakes, if desired. Toss to coat.
8. Serve the roasted vegetables alongside your favorite chicken or fish dish.
Per Serving:calories: 412 / fat: 30g / protein: 9g / carbs: 31g / fiber: 9g / sodium: 148mg

Cauliflower Steaks Gratin

Prep time: 10 minutes / Cook time: 13 minutes / Serves 2
- 1 head cauliflower
- 1 tablespoon olive oil
- Salt and freshly ground black pepper, to taste
- ½ teaspoon chopped fresh thyme leaves
- 3 tablespoons grated Parmigiano-Reggiano cheese
- 2 tablespoons panko bread crumbs
1. Preheat the air fryer to 370ºF (188ºC).
2. Cut two steaks out of the center of the cauliflower. To do this, cut the cauliflower in half and then cut one slice about 1-inch thick off each half. The rest of the cauliflower will fall apart into florets, which you can roast on their own or save for another meal.
3. Brush both sides of the cauliflower steaks with olive oil and season with salt, freshly ground black pepper and fresh thyme. Place the cauliflower steaks into the air fryer basket and air fry for 6 minutes. Turn the steaks over and air fry for another 4 minutes. Combine the Parmesan cheese and panko bread crumbs and sprinkle the mixture over the tops of both steaks and air fry for another 3 minutes until the cheese has melted and the bread crumbs have browned. Serve this with some sautéed bitter greens and air-fried blistered tomatoes.
Per Serving:calories: 192 / fat: 10g / protein: 9g / carbs: 21g / fiber: 6g / sodium: 273mg

Artichokes Provençal

Prep time: 15 minutes / Cook time: 10 minutes / Serves 4
- 4 large artichokes
- 1 medium lemon, cut in half
- 2 tablespoons olive oil
- ½ medium white onion, peeled and sliced
- 4 cloves garlic, peeled and chopped
- 2 tablespoons chopped fresh oregano
- 2 tablespoons chopped fresh basil
- 2 sprigs fresh thyme
- 2 medium tomatoes, seeded and chopped
- ¼ cup chopped Kalamata olives
- ¼ cup red wine
- ¼ cup water
- ¼ teaspoon salt
- ¼ teaspoon ground black pepper
1. Run artichokes under running water, making sure water runs between leaves to flush out any debris. Slice off top ⅓ of artichoke, trim stem, and pull away any tough outer leaves. Rub all cut surfaces with lemon.
2. Press the Sauté button on the Instant Pot® and heat oil. Add onion and cook until just tender, about 2 minutes. Add garlic, oregano, basil, and thyme, and cook until fragrant, about 30 seconds. Add tomatoes and olives and gently mix, then add wine and water and cook for 30 seconds. Press the Cancel button, then add artichokes cut side down to the Instant Pot®.
3. Close lid, set steam release to Sealing, press the Manual button, and set time to 5 minutes. When the timer beeps, quick-release the pressure until the float valve drops. Open lid and transfer artichokes to a serving platter. Pour sauce over top, then season with salt and pepper. Serve warm.

Per Serving:calories: 449 / fat: 16g / protein: 20g / carbs: 40g / fiber: 12g / sodium: 762mg

Curry Roasted Cauliflower

Prep time: 10 minutes / Cook time: 20 minutes / Serves 4

- ¼ cup olive oil
- 2 teaspoons curry powder
- ½ teaspoon salt
- ¼ teaspoon freshly ground black pepper
- 1 head cauliflower, cut into bite-size florets
- ½ red onion, sliced
- 2 tablespoons freshly chopped parsley, for garnish (optional)

1. Preheat the air fryer to 400ºF (204ºC).
2. In a large bowl, combine the olive oil, curry powder, salt, and pepper. Add the cauliflower and onion. Toss gently until the vegetables are completely coated with the oil mixture. Transfer the vegetables to the basket of the air fryer.
3. Pausing about halfway through the cooking time to shake the basket, air fry for 20 minutes until the cauliflower is tender and beginning to brown. Top with the parsley, if desired, before serving.

Per Serving:calories: 141 / fat: 14g / protein: 2g / carbs: 4g / fiber: 2g / sodium: 312mg

Sautéed Garlic Spinach

Prep time: 5 minutes / Cook time: 10 minutes / Serves 4

- ¼ cup extra-virgin olive oil
- 1 large onion, thinly sliced
- 3 cloves garlic, minced
- 6 (1-pound / 454-g) bags of baby spinach, washed
- ½ teaspoon salt
- 1 lemon, cut into wedges

1. Cook the olive oil, onion, and garlic in a large skillet for 2 minutes over medium heat.
2. Add one bag of spinach and ½ teaspoon of salt. Cover the skillet and let the spinach wilt for 30 seconds. Repeat (omitting the salt), adding 1 bag of spinach at a time.
3. Once all the spinach has been added, remove the cover and cook for 3 minutes, letting some of the moisture evaporate.
4. Serve warm with a generous squeeze of lemon over the top.

Per Serving:calories: 301 / fat: 14g / protein: 17g / carbs: 29g / fiber: 17g / sodium: 812mg

Garlic-Parmesan Crispy Baby Potatoes

Prep time: 10 minutes / Cook time: 15 minutes / Serves 4

- Oil, for spraying
- 1 pound (454 g) baby potatoes
- ½ cup grated Parmesan cheese, divided

- 3 tablespoons olive oil
- 2 teaspoons granulated garlic
- ½ teaspoon onion powder
- ½ teaspoon salt
- ¼ teaspoon freshly ground black pepper
- ¼ teaspoon paprika
- 2 tablespoons chopped fresh parsley, for garnish

1. Line the air fryer basket with parchment and spray lightly with oil.
2. Rinse the potatoes, pat dry with paper towels, and place in a large bowl.
3. In a small bowl, mix together ¼ cup of Parmesan cheese, the olive oil, garlic, onion powder, salt, black pepper, and paprika. Pour the mixture over the potatoes and toss to coat.
4. Transfer the potatoes to the prepared basket and spread them out in an even layer, taking care to keep them from touching. You may need to work in batches, depending on the size of your air fryer.
5. Air fry at 400ºF (204ºC) for 15 minutes, stirring after 7 to 8 minutes, or until easily pierced with a fork. Continue to cook for another 1 to 2 minutes, if needed.
6. Sprinkle with the parsley and the remaining Parmesan cheese and serve.

Per Serving:calories: 234 / fat: 14g / protein: 6g / carbs: 22g / fiber: 3g / sodium: 525mg

Caesar Whole Cauliflower

Prep time: 20 minutes / Cook time: 30 minutes / Serves 2 to 4

- 3 tablespoons olive oil
- 2 tablespoons red wine vinegar
- 2 tablespoons Worcestershire sauce
- 2 tablespoons grated Parmesan cheese
- 1 tablespoon Dijon mustard
- 4 garlic cloves, minced
- 4 oil-packed anchovy fillets, drained and finely minced
- Kosher salt and freshly ground black pepper, to taste
- 1 small head cauliflower (about 1 pound / 454 g), green leaves trimmed and stem trimmed flush with the bottom of the head
- 1 tablespoon roughly chopped fresh flat-leaf parsley (optional)

1. In a liquid measuring cup, whisk together the olive oil, vinegar, Worcestershire, Parmesan, mustard, garlic, anchovies, and salt and pepper to taste. Place the cauliflower head upside down on a cutting board and use a paring knife to make an "x" through the full length of the core. Transfer the cauliflower head to a large bowl and pour half the dressing over it. Turn the cauliflower head to coat it in the dressing, then let it rest, stem-side up, in the dressing for at least 10 minutes and up to 30 minutes to allow the dressing to seep into

all its nooks and crannies.

2. Transfer the cauliflower head, stem-side down, to the air fryer and air fry at 340ºF (171ºC) for 25 minutes. Drizzle the remaining dressing over the cauliflower and air fry at 400ºF (204ºC) until the top of the cauliflower is golden brown and the core is tender, about 5 minutes more.
3. Remove the basket from the air fryer and transfer the cauliflower to a large plate. Sprinkle with the parsley, if you like, and serve hot.

Per Serving:calories: 187 / fat: 15g / protein: 5g / carbs: 9g / fiber: 2g / sodium: 453mg

Saffron Couscous with Almonds, Currants, and Scallions

Prep time: 5 minutes / Cook time: 35 minutes / Serves 8
- 2 cups whole wheat couscous
- 1 tablespoon olive oil
- 5 scallions, thinly sliced, whites and greens kept separate
- 1 large pinch saffron threads, crumbled
- 3 cups low-sodium chicken broth or vegetable broth
- ½ cup slivered almonds
- ¼ cup dried currants
- Kosher salt and ground black pepper, to taste

1. In a medium saucepan over medium heat, toast the couscous, stirring occasionally, until lightly browned, about 5 minutes. Transfer to a bowl.
2. In the same saucepan, add the oil and scallion whites. Cook, stirring, until lightly browned, about 5 minutes. Sprinkle in the saffron and stir to combine. Pour in the broth and bring to a boil.
3. Remove the saucepan from the heat, stir in the couscous, cover, and let sit until all the liquid is absorbed and the couscous is tender, about 15 minutes.
4. Fluff the couscous with a fork. Fluff in the scallion greens, almonds, and currants. Season to taste with the salt and pepper.

Per Serving:calories: 212 / fat: 6g / protein: 8g / carbs: 34g / fiber: 4g / sodium: 148mg

Cauliflower with Lime Juice

Prep time: 10 minutes / Cook time: 7 minutes / Serves 4
- 2 cups chopped cauliflower florets
- 2 tablespoons coconut oil, melted
- 2 teaspoons chili powder
- ½ teaspoon garlic powder
- 1 medium lime
- 2 tablespoons chopped cilantro

1. In a large bowl, toss cauliflower with coconut oil. Sprinkle with chili powder and garlic powder. Place seasoned cauliflower into the air fryer basket.
2. Adjust the temperature to 350ºF (177ºC) and set the timer for 7 minutes.

3. Cauliflower will be tender and begin to turn golden at the edges. Place into a serving bowl.
4. Cut the lime into quarters and squeeze juice over cauliflower. Garnish with cilantro.

Per Serving:calories: 80 / fat: 7g / protein: 1g / carbs: 5g / fiber: 2g / sodium: 55mg

Puréed Cauliflower Soup

Prep time: 15 minutes / Cook time: 11 minutes / Serves 6
- 2 tablespoons olive oil
- 1 medium onion, peeled and chopped
- 1 stalk celery, chopped
- 1 medium carrot, peeled and chopped
- 3 sprigs fresh thyme
- 4 cups cauliflower florets
- 2 cups vegetable stock
- ½ cup half-and-half
- ¼ cup low-fat plain Greek yogurt
- 2 tablespoons chopped fresh chives

1. Press the Sauté button on the Instant Pot® and heat oil. Add onion, celery, and carrot. Cook until just tender, about 6 minutes. Add thyme, cauliflower, and stock. Stir well, then press the Cancel button.
2. Close lid, set steam release to Sealing, press the Manual button, and set time to 5 minutes. When the timer beeps, let pressure release naturally, about 15 minutes.
3. Open lid, remove and discard thyme stems, and with an immersion blender, purée soup until smooth. Stir in half-and-half and yogurt. Garnish with chives and serve immediately.

Per Serving:calories: 113 / fat: 7g / protein: 3g / carbs: 9g / fiber: 2g / sodium: 236mg

Grits Casserole

Prep time: 5 minutes / Cook time: 28 to 30 minutes / Serves 4
- 10 fresh asparagus spears, cut into 1-inch pieces
- 2 cups cooked grits, cooled to room temperature
- 1 egg, beaten
- 2 teaspoons Worcestershire sauce
- ½ teaspoon garlic powder
- ¼ teaspoon salt
- 2 slices provolone cheese (about 1½ ounces / 43 g)
- Oil for misting or cooking spray

1. Mist asparagus spears with oil and air fry at 390ºF (199ºC) for 5 minutes, until crisp-tender.
2. In a medium bowl, mix together the grits, egg, Worcestershire, garlic powder, and salt.
3. Spoon half of grits mixture into a baking pan and top with asparagus.
4. Tear cheese slices into pieces and layer evenly on top of asparagus.
5. Top with remaining grits.
6. Bake at 360ºF (182ºC) for 23 to 25 minutes. The

casserole will rise a little as it cooks. When done, the top will have browned lightly with just a hint of crispiness.

Per Serving:calories: 161 / fat: 6g / protein: 8g / carbs: 20g / fiber: 2g / sodium: 704mg

Tahini-Lemon Kale

Prep time: 5 minutes / Cook time: 15 minutes / Serves 2 to 4

- ¼ cup tahini
- ¼ cup fresh lemon juice
- 2 tablespoons olive oil
- 1 teaspoon sesame seeds
- ½ teaspoon garlic powder
- ¼ teaspoon cayenne pepper
- 4 cups packed torn kale leaves (stems and ribs removed and leaves torn into palm-size pieces; about 4 ounces / 113 g)
- Kosher salt and freshly ground black pepper, to taste

1. In a large bowl, whisk together the tahini, lemon juice, olive oil, sesame seeds, garlic powder, and cayenne until smooth. Add the kale leaves, season with salt and black pepper, and toss in the dressing until completely coated. Transfer the kale leaves to a cake pan.
2. Place the pan in the air fryer and roast at 350ºF (177ºC), stirring every 5 minutes, until the kale is wilted and the top is lightly browned, about 15 minutes. Remove the pan from the air fryer and serve warm.

Per Serving:calories: 221 / fat: 21g / protein: 5g / carbs: 8g / fiber: 3g / sodium: 32mg

Crispy Green Beans

Prep time: 5 minutes / Cook time: 8 minutes / Serves 4

- 2 teaspoons olive oil
- ½ pound (227 g) fresh green beans, ends trimmed
- ¼ teaspoon salt
- ¼ teaspoon ground black pepper

1. In a large bowl, drizzle olive oil over green beans and sprinkle with salt and pepper.
2. Place green beans into ungreased air fryer basket. Adjust the temperature to 350ºF (177ºC) and set the timer for 8 minutes, shaking the basket two times during cooking. Green beans will be dark golden and crispy at the edges when done. Serve warm.

Per Serving:calories: 33 / fat: 3g / protein: 1g / carbs: 3g / fiber: 1g / sodium: 147mg

White Beans with Rosemary, Sage, and Garlic

Prep time: 10 minutes / Cook time: 10 minutes / Serves 2

- 1 tablespoon olive oil
- 2 garlic cloves, minced
- 1 (15-ounce / 425-g) can white cannellini beans, drained and rinsed
- ¼ teaspoon dried sage
- 1 teaspoon minced fresh rosemary (from 1 sprig) plus 1 whole fresh rosemary sprig
- ½ cup low-sodium chicken stock
- Salt

1. Heat the olive oil in a sauté pan over medium-high heat. Add the garlic and sauté for 30 seconds.
2. Add the beans, sage, minced and whole rosemary, and chicken stock and bring the mixture to a boil.
3. Reduce the heat to medium and simmer the beans for 10 minutes, or until most of the liquid is evaporated. If desired, mash some of the beans with a fork to thicken them.
4. Season with salt. Remove the rosemary sprig before serving

Per Serving:calories: 155 / fat: 7g / protein: 6g / carbs: 17g / fiber: 8g / sodium: 153mg

Parmesan-Rosemary Radishes

Prep time: 5 minutes / Cook time: 15 to 20 minutes / Serves 4

- 1 bunch radishes, stemmed, trimmed, and quartered
- 1 tablespoon avocado oil
- 2 tablespoons finely grated fresh Parmesan cheese
- 1 tablespoon chopped fresh rosemary
- Sea salt and freshly ground black pepper, to taste

1. Place the radishes in a medium bowl and toss them with the avocado oil, Parmesan cheese, rosemary, salt, and pepper.
2. Set the air fryer to 375ºF (191ºC). Arrange the radishes in a single layer in the air fryer basket. Roast for 15 to 20 minutes, until golden brown and tender. Let cool for 5 minutes before serving.

Per Serving:calories: 58 / fat: 4g / protein: 1g / carbs: 4g / fiber: 2g / sodium: 63mg

Herbed Shiitake Mushrooms

Prep time: 10 minutes / Cook time: 5 minutes / Serves 4

- 8 ounces (227 g) shiitake mushrooms, stems removed and caps roughly chopped
- 1 tablespoon olive oil
- ½ teaspoon salt
- Freshly ground black pepper, to taste
- 1 teaspoon chopped fresh thyme leaves
- 1 teaspoon chopped fresh oregano
- 1 tablespoon chopped fresh parsley

1. Preheat the air fryer to 400ºF (204ºC).
2. Toss the mushrooms with the olive oil, salt, pepper, thyme and oregano. Air fry for 5 minutes, shaking the basket once or twice during the cooking process. The mushrooms will still be somewhat chewy with a meaty texture. If you'd like them a little more tender, add a couple of minutes to this cooking time.
3. Once cooked, add the parsley to the mushrooms and

toss. Season again to taste and serve.

Per Serving:calories: 50 / fat: 4g / protein: 1g / carbs: 4g / fiber: 2g / sodium: 296mg

Garlicky Sautéed Zucchini with Mint

Prep time: 5 minutes / Cook time: 10 minutes / Serves 4

- 3 large green zucchini
- 3 tablespoons extra-virgin olive oil
- 1 large onion, chopped
- 3 cloves garlic, minced
- 1 teaspoon salt
- 1 teaspoon dried mint

1. Cut the zucchini into ½-inch cubes.
2. In a large skillet over medium heat, cook the olive oil, onions, and garlic for 3 minutes, stirring constantly.
3. Add the zucchini and salt to the skillet and toss to combine with the onions and garlic, cooking for 5 minutes.
4. Add the mint to the skillet, tossing to combine. Cook for another 2 minutes. Serve warm.

Per Serving:calories: 147 / fat: 11g / protein: 4g / carbs: 12g / fiber: 3g / sodium: 607mg

Balsamic Beets

Prep time: 15 minutes / Cook time: 3 to 4 hours / Serves 8

- Cooking spray or 1 tablespoon extra-virgin olive oil
- 3 pounds (1.4 kg) beets, scrubbed, peeled, and cut into wedges
- 2 garlic cloves, minced
- 1 cup white grape or apple juice
- ½ cup balsamic vinegar
- 1 tablespoon honey
- 2 fresh thyme sprigs
- 1 teaspoon kosher salt, plus more for seasoning
- ½ teaspoon freshly ground black pepper, plus more for seasoning
- 1 tablespoon cold water
- 1 tablespoon cornstarch

1. Use the cooking spray or olive oil to coat the inside (bottom and sides) of the slow cooker. Add the beets, garlic, juice, vinegar, honey, thyme, salt, and pepper. Stir to combine. Cover and cook on high for 3 to 4 hours.
2. About 10 minutes before serving, combine the water and cornstarch in a small bowl, stirring until no lumps remain. Add to the slow cooker and continue to cook for 10 minutes, or until the sauce thickens.
3. Discard the thyme. Season with additional salt and pepper, as needed. Serve.

Per Serving:calories: 129 / fat: 2g / protein: 3g / carbs: 26g/ fiber: 5g / sodium: 429mg

Parsnip Fries with Romesco Sauce

Prep time: 20 minutes / Cook time: 24 minutes / Serves 4

- Romesco Sauce:
- 1 red bell pepper, halved and seeded
- 1 (1-inch) thick slice of Italian bread, torn into pieces (about 1 to 1½ cups)
- 1 cup almonds, toasted
- Olive oil
- ½ Jalapeño pepper, seeded
- 1 tablespoon fresh parsley leaves
- 1 clove garlic
- 2 Roma tomatoes, peeled and seeded (or ⅓ cup canned crushed tomatoes)
- 1 tablespoon red wine vinegar
- ¼ teaspoon smoked paprika
- ½ teaspoon salt
- ¾ cup olive oil
- 3 parsnips, peeled and cut into long strips
- 2 teaspoons olive oil
- Salt and freshly ground black pepper, to taste

1. Preheat the air fryer to 400ºF (204ºC).
2. Place the red pepper halves, cut side down, in the air fryer basket and air fry for 8 to 10 minutes, or until the skin turns black all over. Remove the pepper from the air fryer and let it cool. When it is cool enough to handle, peel the pepper.
3. Toss the torn bread and almonds with a little olive oil and air fry for 4 minutes, shaking the basket a couple times throughout the cooking time. When the bread and almonds are nicely toasted, remove them from the air fryer and let them cool for just a minute or two.
4. Combine the toasted bread, almonds, roasted red pepper, Jalapeño pepper, parsley, garlic, tomatoes, vinegar, smoked paprika and salt in a food processor or blender. Process until smooth. With the processor running, add the olive oil through the feed tube until the sauce comes together in a smooth paste that is barely pourable.
5. Toss the parsnip strips with the olive oil, salt and freshly ground black pepper and air fry at 400ºF (204ºC) for 10 minutes, shaking the basket a couple times during the cooking process so they brown and cook evenly. Serve the parsnip fries warm with the Romesco sauce to dip into.

Per Serving:calories: 604 / fat: 55g / protein: 7g / carbs: 55g / fiber: 8g / sodium: 319mg

Roasted Beets with Oranges and Onions

Prep time: 10 minutes / Cook time: 40 minutes / Serves 6

- 4 medium beets, trimmed and scrubbed
- Juice and zest of 2 oranges
- 1 red onion, thinly sliced
- 2 tablespoons olive oil
- 1 tablespoon red wine vinegar
- Juice of 1 lemon

- Sea salt and freshly ground pepper, to taste
1. Preheat oven to 400ºF (205ºC).
2. Wrap the beets in a foil pack and close tightly. Place them on a baking sheet and roast 40 minutes until tender enough to be pierced easily with a knife.
3. Cool until easy to handle.
4. Combine the beets with the orange juice and zest, red onion, olive oil, vinegar, and lemon juice.
5. Season with sea salt and freshly ground pepper to taste, and toss lightly. Allow to sit for about 15 minutes for the flavors to meld before serving.

Per Serving:calories: 86 / fat: 5g / protein: 1g / carbs: 10g / fiber: 2g / sodium: 44mg

Broccoli Tots

Prep time: 15 minutes / Cook time: 10 minutes / Makes 24 tots

- 2 cups broccoli florets (about ½ pound / 227 g broccoli crowns)
- 1 egg, beaten
- ⅛ teaspoon onion powder
- ¼ teaspoon salt
- ⅛ teaspoon pepper
- 2 tablespoons grated Parmesan cheese
- ¼ cup panko bread crumbs
- Oil for misting
1. Steam broccoli for 2 minutes. Rinse in cold water, drain well, and chop finely.
2. In a large bowl, mix broccoli with all other ingredients except the oil.
3. Scoop out small portions of mixture and shape into 24 tots. Lay them on a cookie sheet or wax paper as you work.
4. Spray tots with oil and place in air fryer basket in single layer.
5. Air fry at 390ºF (199ºC) for 5 minutes. Shake basket and spray with oil again. Cook 5 minutes longer or until browned and crispy.

Per Serving:2 tots: calories: 21 / fat: 1g / protein: 1g / carbs: 2g / fiber: 0g / sodium: 88mg

Rice Pilaf with Dill

Prep time: 15 minutes / Cook time: 25 minutes / Serves 6

- 2 tablespoons olive oil
- 1 carrot, finely chopped (about ¾ cup)
- 2 leeks, halved lengthwise, washed, well drained, and sliced in half-moons
- ½ teaspoon salt
- ¼ teaspoon freshly ground black pepper
- 2 tablespoons chopped fresh dill
- 1 cup low-sodium vegetable broth or water
- ½ cup basmati rice
1. In a 2-or 3-quart saucepan, heat the olive oil over medium heat. Add the carrot, leeks, salt, pepper, and 1 tablespoon of the dill. Cover and cook for 6 to 8 minutes, stirring once, to soften all the vegetables but not brown them.
2. Add the broth or water and bring to a boil. Stir in the rice, reduce the heat to maintain a simmer, cover, and cook for 15 minutes. Remove from the heat; let stand, covered, for 10 minutes.
3. Fluff the rice with fork. Stir in the remaining 1 tablespoon dill and serve.

Per Serving:1 cup: calories: 100 / fat: 7g / protein: 2g / carbs: 11g / fiber: 4g / sodium: 209mg

Roasted Broccoli with Tahini Yogurt Sauce

Prep time: 15 minutes / Cook time: 30 minutes / Serves 4

- For the Broccoli:
- 1½ to 2 pounds (680 to 907 g) broccoli, stalk trimmed and cut into slices, head cut into florets
- 1 lemon, sliced into ¼-inch-thick rounds
- 3 tablespoons extra-virgin olive oil
- ½ teaspoon kosher salt
- ¼ teaspoon freshly ground black pepper
- For the Tahini Yogurt Sauce:
- ½ cup plain Greek yogurt
- 2 tablespoons tahini
- 1 tablespoon lemon juice
- ¼ teaspoon kosher salt
- 1 teaspoon sesame seeds, for garnish (optional)
1. Make the Broccoli: 1. Preheat the oven to 425ºF (220ºC). Line a baking sheet with parchment paper or foil.
2. In a large bowl, gently toss the broccoli, lemon slices, olive oil, salt, and black pepper to combine. Arrange the broccoli in a single layer on the prepared baking sheet. Roast 15 minutes, stir, and roast another 15 minutes, until golden brown. Make the Tahini Yogurt Sauce:
3. In a medium bowl, combine the yogurt, tahini, lemon juice, and salt; mix well.
4. Spread the tahini yogurt sauce on a platter or large plate and top with the broccoli and lemon slices. Garnish with the sesame seeds (if desired).

Per Serving:calories: 245 / fat: 16g / protein: 12g / carbs: 20g / fiber: 7g / sodium: 305mg

Roasted Brussels Sprouts with Tahini-Yogurt Sauce

Prep time: 10 minutes / Cook time: 35 minutes / Serves 4

- 1 pound (454 g) Brussels sprouts, trimmed and halved lengthwise
- 6 tablespoons extra-virgin olive oil, divided
- 1 teaspoon salt, divided
- ½ teaspoon garlic powder
- ¼ teaspoon freshly ground black pepper
- ¼ cup plain whole-milk Greek yogurt

- ¼ cup tahini
- Zest and juice of 1 lemon

1. Preheat the oven to 425ºF (220ºC). Line a baking sheet with aluminum foil or parchment paper and set aside.
2. Place the Brussels sprouts in a large bowl. Drizzle with 4 tablespoons olive oil, ½ teaspoon salt, the garlic powder, and pepper and toss well to coat.
3. Place the Brussels sprouts in a single layer on the baking sheet, reserving the bowl, and roast for 20 minutes. Remove from the oven and give the sprouts a toss to flip. Return to the oven and continue to roast until browned and crispy, another 10 to 15 minutes. Remove from the oven and return to the reserved bowl.
4. In a small bowl, whisk together the yogurt, tahini, lemon zest and juice, remaining 2 tablespoons olive oil, and remaining ½ teaspoon salt. Drizzle over the roasted sprouts and toss to coat. Serve warm.

Per Serving:calories: 330 / fat: 29g / protein: 7g / carbs: 15g / fiber: 6g / sodium: 635mg

Zesty Fried Asparagus

Prep time: 3 minutes / Cook time: 10 minutes / Serves 4

- Oil, for spraying
- 10 to 12 spears asparagus, trimmed
- 2 tablespoons olive oil
- 1 tablespoon granulated garlic
- 1 teaspoon chili powder
- ½ teaspoon ground cumin
- ¼ teaspoon salt

1. Line the air fryer basket with parchment and spray lightly with oil.
2. If the asparagus are too long to fit easily in the air fryer, cut them in half.
3. Place the asparagus, olive oil, garlic, chili powder, cumin, and salt in a zip-top plastic bag, seal, and toss until evenly coated.
4. Place the asparagus in the prepared basket.
5. Roast at 390ºF (199ºC) for 5 minutes, flip, and cook for another 5 minutes, or until bright green and firm but tender.

Per Serving:calories: 74 / fat: 7g / protein: 1g / carbs: 3g / fiber: 1g / sodium: 166mg

Sesame-Ginger Broccoli

Prep time: 10 minutes / Cook time: 15 minutes / Serves 4

- 3 tablespoons toasted sesame oil
- 2 teaspoons sesame seeds
- 1 tablespoon chili-garlic sauce
- 2 teaspoons minced fresh ginger
- ½ teaspoon kosher salt
- ½ teaspoon black pepper
- 1 (16-ounce / 454-g) package frozen broccoli florets (do not thaw)

1. In a large bowl, combine the sesame oil, sesame seeds, chili-garlic sauce, ginger, salt, and pepper. Stir until well combined. Add the broccoli and toss until well coated.
2. Arrange the broccoli in the air fryer basket. Set the air fryer to 325ºF (163ºC) for 15 minutes, or until the broccoli is crisp, tender, and the edges are lightly browned, gently tossing halfway through the cooking time.

Per Serving:calories: 143 / fat: 11g / protein: 4g / carbs: 9g / fiber: 4g / sodium: 385mg

Roasted Harissa Carrots

Prep time: 10 minutes / Cook time: 15 minutes / Serves 4

- 1 pound (454 g) carrots, peeled and sliced into 1-inch-thick rounds
- 2 tablespoons extra-virgin olive oil
- 2 tablespoons harissa
- 1 teaspoon honey
- 1 teaspoon ground cumin
- ½ teaspoon kosher salt
- ½ cup fresh parsley, chopped

1. Preheat the oven to 450ºF (235ºC). Line a baking sheet with parchment paper or foil.
2. In a large bowl, combine the carrots, olive oil, harissa, honey, cumin, and salt. Arrange in a single layer on the baking sheet. Roast for 15 minutes. Remove from the oven, add the parsley, and toss together.

Per Serving:calories: 120 / fat: 8g / protein: 1g / carbs: 13g / fiber: 4g / sodium: 255mg

Chapter 8 Vegetarian Mains

Freekeh, Chickpea, and Herb Salad

Prep time: 15 minutes / Cook time: 10 minutes / Serves 4 to 6

- 1 (15-ounce / 425-g) can chickpeas, rinsed and drained
- 1 cup cooked freekeh
- 1 cup thinly sliced celery
- 1 bunch scallions, both white and green parts, finely chopped
- ½ cup chopped fresh flat-leaf parsley
- ¼ cup chopped fresh mint
- 3 tablespoons chopped celery leaves
- ½ teaspoon kosher salt
- ⅓ cup extra-virgin olive oil
- ¼ cup freshly squeezed lemon juice
- ¼ teaspoon cumin seeds
- 1 teaspoon garlic powder

1. In a large bowl, combine the chickpeas, freekeh, celery, scallions, parsley, mint, celery leaves, and salt and toss lightly.
2. In a small bowl, whisk together the olive oil, lemon juice, cumin seeds, and garlic powder. Once combined, add to freekeh salad.

Per Serving:calories: 350 / fat: 19g / protein: 9g / carbs: 38g / fiber: 9g / sodium: 329mg

Moroccan Red Lentil and Pumpkin Stew

Prep time: 10 minutes / Cook time: 30 minutes / Serves 4

- 2 tablespoons olive oil
- 1 teaspoon ground cumin
- 1 teaspoon ground turmeric
- 1 tablespoon curry powder
- 1 large onion, diced
- 1 teaspoon salt
- 2 tablespoons minced fresh ginger
- 4 cloves garlic, minced
- 1 pound (454 g) pumpkin, peeled, seeded, and cut into 1-inch dice
- 1 red bell pepper, seeded and diced
- 1½ cups red lentils, rinsed
- 6 cups vegetable broth
- ¼ cup chopped cilantro, for garnish

1. Heat the olive oil in a stockpot over medium heat. Add the cumin, turmeric, and curry powder and cook, stirring, for 1 minute, until fragrant. Add the onion and salt and cook, stirring frequently, until softened, about 5 minutes. Add the ginger and garlic and cook, stirring frequently, for 2 more minutes. Stir in the pumpkin and bell pepper, and then the lentils and broth and bring to a boil.
2. Reduce the heat to low and simmer, uncovered, for about 20 minutes, until the lentils are very tender. Serve hot, garnished with cilantro.

Per Serving:calories: 405 / fat: 9g / protein: 20g / carbs: 66g / fiber: 11g / sodium: 594mg

Stuffed Portobellos

Prep time: 10 minutes / Cook time: 8 minutes / Serves 4

- 3 ounces (85 g) cream cheese, softened
- ½ medium zucchini, trimmed and chopped
- ¼ cup seeded and chopped red bell pepper
- 1½ cups chopped fresh spinach leaves
- 4 large portobello mushrooms, stems removed
- 2 tablespoons coconut oil, melted
- ½ teaspoon salt

1. In a medium bowl, mix cream cheese, zucchini, pepper, and spinach.
2. Drizzle mushrooms with coconut oil and sprinkle with salt. Scoop ¼ zucchini mixture into each mushroom.
3. Place mushrooms into ungreased air fryer basket. Adjust the temperature to 400°F (204°C) and air fry for 8 minutes. Portobellos will be tender and tops will be browned when done. Serve warm.

Per Serving:calories: 151 / fat: 13g / protein: 4g / carbs: 6g / fiber: 2g / sodium: 427mg

Broccoli-Cheese Fritters

Prep time: 5 minutes / Cook time: 20 to 25 minutes / Serves 4

- 1 cup broccoli florets
- 1 cup shredded Mozzarella cheese
- ¾ cup almond flour
- ½ cup flaxseed meal, divided
- 2 teaspoons baking powder
- 1 teaspoon garlic powder
- Salt and freshly ground black pepper, to taste
- 2 eggs, lightly beaten
- ½ cup ranch dressing

1. Preheat the air fryer to 400°F (204°C).
2. In a food processor fitted with a metal blade, pulse the broccoli until very finely chopped.
3. Transfer the broccoli to a large bowl and add the Mozzarella, almond flour, ¼ cup of the flaxseed meal, baking powder, and garlic powder. Stir until thoroughly combined. Season to taste with salt and black pepper. Add the eggs and stir again to form a sticky dough. Shape the dough into 1¼-inch fritters.
4. Place the remaining ¼ cup flaxseed meal in a shallow bowl and roll the fritters in the meal to form an even coating.
5. Working in batches if necessary, arrange the fritters in a single layer in the basket of the air fryer and spray generously with olive oil. Pausing halfway through the cooking time to shake the basket, air fry for 20 to 25

minutes until the fritters are golden brown and crispy. Serve with the ranch dressing for dipping.

Per Serving:calories: 388 / fat: 30g / protein: 19g / carbs: 14g / fiber: 7g / sodium: 526mg

Baked Tofu with Sun-Dried Tomatoes and Artichokes

Prep time: 15 minutes / Cook time: 30 minutes / Serves 4

- 1 (16-ounce / 454-g) package extra-firm tofu, drained and patted dry, cut into 1-inch cubes
- 2 tablespoons extra-virgin olive oil, divided
- 2 tablespoons lemon juice, divided
- 1 tablespoon low-sodium soy sauce or gluten-free tamari
- 1 onion, diced
- ½ teaspoon kosher salt
- 2 garlic cloves, minced
- 1 (14-ounce / 397-g) can artichoke hearts, drained
- 8 sun-dried tomato halves packed in oil, drained and chopped
- ¼ teaspoon freshly ground black pepper
- 1 tablespoon white wine vinegar
- Zest of 1 lemon
- ¼ cup fresh parsley, chopped

1. Preheat the oven to 400ºF (205ºC). Line a baking sheet with foil or parchment paper.
2. In a bowl, combine the tofu, 1 tablespoon of the olive oil, 1 tablespoon of the lemon juice, and the soy sauce. Allow to sit and marinate for 15 to 30 minutes. Arrange the tofu in a single layer on the prepared baking sheet and bake for 20 minutes, turning once, until light golden brown.
3. Heat the remaining 1 tablespoon olive oil in a large skillet or sauté pan over medium heat. Add the onion and salt; sauté until translucent, 5 to 6 minutes. Add the garlic and sauté for 30 seconds. Add the artichoke hearts, sun-dried tomatoes, and black pepper and sauté for 5 minutes. Add the white wine vinegar and the remaining 1 tablespoon lemon juice and deglaze the pan, scraping up any brown bits. Remove the pan from the heat and stir in the lemon zest and parsley. Gently mix in the baked tofu.

Per Serving:calories: 230 / fat: 14g / protein: 14g / carbs: 13g / fiber: 5g / sodium: 500mg

Cauliflower Steaks with Olive Citrus Sauce

Prep time: 15 minutes / Cook time: 30 minutes / Serves 4

- 1 or 2 large heads cauliflower (at least 2 pounds / 907 g, enough for 4 portions)
- ⅓ cup extra-virgin olive oil
- ¼ teaspoon kosher salt
- ⅛ teaspoon ground black pepper
- Juice of 1 orange
- Zest of 1 orange
- ¼ cup black olives, pitted and chopped
- 1 tablespoon Dijon or grainy mustard
- 1 tablespoon red wine vinegar
- ½ teaspoon ground coriander

1. Preheat the oven to 400ºF (205ºC). Line a baking sheet with parchment paper or foil.

2. Cut off the stem of the cauliflower so it will sit upright. Slice it vertically into four thick slabs. Place the cauliflower on the prepared baking sheet. Drizzle with the olive oil, salt, and black pepper. Bake for about 30 minutes, turning over once, until tender and golden brown.
3. In a medium bowl, combine the orange juice, orange zest, olives, mustard, vinegar, and coriander; mix well.
4. Serve the cauliflower warm or at room temperature with the sauce.

Per Serving:calories: 265 / fat: 21g / protein: 5g / carbs: 19g / fiber: 4g / sodium: 310mg

Pistachio Mint Pesto Pasta

Prep time: 10 minutes / Cook time: 10 minutes / Serves 4

- 8 ounces (227 g) whole-wheat pasta
- 1 cup fresh mint
- ½ cup fresh basil
- ⅓ cup unsalted pistachios, shelled
- 1 garlic clove, peeled
- ½ teaspoon kosher salt
- Juice of ½ lime
- ⅓ cup extra-virgin olive oil

1. Cook the pasta according to the package directions. Drain, reserving ½ cup of the pasta water, and set aside.
2. In a food processor, add the mint, basil, pistachios, garlic, salt, and lime juice. Process until the pistachios are coarsely ground. Add the olive oil in a slow, steady stream and process until incorporated.
3. In a large bowl, mix the pasta with the pistachio pesto; toss well to incorporate. If a thinner, more saucy consistency is desired, add some of the reserved pasta water and toss well.

Per Serving:calories: 420 / fat: 3g / protein: 11g / carbs: 48g / fiber: 2g / sodium: 150mg

Creamy Chickpea Sauce with Whole-Wheat Fusilli

Prep time: 15 minutes / Cook time: 20 minutes / Serves 4

- ¼ cup extra-virgin olive oil
- ½ large shallot, chopped
- 5 garlic cloves, thinly sliced
- 1 (15-ounce / 425-g) can chickpeas, drained and rinsed, reserving ½ cup canning liquid
- Pinch red pepper flakes
- 1 cup whole-grain fusilli pasta
- ¼ teaspoon salt
- ⅛ teaspoon freshly ground black pepper
- ¼ cup shaved fresh Parmesan cheese
- ¼ cup chopped fresh basil
- 2 teaspoons dried parsley
- 1 teaspoon dried oregano
- Red pepper flakes

1. In a medium pan, heat the oil over medium heat, and sauté the shallot and garlic for 3 to 5 minutes, until the garlic is golden. Add ¾ of the chickpeas plus 2 tablespoons of liquid from the can, and bring to a simmer.

2. Remove from the heat, transfer into a standard blender, and blend until smooth. At this point, add the remaining chickpeas. Add more reserved chickpea liquid if it becomes thick.

3. Bring a large pot of salted water to a boil and cook pasta until al dente, about 8 minutes. Reserve ½ cup of the pasta water, drain the pasta, and return it to the pot.

4. Add the chickpea sauce to the hot pasta and add up to ¼ cup of the pasta water. You may need to add more pasta water to reach your desired consistency.

5. Place the pasta pot over medium heat and mix occasionally until the sauce thickens. Season with salt and pepper.

6. Serve, garnished with Parmesan, basil, parsley, oregano, and red pepper flakes.

Per Serving:1 cup pasta: calories: 310 / fat: 17g / protein: 10g / carbs: 33g / fiber: 7g / sodium: 243mg

Vegetable Burgers

Prep time: 10 minutes / Cook time: 12 minutes / Serves 4
- 8 ounces (227 g) cremini mushrooms
- 2 large egg yolks
- ½ medium zucchini, trimmed and chopped
- ¼ cup peeled and chopped yellow onion
- 1 clove garlic, peeled and finely minced
- ½ teaspoon salt
- ¼ teaspoon ground black pepper

1. Place all ingredients into a food processor and pulse twenty times until finely chopped and combined.

2. Separate mixture into four equal sections and press each into a burger shape. Place burgers into ungreased air fryer basket. Adjust the temperature to 375ºF (191ºC) and air fry for 12 minutes, turning burgers halfway through cooking. Burgers will be browned and firm when done.

3. Place burgers on a large plate and let cool 5 minutes before serving.

Per Serving:calories: 50 / fat: 3g / protein: 3g / carbs: 4g / fiber: 1g / sodium: 299mg

Cauliflower Rice-Stuffed Peppers

Prep time: 10 minutes / Cook time: 15 minutes / Serves 4
- 2 cups uncooked cauliflower rice
- ¾ cup drained canned petite diced tomatoes
- 2 tablespoons olive oil
- 1 cup shredded Mozzarella cheese
- ¼ teaspoon salt
- ¼ teaspoon ground black pepper
- 4 medium green bell peppers, tops removed, seeded

1. In a large bowl, mix all ingredients except bell peppers. Scoop mixture evenly into peppers.

2. Place peppers into ungreased air fryer basket. Adjust the temperature to 350ºF (177ºC) and air fry for 15 minutes. Peppers will be tender and cheese will be melted when done. Serve warm.

Per Serving:calories: 144 / fat: 7g / protein: 11g / carbs: 11g / fiber: 5g / sodium: 380mg

Sheet Pan Roasted Chickpeas and Vegetables with Harissa Yogurt

Prep time: 10 minutes / Cook time: 30 minutes / Serves 2
- 4 cups cauliflower florets (about ½ small head)
- 2 medium carrots, peeled, halved, and then sliced into quarters lengthwise
- 2 tablespoons olive oil, divided
- ½ teaspoon garlic powder, divided
- ½ teaspoon salt, divided
- 2 teaspoons za'atar spice mix, divided
- 1 (15-ounce / 425-g) can chickpeas, drained, rinsed, and patted dry
- ¾ cup plain Greek yogurt
- 1 teaspoon harissa spice paste

1. Preheat the oven to 400ºF (205ºC) and set the rack to the middle position. Line a sheet pan with foil or parchment paper.

2. Place the cauliflower and carrots in a large bowl. Drizzle with 1 tablespoon olive oil and sprinkle with ¼ teaspoon of garlic powder, ¼ teaspoon of salt, and 1 teaspoon of za'atar. Toss well to combine.

3. Spread the vegetables onto one half of the sheet pan in a single layer.

4. Place the chickpeas in the same bowl and season with the remaining 1 tablespoon of oil, ¼ teaspoon of garlic powder, and ¼ teaspoon of salt, and the remaining za'atar. Toss well to combine.

5. Spread the chickpeas onto the other half of the sheet pan.

6. Roast for 30 minutes, or until the vegetables are tender and the chickpeas start to turn golden. Flip the vegetables halfway through the cooking time, and give the chickpeas a stir so they cook evenly.

7. The chickpeas may need an extra few minutes if you like them crispy. If so, remove the vegetables and leave the chickpeas in until they're cooked to desired crispiness.

8. While the vegetables are roasting, combine the yogurt and harissa in a small bowl. Taste, and add additional harissa as desired.

Per Serving:calories: 467 / fat: 23g / protein: 18g / carbs: 54g / fiber: 15g / sodium: 632mg

Fava Bean Purée with Chicory

Prep time: 5 minutes / Cook time: 2 hours 10 minutes / Serves 4
- ½ pound (227 g) dried fava beans, soaked in water overnight and drained
- 1 pound (454 g) chicory leaves
- ¼ cup olive oil
- 1 small onion, chopped
- 1 clove garlic, minced
- Salt

1. In a saucepan, cover the fava beans by at least an inch of water and bring to a boil over medium-high heat. Reduce the heat to low, cover, and simmer until very tender, about 2 hours. Check the pot from time to time to

make sure there is enough water and add more as needed.

2. Drain off any excess water and then mash the beans with a potato masher.

3. While the beans are cooking, bring a large pot of salted water to a boil. Add the chicory and cook for about 3 minutes, until tender. Drain.

4. In a medium skillet, heat the olive oil over medium-high heat. Add the onion and a pinch of salt and cook, stirring frequently, until softened and beginning to brown, about 5 minutes. Add the garlic and cook, stirring, for another minute. Transfer half of the onion mixture, along with the oil, to the bowl with the mashed beans and stir to mix. Taste and add salt as needed.

5. Serve the purée topped with some of the remaining onions and oil, with the chicory leaves on the side.

Per Serving:calories: 336 / fat: 14g / protein: 17g / carbs: 40g / fiber: 19g / sodium: 59mg

Mozzarella and Sun-Dried Portobello Mushroom Pizza

Prep time: 10 minutes / Cook time: 10 minutes / Serves 4

- 4 large portobello mushroom caps
- 3 tablespoons extra-virgin olive oil
- Salt
- Freshly ground black pepper
- 4 sun-dried tomatoes
- 1 cup mozzarella cheese, divided
- ½ to ¾ cup low-sodium tomato sauce

1. Preheat the broiler on high.

2. On a baking sheet, drizzle the mushroom caps with the olive oil and season with salt and pepper. Broil the portobello mushrooms for 5 minutes on each side, flipping once, until tender.

3. Fill each mushroom cap with 1 sun-dried tomato, 2 tablespoons of cheese, and 2 to 3 tablespoons of sauce. Top each with 2 tablespoons of cheese. Place the caps back under the broiler for a final 2 to 3 minutes, then quarter the mushrooms and serve.

Per Serving:calories: 218/ fat: 16g / protein: 11g / carbs: 12g / fiber: 2g / sodium: 244mg

Broccoli Crust Pizza

Prep time: 15 minutes / Cook time: 12 minutes / Serves 4

- 3 cups riced broccoli, steamed and drained well
- 1 large egg
- ½ cup grated vegetarian Parmesan cheese
- 3 tablespoons low-carb Alfredo sauce
- ½ cup shredded Mozzarella cheese

1. In a large bowl, mix broccoli, egg, and Parmesan.

2. Cut a piece of parchment to fit your air fryer basket. Press out the pizza mixture to fit on the parchment, working in two batches if necessary. Place into the air fryer basket.

3. Adjust the temperature to 370ºF (188ºC) and air fry for 5 minutes.

4. The crust should be firm enough to flip. If not, add 2

additional minutes. Flip crust.

5. Top with Alfredo sauce and Mozzarella. Return to the air fryer basket and cook an additional 7 minutes or until cheese is golden and bubbling. Serve warm.

Per Serving:calories: 87 / fat: 2g / protein: 11g / carbs: 5g / fiber: 1g / sodium: 253mg

Asparagus and Mushroom Farrotto

Prep time: 20 minutes / Cook time: 45 minutes / Serves 2

- 1½ ounces (43 g) dried porcini mushrooms
- 1 cup hot water
- 3 cups low-sodium vegetable stock
- 2 tablespoons olive oil
- ½ large onion, minced (about 1 cup)
- 1 garlic clove
- 1 cup diced mushrooms (about 4 ounces / 113-g)
- ¾ cup farro
- ½ cup dry white wine
- ½ teaspoon dried thyme
- 4 ounces (113 g) asparagus, cut into ½-inch pieces (about 1 cup)
- 2 tablespoons grated Parmesan cheese
- Salt

1. Soak the dried mushrooms in the hot water for about 15 minutes. When they're softened, drain the mushrooms, reserving the liquid. (I like to strain the liquid through a coffee filter in case there's any grit.) Mince the porcini mushrooms.

2. Add the mushroom liquid and vegetable stock to a medium saucepan and bring it to a boil. Reduce the heat to low just to keep it warm.

3. Heat the olive oil in a Dutch oven over high heat. Add the onion, garlic, and mushrooms, and sauté for 10 minutes.

4. Add the farro to the Dutch oven and sauté it for 3 minutes to toast.

5. Add the wine, thyme, and one ladleful of the hot mushroom and chicken stock. Bring it to a boil while stirring the farro. Do not cover the pot while the farro is cooking.

6. Reduce the heat to medium. When the liquid is absorbed, add another ladleful or two at a time to the pot, stirring occasionally, until the farro is cooked through. Keep an eye on the heat, to make sure it doesn't cook too quickly.

7. When the farro is al dente, add the asparagus and another ladleful of stock. Cook for another 3 to 5 minutes, or until the asparagus is softened.

8. Stir in Parmesan cheese and season with salt.

Per Serving:calories: 341 / fat: 16g / protein: 13g / carbs: 26g / fiber: 5g / sodium: 259mg

Mediterranean Baked Chickpeas

Prep time: 15 minutes / Cook time: 15 minutes / Serves 4

- 1 tablespoon extra-virgin olive oil
- ½ medium onion, chopped
- 3 garlic cloves, chopped
- 2 teaspoons smoked paprika
- ¼ teaspoon ground cumin

- 4 cups halved cherry tomatoes
- 2 (15-ounce / 425-g) cans chickpeas, drained and rinsed
- ½ cup plain, unsweetened, full-fat Greek yogurt, for serving
- 1 cup crumbled feta, for serving

1. Preheat the oven to 425ºF (220ºC).
2. In an oven-safe sauté pan or skillet, heat the oil over medium heat and sauté the onion and garlic. Cook for about 5 minutes, until softened and fragrant. Stir in the paprika and cumin and cook for 2 minutes. Stir in the tomatoes and chickpeas.
3. Bring to a simmer for 5 to 10 minutes before placing in the oven.
4. Roast in oven for 25 to 30 minutes, until bubbling and thickened. To serve, top with Greek yogurt and feta.

Per Serving:calories: 412 / fat: 15g / protein: 20g / carbs: 51g / fiber: 13g / sodium: 444mg

Roasted Veggie Bowl

Prep time: 10 minutes / Cook time: 15 minutes / Serves 2
- 1 cup broccoli florets
- 1 cup quartered Brussels sprouts
- ½ cup cauliflower florets
- ¼ medium white onion, peeled and sliced ¼ inch thick
- ½ medium green bell pepper, seeded and sliced ¼ inch thick
- 1 tablespoon coconut oil
- 2 teaspoons chili powder
- ½ teaspoon garlic powder
- ½ teaspoon cumin

1. Toss all ingredients together in a large bowl until vegetables are fully coated with oil and seasoning.
2. Pour vegetables into the air fryer basket.
3. Adjust the temperature to 360ºF (182ºC) and roast for 15 minutes.
4. Shake two or three times during cooking. Serve warm.

Per Serving:calories: 112 / fat: 8g / protein: 4g / carbs: 11g / sugars: 3g / fiber: 5g / sodium: 106mg

Crispy Cabbage Steaks

Prep time: 5 minutes / Cook time: 10 minutes / Serves 4
- 1 small head green cabbage, cored and cut into ½-inch-thick slices
- ¼ teaspoon salt
- ¼ teaspoon ground black pepper
- 2 tablespoons olive oil
- 1 clove garlic, peeled and finely minced
- ½ teaspoon dried thyme
- ½ teaspoon dried parsley

1. Sprinkle each side of cabbage with salt and pepper, then place into ungreased air fryer basket, working in batches if needed.
2. Drizzle each side of cabbage with olive oil, then sprinkle with remaining ingredients on both sides. Adjust the temperature to 350ºF (177ºC) and air fry for 10 minutes, turning "steaks" halfway through cooking.
3. Cabbage will be browned at the edges and tender when done. Serve warm.

Per Serving:calories: 63 / fat: 7g / protein: 0g / carbs: 1g / fiber: 0g / sodium: 155mg

Beet and Carrot Fritters with Yogurt Sauce

Prep time: 15 minutes / Cook time: 15 minutes / Serves 2
- For the Yogurt Sauce:
- ⅓ cup plain Greek yogurt
- 1 tablespoon freshly squeezed lemon juice
- Zest of ½ lemon
- ¼ teaspoon garlic powder
- ¼ teaspoon salt
- For the Fritters:
- 1 large carrot, peeled
- 1 small potato, peeled
- 1 medium golden or red beet, peeled
- 1 scallion, minced
- 2 tablespoons fresh minced parsley
- ¼ cup brown rice flour or unseasoned bread crumbs
- ¼ teaspoon garlic powder
- ¼ teaspoon salt
- 1 large egg, beaten
- ¼ cup feta cheese, crumbled
- 2 tablespoons olive oil (more if needed)

1. Make the Yogurt Sauce: 1. In a small bowl, mix together the yogurt, lemon juice and zest, garlic powder, and salt. Set aside. Make the Fritters: 1. Shred the carrot, potato, and beet in a food processor with the shredding blade. You can also use a mandoline with a julienne shredding blade or a vegetable peeler. Squeeze out any moisture from the vegetables and place them in a large bowl.
2. Add the scallion, parsley, rice flour, garlic powder, salt, and egg. Stir the mixture well to combine. Add the feta cheese and stir briefly, leaving chunks of feta cheese throughout.
3. Heat a large nonstick sauté pan over medium-high heat and add 1 tablespoon of the olive oil.
4. Make the fritters by scooping about 3 tablespoons of the vegetable mixture into your hands and flattening it into a firm disc about 3 inches in diameter.
5. Place 2 fritters at a time in the pan and let them cook for about two minutes. Check to see if the underside is golden, and then flip and repeat on the other side. Remove from the heat, add the rest of the olive oil to the pan, and repeat with the remaining vegetable mixture.
6. To serve, spoon about 1 tablespoon of the yogurt sauce on top of each fritter.

Per Serving:calories: 295 / fat: 14g / protein: 6g / carbs: 44g / fiber: 5g / sodium: 482mg

Three-Cheese Zucchini Boats

Prep time: 15 minutes / Cook time: 20 minutes / Serves 2
- 2 medium zucchini
- 1 tablespoon avocado oil
- ¼ cup low-carb, no-sugar-added pasta sauce
- ¼ cup full-fat ricotta cheese

- ¼ cup shredded Mozzarella cheese
- ¼ teaspoon dried oregano
- ¼ teaspoon garlic powder
- ½ teaspoon dried parsley
- 2 tablespoons grated vegetarian Parmesan cheese

1. Cut off 1 inch from the top and bottom of each zucchini. Slice zucchini in half lengthwise and use a spoon to scoop out a bit of the inside, making room for filling. Brush with oil and spoon 2 tablespoons pasta sauce into each shell.
2. In a medium bowl, mix ricotta, Mozzarella, oregano, garlic powder, and parsley. Spoon the mixture into each zucchini shell. Place stuffed zucchini shells into the air fryer basket.
3. Adjust the temperature to 350ºF (177ºC) and air fry for 20 minutes.
4. To remove from the basket, use tongs or a spatula and carefully lift out. Top with Parmesan. Serve immediately.

Per Serving:calories: 208 / fat: 14g / protein: 12g / carbs: 11g / fiber: 3g / sodium: 247mg

Farro with Roasted Tomatoes and Mushrooms

Prep time: 20 minutes / Cook time: 1 hour / Serves 4
- For the Tomatoes:
- 2 pints cherry tomatoes
- 1 teaspoon extra-virgin olive oil
- ¼ teaspoon kosher salt
- For the Farro:
- 3 to 4 cups water
- ½ cup farro
- ¼ teaspoon kosher salt
- For the Mushrooms:
- 2 tablespoons extra-virgin olive oil
- 1 onion, julienned
- ½ teaspoon kosher salt
- ¼ teaspoon freshly ground black pepper
- 10 ounces (283 g) baby bella (crimini) mushrooms, stemmed and thinly sliced
- ½ cup no-salt-added vegetable stock
- 1 (15-ounce / 425-g) can no-salt-added or low-sodium cannellini beans, drained and rinsed
- 1 cup baby spinach
- 2 tablespoons fresh basil, cut into ribbons
- ¼ cup pine nuts, toasted
- Aged balsamic vinegar (optional)

1. Make the Tomatoes: 1. Preheat the oven to 400ºF (205ºC). Line a baking sheet with parchment paper or foil. Toss the tomatoes, olive oil, and salt together on the baking sheet and roast for 30 minutes. Make the Farro:
2. Bring the water, farro, and salt to a boil in a medium saucepan or pot over high heat. Cover, reduce the heat to low, and simmer, and cook for 30 minutes, or until the farro is al dente. Drain and set aside. Make the Mushrooms:
3. Heat the olive oil in a large skillet or sauté pan over medium-low heat. Add the onions, salt, and black pepper and sauté until golden brown and starting to caramelize, about 15 minutes. Add the mushrooms, increase the heat to medium, and sauté until the liquid has evaporated and the mushrooms brown, about 10 minutes. Add the vegetable stock and deglaze the pan, scraping up any brown bits, and reduce the liquid for about 5 minutes. Add the beans and warm through, about 3 minutes.
4. Remove from the heat and mix in the spinach, basil, pine nuts, roasted tomatoes, and farro. Garnish with a drizzle of balsamic vinegar, if desired.

Per Serving:calories: 375 / fat: 15g / protein: 14g / carbs: 48g / fiber: 10g / sodium: 305mg

Crustless Spanakopita

Prep time: 15 minutes / Cook time: 45 minutes / Serves 6
- 12 tablespoons extra-virgin olive oil, divided
- 1 small yellow onion, diced
- 1 (32-ounce / 907-g) bag frozen chopped spinach, thawed, fully drained, and patted dry (about 4 cups)
- 4 garlic cloves, minced
- ½ teaspoon salt
- ½ teaspoon freshly ground black pepper
- 1 cup whole-milk ricotta cheese
- 4 large eggs
- ¾ cup crumbled traditional feta cheese
- ¼ cup pine nuts

1. Preheat the oven to 375ºF (190ºC).
2. In a large skillet, heat 4 tablespoons olive oil over medium-high heat. Add the onion and sauté until softened, 6 to 8 minutes.
3. Add the spinach, garlic, salt, and pepper and sauté another 5 minutes. Remove from the heat and allow to cool slightly.
4. In a medium bowl, whisk together the ricotta and eggs. Add to the cooled spinach and stir to combine.
5. Pour 4 tablespoons olive oil in the bottom of a 9-by-13-inch glass baking dish and swirl to coat the bottom and sides. Add the spinach-ricotta mixture and spread into an even layer.
6. Bake for 20 minutes or until the mixture begins to set. Remove from the oven and crumble the feta evenly across the top of the spinach. Add the pine nuts and drizzle with the remaining 4 tablespoons olive oil. Return to the oven and bake for an additional 15 to 20 minutes, or until the spinach is fully set and the top is starting to turn golden brown. Allow to cool slightly before cutting to serve.

Per Serving:calories: 497 / fat: 44g / protein: 18g / carbs: 11g / fiber: 5g / sodium: 561mg

Root Vegetable Soup with Garlic Aioli

Prep time: 10 minutes / Cook time 25 minutes / Serves 4
- For the Soup:

- 8 cups vegetable broth
- ½ teaspoon salt
- 1 medium leek, cut into thick rounds
- 1 pound (454 g) carrots, peeled and diced
- 1 pound (454 g) potatoes, peeled and diced
- 1 pound (454 g) turnips, peeled and cut into 1-inch cubes
- 1 red bell pepper, cut into strips
- 2 tablespoons fresh oregano
- For the Aioli:
- 5 garlic cloves, minced
- ¼ teaspoon salt
- ⅔ cup olive oil
- 1 drop lemon juice

1. Bring the broth and salt to a boil and add the vegetables one at a time, letting the water return to a boil after each addition. Add the carrots first, then the leeks, potatoes, turnips, and finally the red bell peppers. Let the vegetables cook for about 3 minutes after adding the green beans and bringing to a boil. The process will take about 20 minutes in total.
2. Meanwhile, make the aioli. In a mortar and pestle, grind the garlic to a paste with the salt. Using a whisk and whisking constantly, add the olive oil in a thin stream. Continue whisking until the mixture thickens to the consistency of mayonnaise. Add the lemon juice.
3. Serve the vegetables in the broth, dolloped with the aioli and garnished with the fresh oregano.

Per Serving:calories: 538 / fat: 37g / protein: 5g / carbs: 50g / fiber: 9g / sodium: 773mg

Baked Falafel Sliders

Prep time: 10 minutes / Cook time: 30 minutes / Makes 6 sliders

- Olive oil cooking spray
- 1 (15-ounce / 425-g) can no-salt-added or low-sodium chickpeas, drained and rinsed
- 1 onion, roughly chopped
- 2 garlic cloves, peeled
- 2 tablespoons fresh parsley, chopped
- 2 tablespoons whole-wheat flour
- ½ teaspoon ground coriander
- ½ teaspoon ground cumin
- ½ teaspoon baking powder
- ½ teaspoon kosher salt
- ¼ teaspoon freshly ground black pepper

1. Preheat the oven to 350ºF (180ºC). Line a baking sheet with parchment paper or foil and lightly spray with olive oil cooking spray.
2. In a food processor, add the chickpeas, onion, garlic, parsley, flour, coriander, cumin, baking powder, salt, and black pepper. Process until smooth, stopping to scrape down the sides of the bowl.
3. Make 6 slider patties, each with a heaping ¼ cup of mixture, and arrange on the prepared baking sheet. Bake for 30 minutes, turning over halfway through.

Per Serving:1 slider: calories: 90 / fat: 1g / protein: 4g / carbs:17 g / fiber: 3g / sodium: 110mg

Quinoa Lentil "Meatballs" with Quick Tomato Sauce

Prep time: 25 minutes / Cook time: 45 minutes / Serves 4

- For the Meatballs:
- Olive oil cooking spray
- 2 large eggs, beaten
- 1 tablespoon no-salt-added tomato paste
- ½ teaspoon kosher salt
- ½ cup grated Parmesan cheese
- ½ onion, roughly chopped
- ¼ cup fresh parsley
- 1 garlic clove, peeled
- 1½ cups cooked lentils
- 1 cup cooked quinoa
- For the Tomato Sauce:
- 1 tablespoon extra-virgin olive oil
- 1 onion, minced
- ½ teaspoon dried oregano
- ½ teaspoon kosher salt
- 2 garlic cloves, minced
- 1 (28-ounce / 794-g) can no-salt-added crushed tomatoes
- ½ teaspoon honey
- ¼ cup fresh basil, chopped

1. Make the Meatballs: 1. Preheat the oven to 400ºF (205ºC). Lightly grease a 12-cup muffin pan with olive oil cooking spray.
2. In a large bowl, whisk together the eggs, tomato paste, and salt until fully combined. Mix in the Parmesan cheese.
3. In a food processor, add the onion, parsley, and garlic. Process until minced. Add to the egg mixture and stir together. Add the lentils to the food processor and process until puréed into a thick paste. Add to the large bowl and mix together. Add the quinoa and mix well.
4. Form balls, slightly larger than a golf ball, with ¼ cup of the quinoa mixture. Place each ball in a muffin pan cup. Note: The mixture will be somewhat soft but should hold together.
5. Bake 25 to 30 minutes, until golden brown. Make the Tomato Sauce:
6. Heat the olive oil in a large saucepan over medium heat. Add the onion, oregano, and salt and sauté until light golden brown, about 5 minutes. Add the garlic and cook for 30 seconds.
7. Stir in the tomatoes and honey. Increase the heat to high and cook, stirring often, until simmering, then decrease the heat to medium-low and cook for 10 minutes. Remove from the heat and stir in the basil. Serve with the meatballs.

Per Serving:3 meatballs: calories: 360 / fat: 10g / protein: 20g / carbs: 48g / fiber: 14g / sodium: 520mg

Chapter 9 Salads

Tossed Green Mediterranean Salad

Prep time: 15 minutes / Cook time: 0 minutes / Serves 4

- 1 medium head romaine lettuce, washed, dried, and chopped into bite-sized pieces
- 2 medium cucumbers, peeled and sliced
- 3 spring onions (white parts only), sliced
- ½ cup finely chopped fresh dill
- ⅓ cup extra virgin olive oil
- 2 tablespoons fresh lemon juice
- ¼ teaspoon fine sea salt
- 4 ounces (113 g) crumbled feta
- 7 Kalamata olives, pitted

1. Add the lettuce, cucumber, spring onions, and dill to a large bowl. Toss to combine.
2. In a small bowl, whisk together the olive oil and lemon juice. Pour the dressing over the salad, toss, then sprinkle the sea salt over the top.
3. Sprinkle the feta and olives over the top and then gently toss the salad one more time. Serve promptly. (This recipe is best served fresh.)

Per Serving:calories: 284 / fat: 25g / protein: 7g / carbs: 10g / fiber: 5g / sodium: 496mg

Arugula Salad with Grapes, Goat Cheese, and Za'atar Croutons

Prep time: 10 minutes / Cook time: 10 minutes / Serves 4

- Croutons:
- 2 slices whole wheat bread, cubed
- 2 teaspoons olive oil, divided
- 1 teaspoon za'atar
- Vinaigrette:
- 2 tablespoons olive oil
- 1 tablespoon red wine vinegar
- ½ teaspoon chopped fresh rosemary
- ¼ teaspoon kosher salt
- ⅛ teaspoon ground black pepper
- Salad:
- 4 cups baby arugula
- 1 cup grapes, halved
- ½ red onion, thinly sliced
- 2 ounces (57 g) goat cheese, crumbled

1. Make the Croutons: Toss the bread cubes with 1 teaspoon of the oil and the za'atar. In a medium skillet over medium heat, warm the remaining 1 teaspoon oil. Cook the bread cubes, stirring frequently, until browned and crispy, 8 to 10 minutes.
2. Make the Vinaigrette: In a small bowl, whisk together the oil, vinegar, rosemary, salt, and pepper.
3. Make the Salad: In a large bowl, toss the arugula, grapes, and onion with the vinaigrette. Top with the cheese and croutons.

Per Serving:calories: 204 / fat: 14g / protein: 6g / carbs: 15g / fiber: 2g / sodium: 283mg

Asparagus Salad

Prep time: 10 minutes / Cook time: 0 minutes / Serves 4

- 1 pound (454 g) asparagus
- Sea salt and freshly ground pepper, to taste
- 4 tablespoons olive oil
- 1 tablespoon balsamic vinegar
- 1 tablespoon lemon zest

1. Either roast the asparagus or, with a vegetable peeler, shave it into thin strips.
2. Season to taste.
3. Toss with the olive oil and vinegar, garnish with a sprinkle of lemon zest, and serve.

Per Serving:calories: 146 / fat: 14g / protein: 3g / carbs: 5g / fiber: 3g / sodium: 4mg

Double-Apple Spinach Salad

Prep time: 15 minutes / Cook time: 0 minutes / Serves 4

- 8 cups baby spinach
- 1 medium Granny Smith apple, diced
- 1 medium red apple, diced
- ½ cup toasted walnuts
- 2 ounces (57 g) low-fat, sharp white cheddar cheese, cubed
- 3 tablespoons olive oil
- 1 tablespoon red wine vinegar or apple cider vinegar

1. Toss the spinach, apples, walnuts, and cubed cheese together. Lightly drizzle olive oil and vinegar over top and serve.

Per Serving:calories: 275 / fat: 22g / protein: 7g / carbs: 16g / fiber: 4g / sodium: 140mg

French Lentil Salad with Parsley and Mint

Prep time: 20 minutes / Cook time:25 minutes / Serves 6

- For the Lentils:
- 1 cup French lentils
- 1 garlic clove, smashed
- 1 dried bay leaf
- For the Salad:
- 2 tablespoons extra-virgin olive oil
- 2 tablespoons red wine vinegar
- ½ teaspoon ground cumin
- ½ teaspoon kosher salt
- ¼ teaspoon freshly ground black pepper
- 2 celery stalks, diced small
- 1 bell pepper, diced small
- ½ red onion, diced small

- ¼ cup fresh parsley, chopped
- ¼ cup fresh mint, chopped
1. Make the Lentils: 1. Put the lentils, garlic, and bay leaf in a large saucepan. Cover with water by about 3 inches and bring to a boil. Reduce the heat, cover, and simmer until tender, 20 to 30 minutes.
2. Drain the lentils to remove any remaining water after cooking. Remove the garlic and bay leaf. Make the Salad:
3. In a large bowl, whisk together the olive oil, vinegar, cumin, salt, and black pepper. Add the celery, bell pepper, onion, parsley, and mint and toss to combine.
4. Add the lentils and mix well.

Per Serving:calories: 200 / fat: 8g / protein: 10g / carbs: 26g / fiber: 10g / sodium: 165mg

Watermelon Burrata Salad

Prep time: 10 minutes / Cook time: 0 minutes / Serves 4
- 2 cups cubes or chunks watermelon
- 1½ cups small burrata cheese balls, cut into medium chunks
- 1 small red onion or 2 shallots, thinly sliced into half-moons
- ¼ cup olive oil
- ¼ cup balsamic vinegar
- 4 fresh basil leaves, sliced chiffonade-style (roll up leaves of basil, and slice into thin strips)
- 1 tablespoon lemon zest
- Salt and freshly ground black pepper, to taste
1. In a large bowl, mix all the ingredients. Refrigerate until chilled before serving.

Per Serving:1 cup: calories: 224 / fat: 14g / protein: 14g / carbs: 12g / fiber: 1g / sodium: 560mg

Greek Potato Salad

Prep time: 15 minutes / Cook time: 15 to 18 minutes / Serves 6
- 1½ pounds (680 g) small red or new potatoes
- ½ cup olive oil
- ⅓ cup red wine vinegar
- 1 teaspoon fresh Greek oregano
- 4 ounces (113 g) feta cheese, crumbled, if desired, or 4 ounces (113 g) grated Swiss cheese (for a less salty option)
- 1 green bell pepper, seeded and chopped (1¼ cups)
- 1 small red onion, halved and thinly sliced (generous 1 cup)
- ½ cup Kalamata olives, pitted and halved
1. Put the potatoes in a large saucepan and add water to cover. Bring the water to a boil and cook until tender, 15 to 18 minutes. Drain and set aside until cool enough to handle.
2. Meanwhile, in a large bowl, whisk together the olive oil, vinegar, and oregano.
3. When the potatoes are just cool enough to handle, cut them into 1-inch pieces and add them to the bowl with

the dressing. Toss to combine. Add the cheese, bell pepper, onion, and olives and toss gently. Let stand for 30 minutes before serving.

Per Serving:calories: 315 / fat: 23g / protein: 5g / carbs: 21g / fiber: 3g / sodium: 360mg

Roasted Cauliflower "Steak" Salad

Prep time: 10 minutes / Cook time: 50 minutes / Serves 4
- 2 tablespoons olive oil, divided
- 2 large heads cauliflower (about 3 pounds / 1.4 kg each), trimmed of outer leaves
- 2 teaspoons za'atar
- 1½ teaspoons kosher salt, divided
- 1¼ teaspoons ground black pepper, divided
- 1 teaspoon ground cumin
- 2 large carrots
- 8 ounces (227 g) dandelion greens, tough stems removed
- ½ cup low-fat plain Greek yogurt
- 2 tablespoons tahini
- 2 tablespoons fresh lemon juice
- 1 tablespoon water
- 1 clove garlic, minced
1. Preheat the oven to 450°F(235°C). Brush a large baking sheet with some of the oil.
2. Place the cauliflower on a cutting board, stem side down. Cut down the middle, through the core and stem, and then cut two 1'-thick "steaks" from the middle. Repeat with the other cauliflower head. Set aside the remaining cauliflower for another use. Brush both sides of the steaks with the remaining oil and set on the baking sheet.
3. Combine the za'atar, 1 teaspoon of the salt, 1 teaspoon of the pepper, and the cumin. Sprinkle on the cauliflower steaks. Bake until the bottom is deeply golden, about 30 minutes. Flip and bake until tender, 10 to 15 minutes.
4. Meanwhile, set the carrots on a cutting board and use a vegetable peeler to peel them into ribbons. Add to a large bowl with the dandelion greens.
5. In a small bowl, combine the yogurt, tahini, lemon juice, water, garlic, the remaining ½ teaspoon salt, and the remaining ¼ teaspoon pepper.
6. Dab 3 tablespoons of the dressing onto the carrot-dandelion mix. With a spoon or your hands, massage the dressing into the mix for 5 minutes.
7. Remove the steaks from the oven and transfer to individual plates. Drizzle each with 2 tablespoons of the dressing and top with 1 cup of the salad.

Per Serving:calories: 214 / fat: 12g / protein: 9g / carbs: 21g / fiber: 7g / sodium: 849mg

Turkish Shepherd'S Salad

Prep time: 15 minutes / Cook time: 0 minutes / Serves 6
- ¼ cup extra-virgin olive oil
- 2 tablespoons apple cider vinegar

- 2 tablespoons lemon juice
- ½ teaspoon kosher salt
- ¼ teaspoon ground black pepper
- 3 plum tomatoes, seeded and chopped
- 2 cucumbers, seeded and chopped
- 1 red bell pepper, seeded and chopped
- 1 green bell pepper, seeded and chopped
- 1 small red onion, chopped
- ⅓ cup pitted black olives (such as kalamata), halved
- ½ cup chopped fresh flat-leaf parsley
- ¼ cup chopped fresh mint
- ¼ cup chopped fresh dill
- 6 ounces (170 g) feta cheese, cubed

1. In a small bowl, whisk together the oil, vinegar, lemon juice, salt, and black pepper.
2. In a large serving bowl, combine the tomatoes, cucumber, bell peppers, onion, olives, parsley, mint, and dill. Pour the dressing over the salad, toss gently, and sprinkle with the cheese.

Per Serving:calories: 238 / fat: 20g / protein: 6g / carbs: 10g / fiber: 2g / sodium: 806mg

Panzanella (Tuscan Bread and Tomatoes Salad)

Prep time: 10 minutes / Cook time: 20 minutes / Serves 6
- 4 ounces (113 g) sourdough bread, cut into 1' slices
- 3 tablespoons extra-virgin olive oil, divided
- 2 tablespoons red wine vinegar
- 2 cloves garlic, mashed to a paste
- 1 teaspoon finely chopped fresh oregano or ½ teaspoon dried
- 1 teaspoon fresh thyme leaves
- ½ teaspoon Dijon mustard
- Pinch of kosher salt
- Few grinds of ground black pepper
- 2 pounds (907 g) ripe tomatoes (mixed colors)
- 6 ounces (170 g) fresh mozzarella pearls
- 1 cucumber, cut into ½'-thick half-moons
- 1 small red onion, thinly sliced
- 1 cup baby arugula
- ½ cup torn fresh basil

1. Coat a grill rack or grill pan with olive oil and prepare to medium-high heat.
2. Brush 1 tablespoon of the oil all over the bread slices. Grill the bread on both sides until grill marks appear, about 2 minutes per side. Cut the bread into 1' cubes.
3. In a large bowl, whisk together the vinegar, garlic, oregano, thyme, mustard, salt, pepper, and the remaining 2 tablespoons oil until emulsified.
4. Add the bread, tomatoes, mozzarella, cucumber, onion, arugula, and basil. Toss to combine and let sit for 10 minutes to soak up the flavors.

Per Serving:calories: 219 / fat: 12g / protein: 10g / carbs: 19g / fiber: 3g / sodium: 222mg

Quinoa with Zucchini, Mint, and Pistachios

Prep time: 20 to 30 minutes / Cook time: 20 minutes / Serves 4
- For the Quinoa:
- 1½ cups water
- 1 cup quinoa
- ¼ teaspoon kosher salt
- For the Salad:
- 2 tablespoons extra-virgin olive oil
- 1 zucchini, thinly sliced into rounds
- 6 small radishes, sliced
- 1 shallot, julienned
- ¾ teaspoon kosher salt
- ¼ teaspoon freshly ground black pepper
- 2 garlic cloves, sliced
- Zest of 1 lemon
- 2 tablespoons lemon juice
- ¼ cup fresh mint, chopped
- ¼ cup fresh basil, chopped
- ¼ cup pistachios, shelled and toasted

1. Make the Quinoa: Bring the water, quinoa, and salt to a boil in a medium saucepan. Reduce to a simmer, cover, and cook for 10 to 12 minutes. Fluff with a fork. Make the Salad: 1. Heat the olive oil in a large skillet or sauté pan over medium-high heat. Add the zucchini, radishes, shallot, salt, and black pepper, and sauté for 7 to 8 minutes. Add the garlic and cook 30 seconds to 1 minute more.
2. In a large bowl, combine the lemon zest and lemon juice. Add the quinoa and mix well. Add the cooked zucchini mixture and mix well. Add the mint, basil, and pistachios and gently mix.

Per Serving:calories: 220 / fat: 12g / protein: 6g / carbs: 25g / fiber: 5g / sodium: 295mg

Tuscan Kale Salad with Anchovies

Prep time: 15 minutes / Cook time: 0 minutes / Serves 4
- 1 large bunch lacinato or dinosaur kale
- ¼ cup toasted pine nuts
- 1 cup shaved or coarsely shredded fresh Parmesan cheese
- ¼ cup extra-virgin olive oil
- 8 anchovy fillets, roughly chopped
- 2 to 3 tablespoons freshly squeezed lemon juice (from 1 large lemon)
- 2 teaspoons red pepper flakes (optional)

1. Remove the rough center stems from the kale leaves and roughly tear each leaf into about 4-by-1-inch strips. Place the torn kale in a large bowl and add the pine nuts and cheese.
2. In a small bowl, whisk together the olive oil, anchovies, lemon juice, and red pepper flakes (if using). Drizzle over the salad and toss to coat well. Let sit at room temperature 30 minutes before serving, tossing again just prior to serving.

Per Serving:calories: 333 / fat: 27g / protein: 16g / carbs:

12g / fiber: 4g / sodium: 676mg

Citrus Fennel Salad

Prep time: 15 minutes / Cook time: 0 minutes / Serves 2

- For the Dressing:
- 2 tablespoons fresh orange juice
- 3 tablespoons olive oil
- 1 tablespoon blood orange vinegar, other orange vinegar, or cider vinegar
- 1 tablespoon honey
- Salt
- Freshly ground black pepper
- For the Salad:
- 2 cups packed baby kale
- 1 medium navel or blood orange, segmented
- ½ small fennel bulb, stems and leaves removed, sliced into matchsticks
- 3 tablespoons toasted pecans, chopped
- 2 ounces (57 g) goat cheese, crumbled

1. Make the Dressing: Combine the orange juice, olive oil, vinegar, and honey in a small bowl and whisk to combine. Season with salt and pepper. Set the dressing aside. Make the Salad: 1. Divide the baby kale, orange segments, fennel, pecans, and goat cheese evenly between two plates.
2. Drizzle half of the dressing over each salad.

Per Serving:calories: 502 / fat: 39g / protein: 13g / carbs: 31g / fiber: 6g / sodium: 158mg

Greek Salad with Lemon-Oregano Vinaigrette

Prep time: 15 minutes / Cook time: 15 minutes / Serves 8

- ½ red onion, thinly sliced
- ¼ cup extra-virgin olive oil
- 3 tablespoons fresh lemon juice or red wine vinegar
- 1 clove garlic, minced
- 1 teaspoon chopped fresh oregano or ½ teaspoon dried
- ½ teaspoon ground black pepper
- ¼ teaspoon kosher salt
- 4 tomatoes, cut into large chunks
- 1 large English cucumber, peeled, seeded (if desired), and diced
- 1 large yellow or red bell pepper, chopped
- ½ cup pitted kalamata or Niçoise olives, halved
- ¼ cup chopped fresh flat-leaf parsley
- 4 ounces (113 g) Halloumi or feta cheese, cut into ½' cubes

1. In a medium bowl, soak the onion in enough water to cover for 10 minutes.
2. In a small bowl, combine the oil, lemon juice or vinegar, garlic, oregano, black pepper, and salt.
3. Drain the onion and add to a large bowl with the tomatoes, cucumber, bell pepper, olives, and parsley. Gently toss to mix the vegetables.

4. Pour the vinaigrette over the salad. Add the cheese and toss again to distribute.
5. Serve immediately, or chill for up to 30 minutes.

Per Serving:calories: 190 / fat: 16g / protein: 5g / carbs: 8g / fiber: 2g / sodium: 554mg

Citrus Avocado Salad

Prep time: 5 minutes / Cook time: 0 minutes / Serves 2

- ½ medium orange (any variety), peeled and cut into bite-sized chunks
- 1 medium tangerine, peeled and sectioned
- ½ medium white grapefruit, peeled and cut into bite-sized chunks
- 2 thin slices red onion
- 1 medium avocado, peeled, pitted, and sliced
- Pinch of freshly ground black pepper
- For the Dressing:
- 3 tablespoons extra virgin olive oil
- 1 tablespoon fresh lemon juice
- ½ teaspoon ground cumin
- ½ teaspoon coarse sea salt
- Pinch of freshly ground black pepper

1. Make the dressing by combining the olive oil, lemon juice, cumin, sea salt, and black pepper in a small jar or bowl. Whisk or shake to combine.
2. Toss the orange, tangerine, and grapefruit in a medium bowl, then place the sliced onion on top. Drizzle half the dressing over the salad.
3. Fan the avocado slices over the top of the salad. Drizzle the remaining dressing over the salad and then sprinkle a pinch of black pepper over the top.
4. Toss gently before serving. (This salad is best eaten fresh, but can be stored in the refrigerator for up to 1 day.)

Per Serving:calories: 448 / fat: 36g / protein: 4g / carbs: 35g / fiber: 11g / sodium: 595mg

Fruited Chicken Salad

Prep time: 10 minutes / Cook time: 0 minutes / Serves 2

- 2 cups chopped cooked chicken breast
- 2 Granny Smith apples, peeled, cored, and diced
- ½ cup dried cranberries
- ¼ cup diced red onion
- ¼ cup diced celery
- 2 tablespoons honey Dijon mustard
- 1 tablespoon olive oil mayonnaise
- ½ teaspoon salt
- ¼ teaspoon freshly ground black pepper

1. In a medium bowl, combine the chicken, apples, cranberries, onion, and celery and mix well.
2. In a small bowl, combine the mustard, mayonnaise, salt, and pepper and whisk together until well blended.
3. Stir the dressing into the chicken mixture until thoroughly combined.

Per Serving:calories: 384 / fat: 9g / protein: 45g / carbs: 28g / fiber: 7g / sodium: 638mg

Classic Tabouli

Prep time: 30 minutes / Cook time: 0 minutes / Serves 8 to 10

- 1 cup bulgur wheat, grind
- 4 cups Italian parsley, finely chopped
- 2 cups ripe tomato, finely diced
- 1 cup green onion, finely chopped
- ½ cup lemon juice
- ½ cup extra-virgin olive oil
- 1½ teaspoons salt
- 1 teaspoon dried mint

1. Before you chop the vegetables, put the bulgur in a small bowl. Rinse with water, drain, and let stand in the bowl while you prepare the other ingredients.
2. Put the parsley, tomatoes, green onion, and bulgur into a large bowl.
3. In a small bowl, whisk together the lemon juice, olive oil, salt, and mint.
4. Pour the dressing over the tomato, onion, and bulgur mixture, tossing everything together. Add additional salt to taste. Serve immediately or store in the fridge for up to 2 days.

Per Serving:calories: 207 / fat: 14g / protein: 4g / carbs: 20g / fiber: 5g / sodium: 462mg

Greek Black-Eyed Pea Salad

Prep time: 10 minutes / Cook time: 0 minutes / Serves 4

- 2 tablespoons olive oil
- Juice of 1 lemon (about 2 tablespoons)
- 1 garlic clove, minced
- 1 teaspoon ground cumin
- 1 (15½-ounce / 439-g) can no-salt-added black-eyed peas, drained and rinsed
- 1 red bell pepper, seeded and chopped
- 1 shallot, finely chopped
- 2 scallions (green onions), chopped
- 2 tablespoons chopped fresh dill
- ¼ cup chopped fresh parsley
- ½ cup pitted Kalamata olives, sliced
- ½ cup crumbled feta cheese (optional)

1. In a large bowl, whisk together the olive oil, lemon juice, garlic, and cumin.
2. Add the black-eyed peas, bell pepper, shallot, scallions, dill, parsley, olives, and feta (if using) and toss to combine. Serve.

Per Serving:calories: 213 / fat: 14g / protein: 7g / carbs: 16g / fiber: 5g / sodium: 426mg

Caprese Salad with Fresh Mozzarella

Prep time: 10 minutes / Cook time: 0 minutes / Serves 6

- For the Pesto:
- 2 cups (packed) fresh basil leaves, plus more for garnish
- ⅓ cup pine nuts
- 3 garlic cloves, minced
- ½ cup (about 2 ounces / 57 g) freshly grated Parmesan cheese
- ½ cup extra-virgin olive oil
- Salt
- Freshly ground black pepper
- For the Salad:
- 4 to 6 large, ripe tomatoes, cut into thick slices
- 1 pound (454 g) fresh mozzarella, cut into thick slices
- 3 tablespoons balsamic vinegar
- Salt
- Freshly ground black pepper

1. To make the pesto, in a food processor combine the basil, pine nuts, and garlic and pulse several times to chop. Add the Parmesan cheese and pulse again until well combined. With the food processor running, add the olive oil in a slow, steady stream. Transfer to a small bowl, taste, and add salt and pepper as needed. Slice, quarter, or halve the tomatoes, based on your preferred salad presentation.
2. To make the salad, on a large serving platter arrange the tomato slices and cheese slices, stacking them like fallen dominoes.
3. Dollop the pesto decoratively on top of the tomato and cheese slices. (You will likely have extra pesto. Refrigerate the extra in a tightly sealed container and use within 3 days, or freeze it for up to 3 months.)
4. Drizzle the balsamic vinegar over the top, garnish with basil leaves, sprinkle with salt and pepper to taste, and serve immediately.

Per Serving:calories: 398 / fat: 32g / protein: 23g / carbs: 8g / fiber: 1g / sodium: 474mg

Taverna-Style Greek Salad

Prep time: 20 minutes / Cook time: 0 minutes / Serves 4

- 4 to 5 medium tomatoes, roughly chopped
- 1 large cucumber, peeled and roughly chopped
- 1 medium green bell pepper, sliced
- 1 small red onion, sliced
- 16 pitted Kalamata olives
- ¼ cup capers, or more olives
- 1 teaspoon dried oregano or fresh herbs of your choice, such as parsley, cilantro, chives, or basil, divided
- ½ cup extra-virgin olive oil, divided
- 1 pack feta cheese
- Optional: salt, pepper, and fresh oregano, for garnish

1. Place the vegetables in a large serving bowl. Add the olives, capers, feta, half of the dried oregano and half of the olive oil. Mix to combine. Place the whole piece of feta cheese on top, sprinkle with the remaining dried oregano, and drizzle with the remaining olive oil. Season to taste and serve immediately, or store in the fridge for up to 1 day.

Per Serving:calories: 320 / fat: 31g / protein: 3g / carbs: 11g / fiber: 4g / sodium: 445mg

Chapter 10 Pizzas, Wraps, and Sandwiches

Dill Salmon Salad Wraps

Prep time: 10 minutes /Cook time: 10 minutes/ Serves:6

- 1 pound (454 g) salmon filet, cooked and flaked, or 3 (5-ounce / 142-g) cans salmon
- ½ cup diced carrots (about 1 carrot)
- ½ cup diced celery (about 1 celery stalk)
- 3 tablespoons chopped fresh dill
- 3 tablespoons diced red onion (a little less than ⅛ onion)
- 2 tablespoons capers
- 1½ tablespoons extra-virgin olive oil
- 1 tablespoon aged balsamic vinegar
- ½ teaspoon freshly ground black pepper
- ¼ teaspoon kosher or sea salt
- 4 whole-wheat flatbread wraps or soft whole-wheat tortillas

1. In a large bowl, mix together the salmon, carrots, celery, dill, red onion, capers, oil, vinegar, pepper, and salt.
2. Divide the salmon salad among the flatbreads. Fold up the bottom of the flatbread, then roll up the wrap and serve.

Per Serving:calories: 185 / fat: 8g / protein: 17g / carbs: 12g / fiber: 2g / sodium: 237mg

Beans and Greens Pizza

Prep time: 11 minutes / Cook time: 14 to 19 minutes / Serves 4

- ¾ cup whole-wheat pastry flour
- ½ teaspoon low-sodium baking powder
- 1 tablespoon olive oil, divided
- 1 cup chopped kale
- 2 cups chopped fresh baby spinach
- 1 cup canned no-salt-added cannellini beans, rinsed and drained
- ½ teaspoon dried thyme
- 1 piece low-sodium string cheese, torn into pieces

1. In a small bowl, mix the pastry flour and baking powder until well combined.
2. Add ¼ cup of water and 2 teaspoons of olive oil. Mix until a dough forms.
3. On a floured surface, press or roll the dough into a 7-inch round. Set aside while you cook the greens.
4. In a baking pan, mix the kale, spinach, and remaining teaspoon of the olive oil. Air fry at 350ºF (177ºC) for 3 to 5 minutes, until the greens are wilted. Drain well.
5. Put the pizza dough into the air fryer basket. Top with the greens, cannellini beans, thyme, and string cheese. Air fry for 11 to 14 minutes, or until the crust is golden

brown and the cheese is melted. Cut into quarters to serve.

Per Serving:calories: 181 / fat: 6g / protein: 8g / carbs: 27g / fiber: 6g / sodium: 103mg

Jerk Chicken Wraps

Prep time: 30 minutes / Cook time: 15 minutes / Serves 4

- 1 pound (454 g) boneless, skinless chicken tenderloins
- 1 cup jerk marinade
- Olive oil
- 4 large low-carb tortillas
- 1 cup julienned carrots
- 1 cup peeled cucumber ribbons
- 1 cup shredded lettuce
- 1 cup mango or pineapple chunks

1. In a medium bowl, coat the chicken with the jerk marinade, cover, and refrigerate for 1 hour.
2. Spray the air fryer basket lightly with olive oil.
3. Place the chicken in the air fryer basket in a single layer and spray lightly with olive oil. You may need to cook the chicken in batches. Reserve any leftover marinade.
4. Air fry at 375ºF (191ºC) for 8 minutes. Turn the chicken over and brush with some of the remaining marinade. Cook until the chicken reaches an internal temperature of at least 165ºF (74ºC), an additional 5 to 7 minutes.
5. To assemble the wraps, fill each tortilla with ¼ cup carrots, ¼ cup cucumber, ¼ cup lettuce, and ¼ cup mango. Place one quarter of the chicken tenderloins on top and roll up the tortilla. These are great served warm or cold.

Per Serving:calories: 241 / fat: 4g / protein: 28g / carbs: 23g / fiber: 4g / sodium: 85mg

Herbed Focaccia Panini with Anchovies and Burrata

Prep time: 5 minutes / Cook time: 8 minutes / Serves 4

- 8 ounces (227 g) burrata cheese, chilled and sliced
- 1 pound (454 g) whole-wheat herbed focaccia, cut crosswise into 4 rectangles and split horizontally
- 1 can anchovy fillets packed in oil, drained
- 8 slices tomato, sliced
- 2 cups arugula
- 1 tablespoon olive oil

1. Divide the cheese evenly among the bottom halves of the focaccia rectangles. Top each with 3 or 4 anchovy fillets, 2 slices of tomato, and ½ cup arugula. Place the top halves of the focaccia on top of the sandwiches.
2. To make the panini, heat a skillet or grill pan over high heat and brush with the olive oil.

3. Place the sandwiches in the hot pan and place another heavy pan, such as a cast-iron skillet, on top to weigh them down. Cook for about 3 to 4 minutes, until crisp and golden on the bottom, and then flip over and repeat on the second side, cooking for an additional 3 to 4 minutes until golden and crisp. Slice each sandwich in half and serve hot.

Per Serving:calories: 596 / fat: 30g / protein: 27g / carbs: 58g / fiber: 5g / sodium: 626mg

Moroccan Lamb Flatbread with Pine Nuts, Mint, and Ras Al Hanout

Prep time: 10 minutes / Cook time: 20 minutes / Serves 4
- 1⅓ cups plain Greek yogurt
- Juice of 1½ lemons, divided
- 1¼ teaspoons salt, divided
- 1 pound (454 g) ground lamb
- 1 medium red onion, diced
- 1 clove garlic, minced
- 1 tablespoon ras al hanout
- ¼ cup chopped fresh mint leaves
- Freshly ground black pepper
- 4 Middle Eastern-style flatbread rounds
- 2 tablespoons toasted pine nuts
- 16 cherry tomatoes, halved
- 2 tablespoons chopped cilantro

1. Preheat the oven to 450°F(235°C).
2. In a small bowl, stir together the yogurt, the juice of ½ lemon, and ¼ teaspoon salt.
3. Heat a large skillet over medium-high heat. Add the lamb and cook, stirring frequently, until browned, about 5 minutes. Drain any excess rendered fat from the pan and then stir in the onion and garlic and cook, stirring, until softened, about 3 minutes more. Stir in the ras al hanout, mint, the remaining teaspoon of salt, and pepper.
4. Place the flatbread rounds on a baking sheet (or two if necessary) and top with the lamb mixture, pine nuts, and tomatoes, dividing equally. Bake in the preheated oven until the crust is golden brown and the tomatoes have softened, about 10 minutes. Scatter the cilantro over the flatbreads and squeeze the remaining lemon juice over them. Cut into wedges and serve dolloped with the yogurt sauce.

Per Serving:calories: 463 / fat: 22g / protein: 34g / carbs: 34g / fiber: 3g / sodium: 859mg

Flatbread Pizza with Roasted Cherry Tomatoes, Artichokes, and Feta

Prep time: 5 minutes / Cook time: 20 minutes / Serves 4
- 1½ pounds (680 g) cherry or grape tomatoes, halved
- 3 tablespoons olive oil, divided
- ½ teaspoon salt
- ½ teaspoon freshly ground black pepper
- 4 Middle Eastern–style flatbread rounds
- 1 can artichoke hearts, rinsed, well drained, and cut into thin wedges
- 8 ounces (227 g) crumbled feta cheese
- ¼ cup chopped fresh Greek oregano

1. Preheat the oven to 500°F(260°C).
2. In a medium bowl, toss the tomatoes with 1 tablespoon olive oil, the salt, and the pepper. Spread out on a large baking sheet. Roast in the preheated oven until the tomato skins begin to blister and crack, about 10 to 12 minutes. Remove the tomatoes from the oven and reduce the heat to 450°F(235°C).
3. Place the flatbreads on a large baking sheet (or two baking sheets if necessary) and brush the tops with the remaining 2 tablespoons of olive oil. Top with the artichoke hearts, roasted tomatoes, and cheese, dividing equally.
4. Bake the flatbreads in the oven for about 8 to 10 minutes, until the edges are lightly browned and the cheese is melted. Sprinkle the oregano over the top and serve immediately.

Per Serving:calories: 436 / fat: 27g / protein: 16g / carbs: 34g / fiber: 6g / sodium: 649mg

Mediterranean-Pita Wraps

Prep time: 5 minutes / Cook time: 14 minutes / Serves 4
- 1 pound (454 g) mackerel fish fillets
- 2 tablespoons olive oil
- 1 tablespoon Mediterranean seasoning mix
- ½ teaspoon chili powder
- Sea salt and freshly ground black pepper, to taste
- 2 ounces (57 g) feta cheese, crumbled
- 4 tortillas

1. Toss the fish fillets with the olive oil; place them in the lightly oiled air fryer basket.
2. Air fry the fish fillets at 400ºF (204ºC) for about 14 minutes, turning them over halfway through the cooking time.
3. Assemble your pitas with the chopped fish and remaining ingredients and serve warm.

Per Serving:calories: 275 / fat: 13g / protein: 27g / carbs: 13g / fiber: 2g / sodium: 322mg

Cucumber Basil Sandwiches

Prep time: 10 minutes / Cook time: 0 minutes / Serves 2
- Cucumber Basil Sandwiches
- 4 slices whole-grain bread
- ¼ cup hummus
- 1 large cucumber, thinly sliced
- 4 whole basil leaves

1. Spread the hummus on 2 slices of bread, and layer the cucumbers onto it. Top with the basil leaves and close the sandwiches.
2. Press down lightly and serve immediately.

Per Serving:calories: 209 / fat: 5g / protein: 9g / carbs: 32g / fiber: 6g / sodium: 275mg

Za'atar Pizza

Prep time: 10 minutes / Cook time: 15 minutes / Serves 4 to 6

- 1 sheet puff pastry
- ¼ cup extra-virgin olive oil
- ⅓ cup za'atar seasoning
1. Preheat the oven to 350°F(180°C).
2. Put the puff pastry on a parchment-lined baking sheet. Cut the pastry into desired slices.
3. Brush the pastry with olive oil. Sprinkle with the za'atar.
4. Put the pastry in the oven and bake for 10 to 12 minutes or until edges are lightly browned and puffed up. Serve warm or at room temperature.

Per Serving:calories: 374 / fat: 30g / protein: 3g / carbs: 20g / fiber: 1g / sodium: 166mg

Mediterranean Tuna Salad Sandwiches

Prep time: 10 minutes / Cook time: 5 minutes / Serves 2

- 1 can white tuna, packed in water or olive oil, drained
- 1 roasted red pepper, diced
- ½ small red onion, diced
- 10 low-salt olives, pitted and finely chopped
- ¼ cup plain Greek yogurt
- 1 tablespoon flat-leaf parsley, chopped
- Juice of 1 lemon
- Sea salt and freshly ground pepper, to taste
- 4 whole-grain pieces of bread
1. In a small bowl, combine all of the ingredients except the bread, and mix well.
2. Season with sea salt and freshly ground pepper to taste. Toast the bread or warm in a pan.
3. Make the sandwich and serve immediately.

Per Serving:calories: 307 / fat: 7g / protein: 30g / carbs: 31g / fiber: 5g / sodium: 564mg

Chicken and Goat Cheese Pizza

Prep time: 10 minutes / Cook time: 10 minutes / Serves 4

- All-purpose flour, for dusting
- 1 pound (454 g) premade pizza dough
- 2 tablespoons olive oil
- 1 cup shredded cooked chicken
- 3 ounces (85 g) goat cheese, crumbled
- Sea salt
- Freshly ground black pepper
1. Preheat the oven to 475°F (245°C) .
2. On a floured surface, roll out the dough to a 12-inch round and place it on a lightly floured pizza pan or baking sheet. Drizzle the dough with the olive oil and spread it out evenly. Top the dough with the chicken and goat cheese.
3. Bake the pizza for 8 to 10 minutes, until the crust is cooked through and golden.
4. Season with salt and pepper and serve.

Per Serving:calories: 555 / fat: 23g / protein: 24g / carbs: 60g / fiber: 2g / sodium: 660mg

Turkish Pizza

Prep time: 20 minutes / Cook time: 10 minutes / Serves 4

- 4 ounces (113 g) ground lamb or 85% lean ground beef
- ¼ cup finely chopped green bell pepper
- ¼ cup chopped fresh parsley
- 1 small plum tomato, seeded and finely chopped
- 2 tablespoons finely chopped yellow onion
- 1 garlic clove, minced
- 2 teaspoons tomato paste
- ¼ teaspoon sweet paprika
- ¼ teaspoon ground cumin
- ⅛ to ¼ teaspoon red pepper flakes
- ⅛ teaspoon ground allspice
- ⅛ teaspoon kosher salt
- ⅛ teaspoon black pepper
- 4 (6-inch) flour tortillas
- For Serving:
- Chopped fresh mint
- Extra-virgin olive oil
- Lemon wedges
1. In a medium bowl, gently mix the ground lamb, bell pepper, parsley, chopped tomato, onion, garlic, tomato paste, paprika, cumin, red pepper flakes, allspice, salt, and black pepper until well combined.
2. Divide the meat mixture evenly among the tortillas, spreading it all the way to the edge of each tortilla.
3. Place 1 tortilla in the air fryer basket. Set the air fryer to 400°F (204°C) for 10 minutes, or until the meat topping has browned and the edge of the tortilla is golden. Transfer to a plate and repeat to cook the remaining tortillas.
4. Serve the pizzas warm, topped with chopped fresh mint and a drizzle of extra-virgin olive oil and with lemon wedges alongside.

Per Serving:calories: 172 / fat: 8g / protein: 8g / carbs: 18g / fiber: 2g / sodium: 318mg

Greek Salad Pita

Prep time: 15 minutes / Cook time: 0 minutes / Serves 4

- 1 cup chopped romaine lettuce
- 1 tomato, chopped and seeded
- ½ cup baby spinach leaves
- ½ small red onion, thinly sliced
- ½ small cucumber, chopped and deseeded
- 2 tablespoons olive oil
- 1 tablespoon crumbled feta cheese

- ½ tablespoon red wine vinegar
- 1 teaspoon Dijon mustard
- Sea salt and freshly ground pepper, to taste
- 1 whole-wheat pita
1. Combine everything except the sea salt, freshly ground pepper, and pita bread in a medium bowl.
2. Toss until the salad is well combined.
3. Season with sea salt and freshly ground pepper to taste. Fill the pita with the salad mixture, serve, and enjoy!

Per Serving:calories: 123 / fat: 8g / protein: 3g / carbs: 12g / fiber: 2g / sodium: 125mg

Classic Margherita Pizza

Prep time: 10 minutes / Cook time: 10 minutes / Serves 4
- All-purpose flour, for dusting
- 1 pound (454 g) premade pizza dough
- 1 (15-ounce / 425-g) can crushed San Marzano tomatoes, with their juices
- 2 garlic cloves
- 1 teaspoon Italian seasoning
- Pinch sea salt, plus more as needed
- 1½ teaspoons olive oil, for drizzling
- 10 slices mozzarella cheese
- 12 to 15 fresh basil leaves
1. Preheat the oven to 475ºF (245ºC).
2. On a floured surface, roll out the dough to a 12-inch round and place it on a lightly floured pizza pan or baking sheet.
3. In a food processor, combine the tomatoes with their juices, garlic, Italian seasoning, and salt and process until smooth. Taste and adjust the seasoning.
4. Drizzle the olive oil over the pizza dough, then spoon the pizza sauce over the dough and spread it out evenly with the back of the spoon, leaving a 1-inch border. Evenly distribute the mozzarella over the pizza.
5. Bake until the crust is cooked through and golden, 8 to 10 minutes. Remove from the oven and let sit for 1 to 2 minutes. Top with the basil right before serving.

Per Serving:calories: 570 / fat: 21g / protein: 28g / carbs: 66g / fiber: 4g / sodium: 570mg

Grilled Chicken Salad Pita

Prep time: 15 minutes / Cook time: 16 minutes / Serves 1
- 1 boneless, skinless chicken breast
- Sea salt and freshly ground pepper, to taste
- 1 cup baby spinach
- 1 roasted red pepper, sliced
- 1 tomato, chopped
- ½ small red onion, thinly sliced
- ½ small cucumber, chopped
- 1 tablespoon olive oil
- Juice of 1 lemon
- 1 whole-wheat pita pocket
- 2 tablespoons crumbled feta cheese

1. Preheat a gas or charcoal grill to medium-high heat.
2. Season the chicken breast with sea salt and freshly ground pepper, and grill until cooked through, about 7–8 minutes per side.
3. Allow chicken to rest for 5 minutes before slicing into strips.
4. While the chicken is cooking, put all the chopped vegetables into a medium-mixing bowl and season with sea salt and freshly ground pepper.
5. Chop the chicken into cubes and add to salad. Add the olive oil and lemon juice and toss well.
6. Stuff the mixture onto a pita pocket and top with the feta cheese. Serve immediately.

Per Serving:calories: 653 / fat: 26g / protein: 71g / carbs: 34g / fiber: 6g / sodium: 464mg

Moroccan Lamb Wrap with Harissa

Prep time: 10 minutes / Cook time: 10 minutes / Serves 4
- 1 clove garlic, minced
- 2 teaspoons ground cumin
- 2 teaspoons chopped fresh thyme
- ¼ cup olive oil, divided
- 1 lamb leg steak, about 12 ounces (340 g)
- 4 (8-inch) pocketless pita rounds or naan, preferably whole-wheat
- 1 medium eggplant, sliced ½-inch thick
- 1 medium zucchini, sliced lengthwise into 4 slices
- 1 bell pepper (any color), roasted and skinned
- 6 to 8 Kalamata olives, sliced
- Juice of 1 lemon
- 2 to 4 tablespoons harissa
- 2 cups arugula
1. In a large bowl, combine the garlic, cumin, thyme, and 1 tablespoon of the olive oil. Add the lamb, turn to coat, cover, refrigerate, and marinate for at least an hour.
2. Preheat the oven to 400ºF(205ºC).
3. Heat a grill or grill pan to high heat. Remove the lamb from the marinade and grill for about 4 minutes per side, until medium-rare. Transfer to a plate and let rest for about 10 minutes before slicing thinly across the grain.
4. While the meat is resting, wrap the bread rounds in aluminum foil and heat in the oven for about 10 minutes.
5. Meanwhile, brush the eggplant and zucchini slices with the remaining olive oil and grill until tender, about 3 minutes. Dice them and the bell pepper. Toss in a large bowl with the olives and lemon juice.
6. Spread some of the harissa onto each warm flatbread round and top each evenly with roasted vegetables, a few slices of lamb, and a handful of the arugula.
7. Roll up the wraps, cut each in half crosswise, and serve immediately.

Per Serving:calories: 553 / fat: 24g / protein: 33g / carbs:

53g / fiber: 11g / sodium: 531mg

Greek Salad Wraps

Prep time: 15 minutes /Cook time: 0 minutes/ Serves: 4

- 1½ cups seedless cucumber, peeled and chopped (about 1 large cucumber)
- 1 cup chopped tomato (about 1 large tomato)
- ½ cup finely chopped fresh mint
- 1 (2¼ ounces / 64 g) can sliced black olives (about ½ cup), drained
- ¼ cup diced red onion (about ¼ onion)
- 2 tablespoons extra-virgin olive oil
- 1 tablespoon red wine vinegar
- ¼ teaspoon freshly ground black pepper
- ¼ teaspoon kosher or sea salt
- ½ cup crumbled goat cheese (about 2 ounces / 57 g)
- 4 whole-wheat flatbread wraps or soft whole-wheat tortillas

1. In a large bowl, mix together the cucumber, tomato, mint, olives, and onion until well combined.
2. In a small bowl, whisk together the oil, vinegar, pepper, and salt. Drizzle the dressing over the salad, and mix gently.
3. With a knife, spread the goat cheese evenly over the four wraps. Spoon a quarter of the salad filling down the middle of each wrap.
4. Fold up each wrap: Start by folding up the bottom, then fold one side over and fold the other side over the top. Repeat with the remaining wraps and serve.

Per Serving:calories: 217 / fat: 14g / protein: 7g / carbs: 17g / fiber: 3g / sodium: 329mg

Turkey Burgers with Feta and Dill

Prep time: 5 minutes / Cook time: 15 minutes / Serves 4

- 1 pound (454 g) ground turkey breast
- 1 small red onion, ½ finely chopped, ½ sliced
- ½ cup crumbled feta cheese
- ¼ cup chopped fresh dill
- 1 clove garlic, minced
- ½ teaspoon kosher salt
- ¼ teaspoon ground black pepper
- 4 whole grain hamburger rolls
- 4 thick slices tomato
- 4 leaves lettuce

1. Coat a grill rack or grill pan with olive oil and prepare to medium-high heat.
2. In a large bowl, use your hands to combine the turkey, chopped onion, cheese, dill, garlic, salt, and pepper. Do not overmix. Divide into 4 patties, 4' in diameter.
3. Grill the patties, covered, until a thermometer inserted in the center registers 165°F(74°C), 5 to 6 minutes per side.
4. Serve each patty on a roll with the sliced onion, 1 slice of the tomato, and 1 leaf of the lettuce.

Per Serving:calories: 305 / fat: 7g / protein: 35g / carbs: 26g / fiber: 3g / sodium: 708mg

Chapter 11 Pasta

Tahini Soup

Prep time: 5 minutes / Cook time: 4 minutes / Serves 6

- 2 cups orzo
- 8 cups water
- 1 tablespoon olive oil
- 1 teaspoon salt
- ½ teaspoon ground black pepper
- ½ cup tahini
- ¼ cup lemon juice

1. Add pasta, water, oil, salt, and pepper to the Instant Pot®. Close lid, set steam release to Sealing, press the Manual button, and set time to 4 minutes. When the timer beeps, quick-release the pressure until the float valve drops, and open lid. Set aside.
2. Add tahini to a small mixing bowl and slowly add lemon juice while whisking constantly. Once lemon juice has been incorporated, take about ½ cup hot broth from the pot and slowly add to tahini mixture while whisking, until creamy smooth.
3. Pour mixture into the soup and mix well. Serve immediately.

Per Serving:calories: 338 / fat: 13g / protein: 12g / carbs: 49g / fiber: 5g / sodium: 389mg

Penne with Broccoli and Anchovies

Prep time: 10 minutes / Cook time: 10 minutes / Serves 4

- ¼ cup olive oil
- 1 pound (454 g) whole-wheat pasta
- ½ pound (227 g) broccoli or broccoli rabe cut into 1-inch florets
- 3 to 4 anchovy fillets, packed in olive oil
- 2 cloves garlic, sliced
- Pinch red pepper flakes
- ¼ cup freshly grated, lowfat Parmesan
- Sea salt and freshly ground pepper, to taste

1. Heat the olive oil in a deep skillet on medium heat.
2. In the meantime, prepare the pasta al dente, according to the package directions.
3. Fry the broccoli, anchovies, and garlic in the oil until the broccoli is almost tender and the garlic is slightly browned, about 5 minutes or so.
4. Rinse and drain the pasta, and add it to the broccoli mixture. Stir to coat the pasta with the garlic oil. Transfer to a serving dish, toss with red pepper flakes and Parmesan, and season.

Per Serving:calories: 568 / fat: 17g / protein: 21g / carbs: 89g / fiber: 11g / sodium: 203mg

No-Drain Pasta alla Norma

Prep time: 5 minutes /Cook time: 25 minutes/ Serves: 6

- 1 medium globe eggplant (about 1 pound / 454 g), cut into ¾-inch cubes

- 1 tablespoon extra-virgin olive oil
- 1 cup chopped onion (about ½ medium onion)
- 8 ounces (227 g) uncooked thin spaghetti
- 1 (15-ounce / 425-g) container part-skim ricotta cheese
- 3 Roma tomatoes, chopped (about 2 cups)
- 2 garlic cloves, minced (about 1 teaspoon)
- ¼ teaspoon kosher or sea salt
- ½ cup loosely packed fresh basil leaves
- Grated Parmesan cheese, for serving (optional)

1. Lay three paper towels on a large plate, and pile the cubed eggplant on top. (Don't cover the eggplant.) Microwave the eggplant on high for 5 minutes to dry and partially cook it.
2. In a large stockpot over medium-high heat, heat the oil. Add the eggplant and the onion and cook for 5 minutes, stirring occasionally.
3. Add the spaghetti, ricotta, tomatoes, garlic, and salt. Cover with water by a ½ inch (about 4 cups of water). Cook uncovered for 12 to 15 minutes, or until the pasta is just al dente (tender with a bite), stirring occasionally to prevent the pasta from sticking together or sticking to the bottom of the pot.
4. Remove the pot from the heat and let the pasta stand for 3 more minutes to absorb more liquid while you tear the basil into pieces. Sprinkle the basil over the pasta and gently stir. Serve with Parmesan cheese, if desired.

Per Serving:calories: 299 / fat: 9g / protein: 15g / carbs: 41g / fiber: 5g / sodium: 174mg

Simple Pesto Pasta

Prep time: 10 minutes / Cook time: 10 minutes / Serves 4 to 6

- 1 pound (454 g) spaghetti
- 4 cups fresh basil leaves, stems removed
- 3 cloves garlic
- 1 teaspoon salt
- ½ teaspoon freshly ground black pepper
- ¼ cup lemon juice
- ½ cup pine nuts, toasted
- ½ cup grated Parmesan cheese
- 1 cup extra-virgin olive oil

1. Bring a large pot of salted water to a boil. Add the spaghetti to the pot and cook for 8 minutes.
2. Put basil, garlic, salt, pepper, lemon juice, pine nuts, and Parmesan cheese in a food processor bowl with chopping blade and purée.
3. While the processor is running, slowly drizzle the olive oil through the top opening. Process until all the olive oil has been added.
4. Reserve ½ cup of the pasta water. Drain the pasta and put it into a bowl. Immediately add the pesto and pasta water

to the pasta and toss everything together. Serve warm.

Per Serving:calories: 1067 / fat: 72g / protein: 23g / carbs: 91g / fiber: 6g / sodium: 817mg

Roasted Asparagus Caprese Pasta

Prep time: 10 minutes /Cook time: 15 minutes/ Serves: 6

- 8 ounces (227 g) uncooked small pasta, like orecchiette (little ears) or farfalle (bow ties)
- 1½ pounds (680 g) fresh asparagus, ends trimmed and stalks chopped into 1-inch pieces (about 3 cups)
- 1 pint grape tomatoes, halved (about 1½ cups)
- 2 tablespoons extra-virgin olive oil
- ¼ teaspoon freshly ground black pepper
- ¼ teaspoon kosher or sea salt
- 2 cups fresh mozzarella, drained and cut into bite-size pieces (about 8 ounces / 227 g)
- ⅓ cup torn fresh basil leaves
- 2 tablespoons balsamic vinegar

1. Preheat the oven to 400°F(205°C).
2. In a large stockpot, cook the pasta according to the package directions. Drain, reserving about ¼ cup of the pasta water.
3. While the pasta is cooking, in a large bowl, toss the asparagus, tomatoes, oil, pepper, and salt together. Spread the mixture onto a large, rimmed baking sheet and bake for 15 minutes, stirring twice as it cooks.
4. Remove the vegetables from the oven, and add the cooked pasta to the baking sheet. Mix with a few tablespoons of pasta water to help the sauce become smoother and the saucy vegetables stick to the pasta.
5. Gently mix in the mozzarella and basil. Drizzle with the balsamic vinegar. Serve from the baking sheet or pour the pasta into a large bowl.
6. If you want to make this dish ahead of time or to serve it cold, follow the recipe up to step 4, then refrigerate the pasta and vegetables. When you are ready to serve, follow step 5 either with the cold pasta or with warm pasta that's been gently reheated in a pot on the stove.

Per Serving:calories: 317 / fat: 12g / protein: 16g / carbs: 38g / fiber: 7g / sodium: 110mg

Whole-Wheat Spaghetti à la Puttanesca

Prep time: 5 minutes / Cook time: 20 minutes / Serves 6

- 1 pound (454 g) dried whole-wheat spaghetti
- ⅓ cup olive oil
- 5 garlic cloves, minced or pressed
- 4 anchovy fillets, chopped
- ½ teaspoon red pepper flakes
- 1 teaspoon salt
- ½ teaspoon freshly ground black pepper
- 1 (28-ounce / 794-g) can tomato purée
- 1 pint cherry tomatoes, halved
- ½ cup pitted green olives, halved
- 2 tablespoons drained capers
- ¾ cup coarsely chopped basil

1. Cook the pasta according to the package instructions.
2. Meanwhile, heat the oil in a large skillet over medium-high heat. Add the garlic, anchovies, red pepper flakes, salt, and pepper. Cook, stirring frequently, until the garlic just begins to turn golden brown, 2 to 3 minutes. Add the tomato purée, olives, cherry tomatoes, and capers and let the mixture simmer, reducing the heat if necessary, and stirring occasionally, until the pasta is done, about 10 minutes.
3. Drain the pasta in a colander and then add it to the sauce, tossing with tongs until the pasta is well coated. Serve hot, garnished with the basil.

Per Serving:calories: 464 / fat: 17g / protein: 12g / carbs: 70g / fiber: 12g / sodium: 707mg

Rotini with Walnut Pesto, Peas, and Cherry Tomatoes

Prep time: 10 minutes / Cook time: 4 minutes / Serves 8

- 1 cup packed fresh basil leaves
- ⅓ cup chopped walnuts
- ¼ cup grated Parmesan cheese
- ¼ cup plus 1 tablespoon extra-virgin olive oil, divided
- 1 clove garlic, peeled
- 1 tablespoon lemon juice
- ¼ teaspoon salt
- 1 pound (454 g) whole-wheat rotini pasta
- 4 cups water
- 1 pint cherry tomatoes
- 1 cup fresh or frozen green peas
- ½ teaspoon ground black pepper

1. In a food processor, add basil and walnuts. Pulse until finely chopped, about 12 pulses. Add cheese, ¼ cup oil, garlic, lemon juice, and salt, and pulse until a rough paste forms, about 10 pulses. Refrigerate until ready to use.
2. Add pasta, water, and remaining 1 tablespoon oil to the Instant Pot®. Close lid, set steam release to Sealing, press the Manual button, and set time to 4 minutes.
3. When the timer beeps, quick-release the pressure until the float valve drops and open lid. Drain off any excess liquid. Allow pasta to cool to room temperature, about 30 minutes. Stir in basil mixture until pasta is well coated. Add tomatoes, peas, and pepper and toss to coat. Refrigerate for 2 hours. Stir well before serving.

Per Serving:calories: 371 / fat: 15g / protein: 12g / carbs: 47g / fiber: 7g / sodium: 205mg

Israeli Pasta Salad

Prep time: 15 minutes / Cook time: 4 minutes / Serves 6

- ½ pound (227 g) whole-wheat penne pasta
- 4 cups water
- 1 tablespoon plus ¼ cup extra-virgin olive oil, divided
- 1 cup quartered cherry tomatoes
- ½ English cucumber, chopped
- ½ medium orange bell pepper, seeded and chopped
- ½ medium red onion, peeled and chopped

- ½ cup crumbled feta cheese
- 1 teaspoon fresh thyme leaves
- 1 teaspoon chopped fresh oregano
- ½ teaspoon ground black pepper
- ¼ cup lemon juice
1. Add pasta, water, and 1 tablespoon oil to the Instant Pot®. Close lid, set steam release to Sealing, press the Manual button, and set time to 4 minutes.
2. When the timer beeps, quick-release the pressure until the float valve drops and open lid. Drain and set aside to cool for 30 minutes. Stir in tomatoes, cucumber, bell pepper, onion, feta, thyme, oregano, black pepper, lemon juice, and remaining ¼ cup oil. Refrigerate for 2 hours.

Per Serving:calories: 243 / fat: 16g / protein: 7g / carbs: 20g / fiber: 3g / sodium: 180mg

Mixed Vegetable Couscous

Prep time: 20 minutes / Cook time: 10 minutes / Serves 8
- 1 tablespoon light olive oil
- 1 medium zucchini, trimmed and chopped
- 1 medium yellow squash, chopped
- 1 large red bell pepper, seeded and chopped
- 1 large orange bell pepper, seeded and chopped
- 2 tablespoons chopped fresh oregano
- 2 cups Israeli couscous
- 3 cups vegetable broth
- ½ cup crumbled feta cheese
- ¼ cup red wine vinegar
- ¼ cup extra-virgin olive oil
- ½ teaspoon ground black pepper
- ¼ cup chopped fresh basil
1. Press the Sauté button on the Instant Pot® and heat light olive oil. Add zucchini, squash, bell peppers, and oregano, and sauté 8 minutes. Press the Cancel button. Transfer to a serving bowl and set aside to cool.
2. Add couscous and broth to the Instant Pot® and stir well. Close lid, set steam release to Sealing, press the Manual button, and set time to 2 minutes. When the timer beeps, let pressure release naturally for 5 minutes, then quick-release the remaining pressure and open lid.
3. Fluff with a fork and stir in cooked vegetables, cheese, vinegar, extra-virgin olive oil, black pepper, and basil. Serve warm.

Per Serving:calories: 355 / fat: 9g / protein: 14g / carbs: 61g / fiber: 7g / sodium: 588mg

Bowtie Pesto Pasta Salad

Prep time: 5 minutes / Cook time: 4 minutes / Serves 8
- 1 pound (454 g) whole-wheat bowtie pasta
- 4 cups water
- 1 tablespoon extra-virgin olive oil
- 2 cups halved cherry tomatoes
- 2 cups baby spinach
- ½ cup chopped fresh basil
- ½ cup prepared pesto

- ½ teaspoon ground black pepper
- ½ cup grated Parmesan cheese
1. Add pasta, water, and olive oil to the Instant Pot®. Close lid, set steam release to Sealing, press the Manual button, and set time to 4 minutes.
2. When the timer beeps, quick-release the pressure until the float valve drops and open lid. Drain off any excess liquid. Allow pasta to cool to room temperature, about 30 minutes. Stir in tomatoes, spinach, basil, pesto, pepper, and cheese. Refrigerate for 2 hours. Stir well before serving.

Per Serving:calories: 360 / fat: 13g / protein: 16g / carbs: 44g / fiber: 7g / sodium: 372mg

Whole-Wheat Capellini with Sardines, Olives, and Manchego

Prep time: 5 minutes / Cook time: 15 minutes / Serves 4
- 1 (7-ounce / 198-g) jar Spanish sardines in olive oil, chopped (reserve the oil)
- 1 medium onion, diced
- 4 cloves garlic, minced
- 2 medium tomatoes, sliced
- 1 pound (454 g) whole-wheat capellini pasta, cooked according to package instructions
- 1 cup pitted, chopped cured black olives, such as Kalamata
- 3 ounces (85 g) freshly grated manchego cheese
1. Heat the olive oil from the sardines in a large skillet over medium-high heat. Add the onion and garlic and cook, stirring frequently, until softened, about 5 minutes. Add the tomatoes and sardines and cook, stirring, 2 minutes more.
2. Add the cooked and drained pasta to the skillet with the sauce and toss to combine.
3. Stir in the olives and serve immediately, topped with the grated cheese.

Per Serving:calories: 307 / fat: 11g / protein: 8g / carbs: 38g / fiber: 6g / sodium: 433mg

Greek Spaghetti with Meat Sauce

Prep time: 10 minutes / Cook time: 17 minutes / Serves 6
- 1 pound (454 g) spaghetti
- 4 cups water
- 3 tablespoons olive oil, divided
- 1 medium white onion, peeled and diced
- ½ pound (227 g) lean ground veal
- ½ teaspoon salt
- ¼ teaspoon ground black pepper
- ¼ cup white wine
- ½ cup tomato sauce
- 1 cinnamon stick
- 2 bay leaves
- 1 clove garlic, peeled
- ¼ cup grated aged myzithra or Parmesan cheese
1. Add pasta, water, and 1 tablespoon oil to the Instant Pot®. Close lid, set steam release to Sealing, press the Manual button, and set time to 4 minutes. When

the timer beeps, quick-release the pressure until the float valve drops, open lid, and drain. Press the Cancel button. Set aside.

2. Press the Sauté button and heat remaining 2 tablespoons oil. Add onion and cook until soft, about 3 minutes. Add veal and crumble well. Keep stirring until meat is browned, about 5 minutes. Add salt, pepper, wine, and tomato sauce, and mix well.

3. Stir in cinnamon stick, bay leaves, and garlic. Press the Cancel button. Close lid, set steam release to Sealing, press the Manual button, and set time to 5 minutes. When the timer beeps, quick-release the pressure until the float valve drops and open lid. Remove and discard cinnamon stick and bay leaves.

4. Place pasta in a large bowl. Sprinkle with cheese and spoon meat sauce over top. Serve immediately.

Per Serving:calories: 447 / fat: 15g / protein: 18g / carbs: 60g / fiber: 4g / sodium: 394mg

Quick Shrimp Fettuccine

Prep time: 10 minutes / Cook time: 10 minutes / Serves 4 to 6

- 8 ounces (227 g) fettuccine pasta
- ¼ cup extra-virgin olive oil
- 3 tablespoons garlic, minced
- 1 pound (454 g) large shrimp (21-25), peeled and deveined
- ⅓ cup lemon juice
- 1 tablespoon lemon zest
- ½ teaspoon salt
- ½ teaspoon freshly ground black pepper

1. Bring a large pot of salted water to a boil. Add the fettuccine and cook for 8 minutes.

2. In a large saucepan over medium heat, cook the olive oil and garlic for 1 minute.

3. Add the shrimp to the saucepan and cook for 3 minutes on each side. Remove the shrimp from the pan and set aside.

4. Add the lemon juice and lemon zest to the saucepan, along with the salt and pepper.

5. Reserve ½ cup of the pasta water and drain the pasta.

6. Add the pasta water to the saucepan with the lemon juice and zest and stir everything together. Add the pasta and toss together to evenly coat the pasta. Transfer the pasta to a serving dish and top with the cooked shrimp. Serve warm.

Per Serving:calories: 615 / fat: 17g / protein: 33g / carbs: 89g / fiber: 4g / sodium: 407mg

Baked Ziti

Prep time: 10 minutes / Cook time: 55 minutes / Serves 8

- For the Marinara Sauce:
- 2 tablespoons olive oil
- ¼ medium onion, diced (about 3 tablespoons)
- 3 cloves garlic, chopped
- 1 (28-ounce / 794-g) can whole, peeled tomatoes, roughly chopped
- Sprig of fresh thyme

- ½ bunch fresh basil
- Sea salt and freshly ground pepper, to taste
- For the Ziti:
- 1 pound (454 g) whole-wheat ziti
- 3½ cups marinara sauce
- 1 cup low-fat cottage cheese
- 1 cup grated, low-fat mozzarella cheese, divided
- ¾ cup freshly grated, low-fat Parmesan cheese, divided

1. Make the marinara sauce: 1. Heat the olive oil in a medium saucepan over medium-high heat.

2. Sauté the onion and garlic, stirring until lightly browned, about 3 minutes.

3. Add the tomatoes and the herb sprigs, and bring to a boil. Lower the heat and simmer, covered, for 10 minutes. Remove and discard the herb sprigs.

4. Stir in sea salt and season with freshly ground pepper to taste. Make the ziti: 1. Preheat the oven to 375°F (190°C).

2. Prepare the pasta according to package directions. Drain pasta. Combine the pasta in a bowl with 2 cups marinara sauce, the cottage cheese, and half the mozzarella and Parmesan cheeses.

3. Spread the mixture in a baking dish, and top with the remaining marinara sauce and cheese.

4. Bake for 30–40 minutes, or until bubbly and golden brown.

Per Serving:calories: 389 / fat: 12g / protein: 18g / carbs: 56g / fiber: 9g / sodium: 369mg

Fettuccine with Tomatoes and Pesto

Prep time: 15 minutes / Cook time: 10 minutes / Serves 4

- 1 pound (454 g) whole-grain fettuccine
- 4 Roma tomatoes, diced
- 2 teaspoons tomato paste
- 1 cup vegetable broth
- 2 garlic cloves, minced
- 1 tablespoon chopped fresh oregano
- ½ teaspoon salt
- 1 packed cup fresh basil leaves
- ¼ cup extra-virgin olive oil
- ¼ cup grated Parmesan cheese
- ¼ cup pine nuts

1. Bring a large stockpot of water to a boil over high heat, and cook the fettuccine according to the package instructions until al dente (still slightly firm). Drain but do not rinse.

2. Meanwhile, in a large, heavy skillet, combine the tomatoes, tomato paste, broth, garlic, oregano, and salt and stir well. Cook over medium heat for 10 minutes.

3. In a blender or food processor, combine the basil, olive oil, Parmesan cheese, and pine nuts and blend until smooth.

4. Stir the pesto into the tomato mixture. Add the pasta and cook, stirring frequently, just until the pasta is well coated and heated through.

5. Serve immediately.

Per Serving:calories: 636 / fat: 22g / protein: 11g / carbs: 96g / fiber: 3g / sodium: 741mg

Chapter 12 Desserts

Nut Butter Cup Fat Bomb

Prep time: 5 minutes / Cook time: 0 minutes / Serves 8

- ½ cup crunchy almond butter (no sugar added)
- ½ cup light fruity extra-virgin olive oil
- ¼ cup ground flaxseed
- 2 tablespoons unsweetened cocoa powder
- 1 teaspoon vanilla extract
- 1 teaspoon ground cinnamon (optional)
- 1 to 2 teaspoons sugar-free sweetener of choice (optional)

1. In a mixing bowl, combine the almond butter, olive oil, flaxseed, cocoa powder, vanilla, cinnamon (if using), and sweetener (if using) and stir well with a spatula to combine. Mixture will be a thick liquid.
2. Pour into 8 mini muffin liners and freeze until solid, at least 12 hours. Store in the freezer to maintain their shape.

Per Serving:calories: 239 / fat: 24g / protein: 4g / carbs: 5g / fiber: 3g / sodium: 3mg

Red Wine–Poached Figs with Ricotta and Almond

Prep time: 5 minutes / Cook time: 1 minute / Serves 4

- 2 cups water
- 2 cups red wine
- ¼ cup honey
- 1 cinnamon stick
- 1 star anise
- 1 teaspoon vanilla bean paste
- 12 dried mission figs
- 1 cup ricotta cheese
- 1 tablespoon confectioners' sugar
- ¼ teaspoon almond extract
- 1 cup toasted sliced almonds

1. Add water, wine, honey, cinnamon, star anise, and vanilla to the Instant Pot® and whisk well. Add figs, close lid, set steam release to Sealing, press the Manual button, and set time to 1 minute.
2. When the timer beeps, quick-release the pressure until the float valve drops. Press the Cancel button and open lid. With a slotted spoon, transfer figs to a plate and set aside to cool for 5 minutes.
3. In a small bowl, mix together ricotta, sugar, and almond extract. Serve figs with a dollop of sweetened ricotta and a sprinkling of almonds.

Per Serving:calories: 597 / fat: 21g / protein: 13g / carbs: 56g / fiber: 9g / sodium: 255mg

Almond Cookies

Prep time: 5 minutes / Cook time: 10 minutes / Serves 4 to 6

- ½ cup sugar
- 8 tablespoons (1 stick) room temperature salted butter
- 1 large egg
- 1½ cups all-purpose flour
- 1 cup ground almonds or almond flour

1. Preheat the oven to 375°F(190°C).
2. Using a mixer, cream together the sugar and butter.
3. Add the egg and mix until combined.
4. Alternately add the flour and ground almonds, ½ cup at a time, while the mixer is on slow.
5. Once everything is combined, line a baking sheet with parchment paper. Drop a tablespoon of dough on the baking sheet, keeping the cookies at least 2 inches apart.
6. Put the baking sheet in the oven and bake just until the cookies start to turn brown around the edges, about 5 to 7 minutes.

Per Serving:calories: 604 / fat: 36g / protein: 11g / carbs: 63g / fiber: 4g / sodium: 181mg

Orange–Olive Oil Cupcakes

Prep time: 15 minutes / Cook time: 20 minutes / Makes 6 cupcakes

- 1 large egg
- 2 tablespoons powdered sugar-free sweetener (such as stevia or monk fruit extract)
- ½ cup extra-virgin olive oil
- 1 teaspoon almond extract
- Zest of 1 orange
- 1 cup almond flour
- ¾ teaspoon baking powder
- ⅛ teaspoon salt
- 1 tablespoon freshly squeezed orange juice

1. Preheat the oven to 350°F (180°C). Place muffin liners into 6 cups of a muffin tin.
2. In a large bowl, whisk together the egg and powdered sweetener. Add the olive oil, almond extract, and orange zest and whisk to combine well.
3. In a small bowl, whisk together the almond flour, baking powder, and salt. Add to wet ingredients along with the orange juice and stir until just combined.
4. Divide the batter evenly into 6 muffin cups and bake until a toothpick inserted in the center of the cupcake comes out clean, 15 to 18 minutes.
5. Remove from the oven and cool for 5 minutes in the tin

before transferring to a wire rack to cool completely.

Per Serving:1 cup cake: calories: 280 / fat: 27g / protein: 4g / carbs: 8g / fiber: 2g / sodium: 65mg

Greek Yogurt with Honey and Pomegranates

Prep time: 5 minutes / Cook time: 0 minutes / Serves 4

- 4 cups plain full-fat Greek yogurt
- ½ cup pomegranate seeds
- ¼ cup honey
- Sugar, for topping (optional)

1. Evenly divide the yogurt among four bowls. Evenly divide the pomegranate seeds among the bowls and drizzle each with the honey.
2. Sprinkle each bowl with a pinch of sugar, if desired, and serve.

Per Serving:calories: 232 / fat: 8g / protein: 9g / carbs: 33g / fiber: 1g / sodium: 114mg

Poached Apricots and Pistachios with Greek Yogurt

Prep time: 2 minutes / Cook time: 18 minutes / Serves 4

- ½ cup orange juice
- 2 tablespoons brandy
- 2 tablespoons honey
- ¾ cup water
- 1 cinnamon stick
- 12 dried apricots
- ⅓ cup 2% Greek yogurt
- 2 tablespoons mascarpone cheese
- 2 tablespoons shelled pistachios

1. Place a saucepan over medium heat and add the orange juice, brandy, honey, and water. Stir to combine, then add the cinnamon stick.
2. Once the honey has dissolved, add the apricots. Bring the mixture to a boil, then cover, reduce the heat to low, and simmer for 15 minutes.
3. While the apricots are simmering, combine the Greek yogurt and mascarpone cheese in a small serving bowl. Stir until smooth, then set aside.
4. When the cooking time for the apricots is complete, uncover, add the pistachios, and continue simmering for 3 more minutes. Remove the pan from the heat.
5. To serve, divide the Greek yogurt–mascarpone cheese mixture into 4 serving bowls and top each serving with 3 apricots, a few pistachios, and 1 teaspoon of the syrup. The apricots and syrup can be stored in a jar at room temperature for up to 1 month.

Per Serving:calories: 146 / fat: 3g / protein: 4g / carbs: 28g / fiber: 4g / sodium: 62mg

Olive Oil Ice Cream

Prep time: 5 minutes / Cook time: 25 minutes / Serves 8

- 4 large egg yolks
- ⅓ cup powdered sugar-free sweetener (such as stevia or monk fruit extract)
- 2 cups half-and-half or 1 cup heavy whipping cream and 1 cup whole milk
- 1 teaspoon vanilla extract
- ⅛ teaspoon salt
- ¼ cup light fruity extra-virgin olive oil

1. Freeze the bowl of an ice cream maker for at least 12 hours or overnight.
2. In a large bowl, whisk together the egg yolks and sugar-free sweetener.
3. In a small saucepan, heat the half-and-half over medium heat until just below a boil. Remove from the heat and allow to cool slightly.
4. Slowly pour the warm half-and-half into the egg mixture, whisking constantly to avoid cooking the eggs. Return the eggs and cream to the saucepan over low heat.
5. Whisking constantly, cook over low heat until thickened, 15 to 20 minutes. Remove from the heat and stir in the vanilla extract and salt. Whisk in the olive oil and transfer to a glass bowl. Allow to cool, cover, and refrigerate for at least 6 hours.
6. Freeze custard in an ice cream maker according to manufacturer's directions.

Per Serving:calories: 168 / fat: 15g / protein: 2g / carbs: 8g / fiber: 0g / sodium: 49mg

Toasted Almonds with Honey

Prep time: 15 minutes / Cook time: 5 minutes / Serves 4

- ½ cup raw almonds
- 3 tablespoons good-quality honey, plus more if desired

1. Fill a medium saucepan three-quarters full with water and bring to a boil over high heat. Add the almonds and cook for 1 minute. Drain the almonds in a fine-mesh sieve and rinse them under cold water to cool and stop the cooking. Remove the skins from the almonds by rubbing them in a clean kitchen towel. Place the almonds on a paper towel to dry.
2. In the same saucepan, combine the almonds and honey and cook over medium heat until the almonds get a little golden, 4 to 5 minutes. Remove from the heat and let cool completely, about 15 minutes, before serving or storing.

Per Serving:calories: 151 / fat: 9g / protein: 4g / carbs: 17g / fiber: 2g / sodium: 1mg

Cucumber-Lime Popsicles

Prep time: 5 minutes / Cook time: 0 minutes / Serves 4 to 6

- 2 cups cold water
- 1 cucumber, peeled
- ¼ cup honey
- Juice of 1 lime

1. In a blender, purée the water, cucumber, honey, and lime juice. Pour into popsicle molds, freeze, and enjoy on a hot summer day!

Per Serving:calories: 49 / fat: 0g / protein: 0g / carbs: 13g / fiber: 0g / sodium: 3mg

Fresh Figs with Chocolate Sauce

Prep time: 5 minutes / Cook time: 0 minutes / Serves 4

- ¼ cup honey
- 2 tablespoons cocoa powder
- 8 fresh figs

1. Combine the honey and cocoa powder in a small bowl, and mix well to form a syrup.
2. Cut the figs in half and place cut side up. Drizzle with the syrup and serve.

Per Serving:calories: 112 / fat: 1g / protein: 1g / carbs: 30g / fiber: 3g / sodium: 3mg

Mediterranean Orange Yogurt Cake

Prep time: 10 minutes / Cook time: 3 to 5 hours / Serves 4 to 6

- Nonstick cooking spray
- ¾ cup all-purpose flour
- ¾ cup whole-wheat flour
- 2 teaspoons baking powder
- ¼ teaspoon salt
- 1 cup coconut palm sugar
- ½ cup plain Greek yogurt
- ½ cup mild-flavored, extra-virgin olive oil
- 3 large eggs
- 2 teaspoons vanilla extract
- Grated zest of 1 orange
- Juice of 1 orange

1. Generously coat a slow cooker with cooking spray, or line the bottom and sides with parchment paper or aluminum foil.
2. In a large bowl, whisk together the all-purpose and whole-wheat flours, baking powder, and salt.
3. In another large bowl, whisk together the sugar, yogurt, olive oil, eggs, vanilla, orange zest, and orange juice until smooth.
4. Add the dry ingredients to the wet ingredients and mix together until well-blended. Pour the batter into the prepared slow cooker.
5. Cover the cooker and cook for 3 to 5 hours on Low heat, or until the middle has set and a knife inserted into it comes out clean.

Per Serving:calories: 544 / fat: 33g / protein: 11g / carbs: 53g / fiber: 4g / sodium: 482mg

Mascarpone and Fig Crostini

Prep time: 10 minutes / Cook time: 10 minutes / Serves 6 to 8

- 1 long French baguette
- 4 tablespoons (½ stick) salted butter, melted
- 1 (8-ounce / 227-g) tub mascarpone cheese
- 1 (12-ounce / 340-g) jar fig jam

1. Preheat the oven to 350°F(180°C).
2. Slice the bread into ¼-inch-thick slices.
3. Arrange the sliced bread on a baking sheet and brush each slice with the melted butter.
4. Put the baking sheet in the oven and toast the bread for 5 to 7 minutes, just until golden brown.
5. Let the bread cool slightly. Spread about a teaspoon or so of the mascarpone cheese on each piece of bread.
6. Top with a teaspoon or so of the jam. Serve immediately.

Per Serving:calories: 445 / fat: 24g / protein: 3g / carbs: 48g / fiber: 5g / sodium: 314mg

Strawberry Panna Cotta

Prep time: 10 minutes / Cook time: 10 minutes / Serves 4

- 2 tablespoons warm water
- 2 teaspoons gelatin powder
- 2 cups heavy cream
- 1 cup sliced strawberries, plus more for garnish
- 1 to 2 tablespoons sugar-free sweetener of choice (optional)
- 1½ teaspoons pure vanilla extract
- 4 to 6 fresh mint leaves, for garnish (optional)

1. Pour the warm water into a small bowl. Sprinkle the gelatin over the water and stir well to dissolve. Allow the mixture to sit for 10 minutes.
2. In a blender or a large bowl, if using an immersion blender, combine the cream, strawberries, sweetener (if using), and vanilla. Blend until the mixture is smooth and the strawberries are well puréed.
3. Transfer the mixture to a saucepan and heat over medium-low heat until just below a simmer. Remove from the heat and cool for 5 minutes.
4. Whisking constantly, add in the gelatin mixture until smooth. Divide the custard between ramekins or small glass bowls, cover and refrigerate until set, 4 to 6 hours.
5. Serve chilled, garnishing with additional sliced strawberries or mint leaves (if using).

Per Serving:calories: 229 / fat: 22g / protein: 3g / carbs: 5g / fiber: 1g / sodium: 26mg

Peaches Poached in Rose Water

Prep time: 15 minutes / Cook time: 1 minute / Serves 6

- 1 cup water

- 1 cup rose water
- ¼ cup wildflower honey
- 8 green cardamom pods, lightly crushed
- 1 teaspoon vanilla bean paste
- 6 large yellow peaches, pitted and quartered
- ½ cup chopped unsalted roasted pistachio meats

1. Add water, rose water, honey, cardamom, and vanilla to the Instant Pot®. Whisk well, then add peaches. Close lid, set steam release to Sealing, press the Manual button, and set time to 1 minute.
2. When the timer beeps, quick-release the pressure until the float valve drops. Press the Cancel button and open lid. Allow peaches to stand for 10 minutes. Carefully remove peaches from poaching liquid with a slotted spoon.
3. Slip skins from peach slices. Arrange slices on a plate and garnish with pistachios. Serve warm or at room temperature.

Per Serving:calories: 145 / fat: 3g / protein: 2g / carbs: 28g / fiber: 2g / sodium: 8mg

Whipped Greek Yogurt with Chocolate

Prep time: 10 minutes / Cook time: 0 minutes / Serves 4
- 4 cups plain full-fat Greek yogurt
- ½ cup heavy (whipping) cream
- 2 ounces (57 g) dark chocolate (at least 70% cacao), grated, for topping

1. In the bowl of a stand mixer fitted with the whisk attachment or in a large bowl using a handheld mixer, whip the yogurt and cream for about 5 minutes, or until peaks form.
2. Evenly divide the whipped yogurt mixture among bowls and top with the grated chocolate. Serve.

Per Serving:calories: 337 / fat: 25g / protein: 10g / carbs: 19g / fiber: 2g / sodium: 127mg

Lemon Fool

Prep time: 25minutes /Cook time: 5 minutes/ Serves: 4
- 1 cup 2% plain Greek yogurt
- 1 medium lemon
- ¼ cup cold water
- 1½ teaspoons cornstarch
- 3½ tablespoons honey, divided
- ⅔ cup heavy (whipping) cream
- Fresh fruit and mint leaves, for serving (optional)

1. Place a large glass bowl and the metal beaters from your electric mixer in the refrigerator to chill. Add the yogurt to a medium glass bowl, and place that bowl in the refrigerator to chill as well.
2. Using a Microplane or citrus zester, zest the lemon into a medium, microwave-safe bowl. Halve the lemon, and squeeze 1 tablespoon of lemon juice into the bowl. Add the water and cornstarch, and stir well. Whisk in 3 tablespoons of honey. Microwave the lemon mixture on

high for 1 minute; stir and microwave for an additional 10 to 30 seconds, until the mixture is thick and bubbling.
3. Remove the bowl of yogurt from the refrigerator, and whisk in the warm lemon mixture. Place the yogurt back in the refrigerator.
4. Remove the large chilled bowl and the beaters from the refrigerator. Assemble your electric mixer with the chilled beaters. Pour the cream into the chilled bowl, and beat until soft peaks form—1 to 3 minutes, depending on the freshness of your cream.
5. Take the chilled yogurt mixture out of the refrigerator. Gently fold it into the whipped cream using a rubber scraper; lift and turn the mixture to prevent the cream from deflating. Chill until serving, at least 15 minutes but no longer than 1 hour.
6. To serve, spoon the lemon fool into four glasses or dessert dishes and drizzle with the remaining ½ tablespoon of honey. Top with fresh fruit and mint, if desired.

Per Serving:calories: 172 / fat: 8g / protein: 4g / carbs: 22g / fiber: 1g / sodium: 52mg

Tahini Baklava Cups

Prep time: 10 minutes / Cook time: 25 minutes / Serves 8
- 1 box (about 16) mini phyllo dough cups, thawed
- ⅓ cup tahini
- ¼ cup shelled pistachios or walnuts, chopped, plus more for garnish
- 4 tablespoons honey, divided
- 1 teaspoon ground cinnamon
- Pinch of kosher salt
- ½ teaspoon rosewater (optional)

1. Preheat the oven to 350°F(180°C). Remove the phyllo cups from the packaging and place on a large rimmed baking sheet.
2. In a small bowl, stir together the tahini, nuts, 1 tablespoon of the honey, the cinnamon, and salt. Divide this mixture among the phyllo cups and top each with a few more nuts. Bake until golden and warmed through, 10 minutes. Remove from the oven and cool for 5 minutes.
3. Meanwhile, in a small saucepan or in a microwaveable bowl, stir together the remaining 3 tablespoons honey and the rosewater, if using, and heat until warmed, about 5 minutes over medium heat .

Per Serving:calories: 227 / fat: 9g / protein: 5g / carbs: 32g / fiber: 2g / sodium: 195mg

Banana Cream Pie Parfaits

Prep time: 10 minutes / Cook time: 0 minutes / Serves 2
- 1 cup nonfat vanilla pudding
- 2 low-sugar graham crackers, crushed
- 1 banana, peeled and sliced

- ¼ cup walnuts, chopped
- Honey for drizzling

1. In small parfait dishes or glasses, layer the ingredients, starting with the pudding and ending with chopped walnuts.
2. You can repeat the layers, depending on the size of the glass and your preferences.
3. Drizzle with the honey. Serve chilled.

Per Serving:calories: 312 / fat: 11g / protein: 7g / carbs: 50g / fiber: 3g / sodium: 273mg

Golden Coconut Cream Pops

Prep time: 5 minutes / Cook time: 0 minutes / Makes 8 cream pops

- 1½ cups coconut cream
- ½ cup coconut milk
- 4 egg yolks
- 2 teaspoons ground turmeric
- 1 teaspoon ground ginger
- 1 teaspoon cinnamon
- 1 teaspoon vanilla powder or 1 tablespoon unsweetened vanilla extract
- ¼ teaspoon ground black pepper
- Optional: low-carb sweetener, to taste

1. Place all of the ingredients in a blender (including the optional sweetener) and process until well combined. Pour into eight ⅓-cup (80 ml) ice pop molds. Freeze until solid for 3 hours, or until set.
2. To easily remove the ice pops from the molds, fill a pot as tall as the ice pops with warm (not hot) water and dip the ice pop molds in for 15 to 20 seconds. Remove the ice pops from the molds and then freeze again. Store in the freezer in a resealable bag for up to 3 months.

Per Serving:calories: 281 / fat: 28g / protein: 4g / carbs: 5g / net carbs: 4g / fiber: 1g

Pears with Blue Cheese and Walnuts

Prep time: 10 minutes / Cook time: 0 minutes / Serves 1

- 1 to 2 pears, cored and sliced into 12 slices
- ¼ cup blue cheese crumbles
- 12 walnut halves
- 1 tablespoon honey

1. Lay the pear slices on a plate, and top with the blue cheese crumbles. Top each slice with 1 walnut, and drizzle with honey.
2. Serve and enjoy!

Per Serving:calories: 420 / fat: 29g / protein: 12g / carbs: 35g / fiber: 6g / sodium: 389mg

Blueberry Compote

Prep time: 10 minutes / Cook time: 5 minutes / Serves 8

- 1 (16-ounce/ 454-g) bag frozen blueberries, thawed
- ¼ cup sugar
- 1 tablespoon lemon juice

- 2 tablespoons cornstarch
- 2 tablespoons water
- ¼ teaspoon vanilla extract
- ¼ teaspoon grated lemon zest

1. Add blueberries, sugar, and lemon juice to the Instant Pot®. Close lid, set steam release to Sealing, press the Manual button, and set time to 1 minute.
2. When the timer beeps, quick-release the pressure until the float valve drops. Press the Cancel button and open lid.
3. Press the Sauté button. In a small bowl, combine cornstarch and water. Stir into blueberry mixture and cook until mixture comes to a boil and thickens, about 3–4 minutes. Press the Cancel button and stir in vanilla and lemon zest. Serve immediately or refrigerate until ready to serve.

Per Serving:calories: 57 / fat: 0g / protein: 0g / carbs: 14g / fiber: 2g / sodium: 0mg

Chocolate Pudding

Prep time: 10 minutes / Cook time: 0 minutes / Serves 4

- 2 ripe avocados, halved and pitted
- ¼ cup unsweetened cocoa powder
- ¼ cup heavy whipping cream, plus more if needed
- 2 teaspoons vanilla extract
- 1 to 2 teaspoons liquid stevia or monk fruit extract (optional)
- ½ teaspoon ground cinnamon (optional)
- ¼ teaspoon salt
- Whipped cream, for serving (optional)

1. Using a spoon, scoop out the ripe avocado into a blender or large bowl, if using an immersion blender. Mash well with a fork.
2. Add the cocoa powder, heavy whipping cream, vanilla, sweetener (if using), cinnamon (if using), and salt. Blend well until smooth and creamy, adding additional cream, 1 tablespoon at a time, if the mixture is too thick.
3. Cover and refrigerate for at least 1 hour before serving. Serve chilled with additional whipped cream, if desired.

Per Serving:calories: 205 / fat: 18g / protein: 3g / carbs: 12g / fiber: 9g / sodium: 156mg

Apricot and Mint No-Bake Parfait

Prep time: 10 minutes / Cook time: 0 minutes / Serves 6

- 4 ounces (113 g) Neufchâtel or other light cream cheese
- 1 (7-ounce / 198-g) container 2% Greek yogurt
- ½ cup plus 2 tablespoons sugar
- 2 teaspoons vanilla extract
- 1 tablespoon fresh lemon juice
- 1 pound (454 g) apricots, rinsed, pitted, and cut into bite-size pieces
- 2 tablespoons finely chopped fresh mint, plus whole leaves for garnish if desired

1. In the bowl of a stand mixer fitted with the paddle attachment, beat the Neufchâtel cheese and yogurt on low speed until well combined, about 2 minutes, scraping down the bowl as needed. Add ½ cup of the sugar, the vanilla, and the lemon juice. Mix until smooth and free of lumps, 2 to 3 minutes; set aside.
2. In a medium bowl, combine the apricots, mint, and remaining 2 tablespoons sugar. Stir occasionally, waiting to serve until after the apricots have released their juices and have softened.
3. Line up six 6-to 8-ounce (170-to 227-g) glasses. Using an ice cream scoop, spoon 3 to 4 tablespoons of the cheesecake mixture evenly into the bottom of each glass. (Alternatively, transfer the cheesecake mixture to a piping bag or a small zip-top bag with one corner snipped and pipe the mixture into the glasses.) Add a layer of the same amount of apricots to each glass. Repeat so you have two layers of cheesecake mixture and two layers of the apricots, ending with the apricots.) Garnish with the mint, if desired, and serve.

Per Serving:calories: 132 / fat: 2g / protein: 5g / carbs: 23g / fiber: 2g / sodium: 35mg

Greek Yogurt Chocolate "Mousse" with Berries

Prep time: 15 minutes / Cook time: 0 minutes / Serves 4
- 2 cups plain Greek yogurt
- ¼ cup heavy cream
- ¼ cup pure maple syrup
- 3 tablespoons unsweetened cocoa powder
- 2 teaspoons vanilla extract
- ¼ teaspoon kosher salt
- 1 cup fresh mixed berries
- ¼ cup chocolate chips

1. Place the yogurt, cream, maple syrup, cocoa powder, vanilla, and salt in the bowl of a stand mixer or use a large bowl with an electric hand mixer. Mix at medium-high speed until fluffy, about 5 minutes.
2. Spoon evenly among 4 bowls and put in the refrigerator to set for at least 15 minutes.
3. Serve each bowl with ¼ cup mixed berries and 1 tablespoon chocolate chips.

Per Serving:calories: 300 / fat: 11g / protein: 16g / carbs: 35g / fiber: 3g / sodium: 60mg

Honey Ricotta with Espresso and Chocolate Chips

Prep time: 5 minutes / Cook time: 0 minutes / Serves 2
- 8 ounces (227 g) ricotta cheese
- 2 tablespoons honey
- 2 tablespoons espresso, chilled or room temperature
- 1 teaspoon dark chocolate chips or chocolate shavings

1. In a medium bowl, whip together the ricotta cheese and honey until light and smooth, 4 to 5 minutes.
2. Spoon the ricotta cheese-honey mixture evenly into 2 dessert bowls. Drizzle 1 tablespoon espresso into each dish and sprinkle with chocolate chips or shavings.

Per Serving:calories: 235 / fat: 10g / protein: 13g / carbs: 25g / fiber: 0g / sodium: 115mg

Chapter 13 Staples, Sauces, Dips, and Dressings

Orange Dijon Dressing

Prep time: 5 minutes / Cook time: 0 minutes / Serves 2

- ¼ cup extra-virgin olive oil
- 2 tablespoons freshly squeezed orange juice
- 1 orange, zested
- 1 teaspoon garlic powder
- ¾ teaspoon za'atar seasoning
- ½ teaspoon salt
- ¼ teaspoon Dijon mustard
- Freshly ground black pepper, to taste

1. In a jar, combine the olive oil, orange juice and zest, garlic powder, za'atar, salt, and mustard. Season with pepper and shake vigorously until completely mixed.

Per Serving:calories: 284 / fat: 27g / protein: 1g / carbs: 11g / fiber: 2g / sodium: 590mg

Parsley-Mint Sauce

Prep time: 5 minutes / Cook time: 0 minutes / Serves 6

- ½ cup fresh flat-leaf parsley
- 1 cup fresh mint leaves
- 2 garlic cloves, minced
- 2 scallions (green onions), chopped
- 2 tablespoons pomegranate molasses
- ¼ cup olive oil
- 1 tablespoon fresh lemon juice

1. Combine all the ingredients in a blender and blend until smooth. Transfer to an airtight container and refrigerate until ready to use. Can be refrigerated for 1 day.

Per Serving:calories: 90 / fat: 9g / protein: 1g / carbs: 2g / fiber: 0g / sodium: 5mg

Classic Basil Pesto

Prep time: 5 minutes / Cook time: 13 minutes / Makes about 1½ cups

- 6 garlic cloves, unpeeled
- ½ cup pine nuts
- 4 cups fresh basil leaves
- ¼ cup fresh parsley leaves
- 1 cup extra-virgin olive oil
- 1 ounce (28 g) Parmesan cheese, grated fine (½ cup)

1. Toast garlic in 8-inch skillet over medium heat, shaking skillet occasionally, until softened and spotty brown, about 8 minutes. When garlic is cool enough to handle, remove and discard skins and chop coarsely. Meanwhile, toast pine nuts in now-empty skillet over medium heat, stirring often, until golden and fragrant, 4 to 5 minutes.
2. Place basil and parsley in 1-gallon zipper-lock bag. Pound bag with flat side of meat pounder or with rolling pin until all leaves are bruised.
3. Process garlic, pine nuts, and herbs in food processor until finely chopped, about 1 minute, scraping down sides of bowl as needed. With processor running, slowly add oil until incorporated. Transfer pesto to bowl, stir in Parmesan, and season with salt and pepper to taste. (Pesto can be refrigerated for up to 3 days or frozen for up to 3 months. To prevent browning, press plastic wrap flush to surface or top with thin layer of olive oil. Bring to room temperature before using.)

Per Serving:¼ cup: calories: 423 / fat: 45g / protein: 4g / carbs: 4g / fiber: 1g / sodium: 89mg

Basic Brown-Onion Masala

Prep time: 20 minutes / Cook time: 6½ hours / Makes 4 cups

- 2 tablespoons rapeseed oil
- 6 onions, finely diced
- 8 garlic cloves, finely chopped
- 1¾ pounds (794 g) canned plum tomatoes
- 3-inch piece fresh ginger, grated
- 1 teaspoon salt
- 1½ teaspoons turmeric
- Handful fresh coriander stalks, finely chopped
- 3 fresh green chiles, finely chopped
- 1 teaspoon chili powder
- 1 teaspoon ground cumin seeds
- 1 cup hot water
- 2 teaspoons garam masala

1. Preheat the slow cooker on high (or to the sauté setting, if you have it). Then add the oil and let it heat. Add the onions and cook for a few minutes until they start to brown. Make sure you brown the onions well so you get a deep, flavorsome base.
2. Add the garlic and continue to cook on high for about 10 minutes.
3. Add the tomatoes, ginger, salt, turmeric, coriander stalks, chopped chiles, chili powder, cumin seeds, and water.
4. Cover the slow cooker and cook on low for 6 hours.
5. Remove the lid and stir. Let the masala cook for another 30 minutes uncovered to reduce a little.
6. Add the garam masala after the masala has cooked.
7. Use right away, or freeze it in small tubs or freezer bags. Just defrost what you need, when you need it.

Per Serving:calories: 286 / fat: 8g / protein: 7g / carbs: 52g /fiber: 8g / sodium: 656mg

Tomatillo Salsa

Prep time: 5 minutes / Cook time: 15 minutes / Serves 4

- 12 tomatillos
- 2 fresh serrano chiles
- 1 tablespoon minced garlic
- 1 cup chopped fresh cilantro leaves
- 1 tablespoon vegetable oil
- 1 teaspoon kosher salt

1. Remove and discard the papery husks from the tomatillos and rinse them under warm running water to remove the sticky coating.
2. Place the tomatillos and peppers in a baking pan. Place the pan in the air fryer basket. Air fry at 350ºF (177ºC) for 15 minutes.
3. Transfer the tomatillos and peppers to a blender, add the garlic, cilantro, vegetable oil, and salt, and blend until almost smooth. (If not using immediately, omit the salt and add it just before serving.)
4. Serve or store in an airtight container in the refrigerator for up to 10 days.

Per Serving:calories: 68 / fat: 4g / protein: 1g / carbs: 7g / fiber: 2g / sodium: 585mg

Harissa Spice Mix

Prep time: 5 minutes / Cook time: 0 minutes / Makes about 7 tablespoons

- 2 tablespoons ground cumin
- 4 teaspoons paprika
- 4 teaspoons ground turmeric
- 2 teaspoons ground coriander
- 2 teaspoons chili powder
- 1 teaspoon garlic powder
- 1 teaspoon ground caraway seeds
- ½ teaspoon cayenne powder

1. Place all of the ingredients in a jar. Seal and shake well to combine. Store in a sealed jar at room temperature for up to 6 months.

Per Serving:1 tablespoon: calories: 21 / fat: 1g / protein: 1g / carbs: 4g / fiber: 2g / sodium: 27mg

Pickled Turnips

Prep time: 5 minutes / Cook time: 0 minutes / Serves 2

- 1 pound (454 g) turnips, washed well, peeled, and cut into 1-inch batons
- 1 small beet, roasted, peeled, and cut into 1-inch batons
- 2 garlic cloves, smashed
- 1 teaspoon dried Turkish oregano
- 3 cups warm water
- ½ cup red wine vinegar
- ½ cup white vinegar

1. In a jar, combine the turnips, beet, garlic, and oregano. Pour the water and vinegars over the vegetables, cover, then shake well and put it in the refrigerator. The turnips

will be pickled after 1 hour.

Per Serving:calories: 3 / fat: 0g / protein: 1g / carbs: 0g / fiber: 0g / sodium: 6mg

Sofrito

Prep time: 10 minutes / Cook time: 10 minutes / Serves 8 to 10

- 4 tablespoons olive oil
- 1 small onion, chopped
- 1 medium green bell pepper, seeded and chopped
- ¼ teaspoon salt
- 6 garlic cloves, minced
- ½ teaspoon red pepper flakes
- ¼ teaspoon freshly ground black pepper
- 1 cup finely chopped fresh cilantro
- 2 tablespoons red wine vinegar or sherry vinegar

1. In a 10-inch skillet, heat 2 tablespoons of the olive oil over medium-high heat. Add the onion, bell pepper, and salt. Cook, stirring occasionally, for 6 to 8 minutes, until softened.
2. Add the garlic, red pepper flakes, and black pepper; cook for 1 minute.
3. Transfer the vegetables to a blender or food processor and add the remaining 2 tablespoons olive oil, the cilantro, and the vinegar. Blend until smooth.

Per Serving:calories: 63 / fat: 6g / protein: 0g / carbs: 2g / fiber: 0g / sodium: 67mg

Red Pepper Chimichurri

Prep time: 10 minutes / Cook time: 0 minutes / Serves 4

- 1 garlic clove, minced
- 3 tablespoons olive oil
- 1 tablespoon red wine vinegar or sherry vinegar
- ¼ teaspoon freshly ground black pepper
- 1 shallot, finely chopped
- 1 large red bell pepper, roasted, peeled, seeded, and finely chopped (about 1 cup)
- 3 tablespoons capers, rinsed
- 3 tablespoons chopped fresh parsley
- ½ teaspoon red pepper flakes

1. In a small bowl, stir together all the ingredients until well combined.

Per Serving:calories: 113 / fat: 10g / protein: 1g / carbs: 5g / fiber: 1g / sodium: 157mg

Sherry Vinaigrette

Prep time: 5 minutes / Cook time: 0 minutes / Makes about ¾ cup

- ⅓ cup sherry vinegar
- 1 clove garlic
- 2 teaspoons dried oregano
- 1 teaspoon salt
- ½ teaspoon freshly ground black pepper
- ½ cup olive oil

1. In a food processor or blender, combine the vinegar, garlic, oregano, salt, and pepper and process until the garlic is minced and the ingredients are well combined. With the food processor running, add the olive oil in a thin stream until it is well incorporated. Serve immediately or store, covered, in the refrigerator for up to a week.

Per Serving:calories: 74 / fat: 8g / protein: 0g / carbs: 0g / fiber: 0g / sodium: 194mg

Red Pepper and Tomato Chutney

Prep time: 10 minutes / Cook time: 4 hours / Makes 2 to 3 cups

- 3 tablespoons rapeseed oil
- 1 teaspoon cumin seeds
- 4 garlic cloves, roughly chopped
- 1 large red onion, roughly chopped
- 2 red bell peppers, seeded and roughly chopped
- 1 pound (454 g) fresh tomatoes
- 1 tablespoon malt vinegar
- 1 teaspoon salt
- 1 fresh green chile
- ¼ cup hot water

1. Heat the slow cooker to high and add the oil.
2. Add the cumin seeds and cook until they are fragrant. Then stir in the garlic and cook 1 to 2 minutes.
3. Add the onion, peppers, tomatoes, vinegar, salt, chile, and water.
4. Cook on low for 4 hours, until the peppers are soft and the tomatoes have burst.
5. Using an immersion or regular blender, purée, and then pour the chutney through a colander.
6. Put the chutney into a sterilized glass jar and leave to cool. When cooled, seal the jar. The chutney will keep for 2 weeks in the refrigerator.

Per Serving:calories: 99 / fat: 7g / protein: 2g / carbs: 8g / fiber: 2g / sodium: 423mg

Traditional Caesar Dressing

Prep time: 10 minutes / Cook time: 5 minutes / Makes 1½ cups

- 2 teaspoons minced garlic
- 4 large egg yolks
- ¼ cup wine vinegar
- ½ teaspoon dry mustard
- Dash Worcestershire sauce
- 1 cup extra-virgin olive oil
- ¼ cup freshly squeezed lemon juice
- Sea salt and freshly ground black pepper, to taste

1. To a small saucepan, add the garlic, egg yolks, vinegar, mustard, and Worcestershire sauce and place over low heat.
2. Whisking constantly, cook the mixture until it thickens and is a little bubbly, about 5 minutes.

3. Remove from saucepan from the heat and let it stand for about 10 minutes to cool.
4. Transfer the egg mixture to a large stainless steel bowl. Whisking constantly, add the olive oil in a thin stream.
5. Whisk in the lemon juice and season the dressing with salt and pepper.
6. Transfer the dressing to an airtight container and keep in the refrigerator for up to 3 days.

Per Serving:calories: 202 / fat: 21g / protein: 2g / carbs: 2g / fiber: 0g / sodium: 14mg

Pepper Sauce

Prep time: 10 minutes / Cook time: 20 minutes / Makes 4 cups

- 2 red hot fresh chiles, seeded
- 2 dried chiles
- ½ small yellow onion, roughly chopped
- 2 garlic cloves, peeled
- 2 cups water
- 2 cups white vinegar

1. In a medium saucepan, combine the fresh and dried chiles, onion, garlic, and water. Bring to a simmer and cook for 20 minutes, or until tender. Transfer to a food processor or blender.
2. Add the vinegar and blend until smooth.

Per Serving:1 cup: calories: 41 / fat: 0g / protein: 1g / carbs: 5g / fiber: 1g / sodium: 11mg

Pickled Onions

Prep time: 5 minutes / Cook time: 0 minutes / Serves 8 to 10

- 3 red onions, finely chopped
- ½ cup warm water
- ¼ cup granulated sugar
- ¼ cup red wine vinegar
- 1 teaspoon dried oregano

1. In a jar, combine the onions, water, sugar, vinegar, and oregano, then shake well and put it in the refrigerator. The onions will be pickled after 1 hour.

Per Serving:calories: 40 / fat: 0g / protein: 1g / carbs: 10g / fiber: 1g / sodium: 1mg

Garlic-Rosemary Infused Olive Oil

Prep time: 5 minutes / Cook time: 45 minutes / Makes 1 cup

- 1 cup extra-virgin olive oil
- 4 large garlic cloves, smashed
- 4 (4- to 5-inch) sprigs rosemary

1. In a medium skillet, heat the olive oil, garlic, and rosemary sprigs over low heat. Cook until fragrant and garlic is very tender, 30 to 45 minutes, stirring occasionally. Don't let the oil get too hot or the garlic will burn and become bitter.
2. Remove from the heat and allow to cool slightly.

Remove the garlic and rosemary with a slotted spoon and pour the oil into a glass container. Allow to cool completely before covering. Store covered at room temperature for up to 3 months.

Per Serving: ⅛ cup: calories: 241 / fat: 27g / protein: 0g / carbs: 1g / fiber: 0g / sodium: 1mg

Herbed Oil

Prep time: 5 minutes / Cook time: 0 minutes / Serves 2

- ½ cup extra-virgin olive oil
- 1 teaspoon dried basil
- 1 teaspoon dried parsley
- 1 teaspoon fresh rosemary leaves
- 2 teaspoons dried oregano
- ⅛ teaspoon salt

1. Pour the oil into a small bowl and stir in the basil, parsley, rosemary, oregano, and salt while whisking the oil with a fork.

Per Serving: calories: 486 / fat: 54g / protein: 1g / carbs: 2g / fiber: 1g / sodium: 78mg

Berry and Honey Compote

Prep time: 5 minutes / Cook time: 15 minutes / Serves 2

- ½ cup honey
- ¼ cup fresh berries
- 2 tablespoons grated orange zest

1. In a small saucepan, heat the honey, berries, and orange zest over medium-low heat for 2 to 5 minutes, until the sauce thickens, or heat for 15 seconds in the microwave. Serve the compote drizzled over pancakes, muffins, or French toast.

Per Serving: calories: 272 / fat: 0g / protein: 1g / carbs: 74g / fiber: 1g / sodium: 4mg

Mint Pesto

Prep time: 5 minutes / Cook time: 0 minutes / Makes about 1 cup

- 1 tablespoon toasted walnuts
- 2 cups packed fresh mint leaves
- 1 clove garlic
- 1 tablespoon lemon juice
- ½ teaspoon lemon zest
- ¼ teaspoon salt
- ⅔ cup olive oil
- ½ cup grated Pecorino cheese

1. Place the walnuts, mint, and garlic in a food processor and pulse to mince finely. Add the lemon juice, lemon zest, and salt and pulse to grind to a paste.
2. With the processor running, add the olive oil in a thin stream. Process until the mixture is well combined.
3. Add the cheese and pulse to combine.

Per Serving: calories: 113 / fat: 12g / protein: 3g / carbs: 1g / fiber: 0g / sodium: 234mg

Artichoke Dip

Prep time: 15 minutes / Cook time: 0 minutes / Serves 3

- 1 (14-ounce / 397-g) can artichoke hearts, drained
- 1 pound (454 g) goat cheese
- 2 tablespoons extra-virgin olive oil
- 2 teaspoons lemon juice
- 1 garlic clove, minced
- 1 tablespoon chopped parsley
- 1 tablespoon chopped chives
- ½ tablespoon chopped basil
- ½ teaspoon sea salt
- ½ teaspoon freshly ground black pepper
- Dash of cayenne pepper (optional)
- ½ cup freshly grated Pecorino Romano

1. In a food processor, combine all the ingredients, except the Pecorino Romano, and process until well incorporated and creamy.
2. Top with the freshly grated Pecorino Romano. Store in an airtight container in the refrigerator for up to 3 days.

Per Serving: calories: 588 / fat: 44g / protein: 36g / carbs: 15g / fiber: 7g / sodium: 513mg

30-Day Meal Plan

	Breakfast	Lunch	Dinner	Snack/Dessert
Day 1	Cauliflower Avocado Toast	Chicken Gyros with Grilled Vegetables and Tzatziki Sauce	Ground Lamb with Lentils and Pomegranate Seeds	Nut Butter Cup Fat Bomb
Day 2	Avocado Toast with Smoked Trout	Lamb with Olives and Potatoes	Mediterranean Cod	Almond Cookies
Day 3	Greek Yogurt and Berries	Seared Duck Breast with Orange Ouzo Sauce	Smoky Pork Tenderloin	Orange–Olive Oil Cupcakes
Day 4	Tiropita (Greek Cheese Pie)	Fried Fresh Sardines	Cajun-Breaded Chicken Bites	Greek Yogurt with Honey and Pomegranates
Day 5	Spiced Scrambled Eggs	Short Ribs with Chimichurri	Mediterranean Cod Stew	Poached Apricots and Pistachios with Greek Yogurt
Day 6	Turkish Egg Bowl	Jerk Chicken Thighs	Lamb Shanks and Potatoes	Olive Oil Ice Cream
Day 7	Spinach and Feta Frittata	Mustard Lamb Chops	Bruschetta Chicken Burgers	Toasted Almonds with Honey
Day 8	Herb & Cheese Fritters	Garlicky Split Chickpea Curry	Steamed Clams	Cucumber-Lime Popsicles
Day 9	Hearty Berry Breakfast Oats	Mediterranean Roasted Turkey Breast	Mediterranean Pork Chops	Fresh Figs with Chocolate Sauce
Day 10	Black Olive Toast with Herbed Hummus	Shrimp with Arugula Pesto and Zucchini Noodles	Puréed Red Lentil Soup	Mediterranean Orange Yogurt Cake
Day 11	Spiced Antioxidant Granola Clusters	Braised Pork Loin with Port and Dried Plums	Turkey Thighs in Fig Sauce	Mascarpone and Fig Crostini
Day 12	Spanish Tortilla with Potatoes and Peppers	Shrimp Foil Packets	Sage-Stuffed Whole Trout with Roasted Vegetables	Strawberry Panna Cotta
Day 13	Nuts and Fruit Oatmeal	Gingery Quinoa Chicken	Garlic-Marinated Flank Steak	Peaches Poached in Rose Water
Day 14	Peachy Green Smoothie	Paprika Crab Burgers	Farro Salad with Tomatoes and Olives	Whipped Greek Yogurt with Chocolate
Day 15	Amaranth Breakfast Bowl with Chocolate and Almonds	Indian Mint and Chile Kebabs	Pesto-Glazed Chicken Breasts	Lemon Fool

	Breakfast	Lunch	Dinner	Snack/Dessert
Day 16	Buffalo Egg Cups	Easy Turkey Tenderloin	Salmon with Provolone Cheese	Tahini Baklava Cups
Day 17	Strawberry Basil Honey Ricotta Toast	Spiced Quinoa Salad	Greek-Style Ground Beef Pita Sandwiches	Banana Cream Pie Parfaits
Day 18	Savory Cottage Cheese Breakfast Bowl	Rosemary Baked Chicken Thighs	Barley and Vegetable Casserole	Golden Coconut Cream Pops
Day 19	Baked Ricotta with Pears	Cod with Tomatoes and Garlic	Apricot-Glazed Turkey Tenderloin	Pears with Blue Cheese and Walnuts
Day 20	Berry Baked Oatmeal	Greek-Style Roast Turkey Breast	Greek-Style Black-Eyed Pea Soup	Blueberry Compote
Day 21	Almond Butter Banana Chocolate Smoothie	Roasted Red Snapper	Lebanese Ground Meat with Rice	Chocolate Pudding
Day 22	Mediterranean-Inspired White Smoothie	Baked Halibut with Cherry Tomatoes	Fiesta Chicken Plate	Apricot and Mint No-Bake Parfait
Day 23	Spiced Potatoes with Chickpeas	Classic Whole Chicken	Lentil Chili	Honey Ricotta with Espresso and Chocolate Chips
Day 24	Harissa Shakshuka with Bell Peppers and Tomatoes	Italian Steak Rolls	Herb-Crusted Lamb Chops	Garlic Edamame
Day 25	Smoky Sausage Patties	Turkey Meatloaf	Asparagus-Spinach Farro	Ranch Oyster Snack Crackers
Day 26	Jalapeño Popper Egg Cups	Kheema Meatloaf	Italian Herb Grilled Chicken	Black Olive and Lentil Pesto
Day 27	Greek Yogurt Parfait	Ahi Tuna Steaks	Lentils with Spinach	Roasted Chickpeas with Herbs and Spices
Day 28	Green Spinach & Salmon Crepes	Roast Chicken	Rosemary Roast Beef	Tuna Croquettes
Day 29	Greek Eggs and Potatoes	Pork with Orzo	Cauliflower Steaks Gratin	Turmeric-Spiced Crunchy Chickpeas
Day 30	Red Pepper and Feta Egg Bites	Beef Whirls	Pork Tenderloin with Chermoula Sauce	Lemon-Pepper Chicken Drumsticks

INDEX

MEASUREMENT CONVERSION CHART

VOLUME EQUIVALENTS(DRY)

US STANDARD	METRIC (APPROXIMATE)
1/8 teaspoon	0.5 mL
1/4 teaspoon	1 mL
1/2 teaspoon	2 mL
3/4 teaspoon	4 mL
1 teaspoon	5 mL
1 tablespoon	15 mL
1/4 cup	59 mL
1/2 cup	118 mL
3/4 cup	177 mL
1 cup	235 mL
2 cups	475 mL
3 cups	700 mL
4 cups	1 L

VOLUME EQUIVALENTS(LIQUID)

US STANDARD	US STANDARD (OUNCES)	METRIC (APPROXIMATE)
2 tablespoons	1 fl.oz.	30 mL
1/4 cup	2 fl.oz.	60 mL
1/2 cup	4 fl.oz.	120 mL
1 cup	8 fl.oz.	240 mL
1 1/2 cup	12 fl.oz.	355 mL
2 cups or 1 pint	16 fl.oz.	475 mL
4 cups or 1 quart	32 fl.oz.	1 L
1 gallon	128 fl.oz.	4 L

TEMPERATURES EQUIVALENTS

FAHRENHEIT(F)	CELSIUS(C) (APPROXIMATE)
225 °F	107 °C
250 °F	120 °C
275 °F	135 °C
300 °F	150 °C
325 °F	160 °C
350 °F	180 °C
375 °F	190 °C
400 °F	205 °C
425 °F	220 °C
450 °F	235 °C
475 °F	245 °C
500 °F	260 °C

WEIGHT EQUIVALENTS

US STANDARD	METRIC (APPROXIMATE)
1 ounce	28 g
2 ounces	57 g
5 ounces	142 g
10 ounces	284 g
15 ounces	425 g
16 ounces (1 pound)	455 g
1.5 pounds	680 g
2 pounds	907 g

The Dirty Dozen and Clean Fifteen

The Environmental Working Group (EWG) is a nonprofit, nonpartisan organization dedicated to protecting human health and the environment Its mission is to empower people to live healthier lives in a healthier environment. This organization publishes an annual list of the twelve kinds of produce, in sequence, that have the highest amount of pesticide residue-the Dirty Dozen-as well as a list of the fifteen kinds ofproduce that have the least amount of pesticide residue-the Clean Fifteen.

THE DIRTY DOZEN	THE CLEAN FIFTEEN
• The 2016 Dirty Dozen includes the following produce. These are considered among the year's most important produce to buy organic:	• The least critical to buy organically are the Clean Fifteen list. The following are on the 2016 list:

THE DIRTY DOZEN

Strawberries	Spinach
Apples	Tomatoes
Nectarines	Bell peppers
Peaches	Cherry tomatoes
Celery	Cucumbers
Grapes	Kale/collard greens
Cherries	Hot peppers

• *The Dirty Dozen list contains two additional itemskale/collard greens and hot peppers-because they tend to contain trace levels of highly hazardous pesticides.*

THE CLEAN FIFTEEN

Avocados	Papayas
Corn	Kiw
Pineapples	Eggplant
Cabbage	Honeydew
Sweet peas	Grapefruit
Onions	Cantaloupe
Asparagus	Cauliflower
Mangos	

• *Some of the sweet corn sold in the United States are made from genetically engineered (GE) seedstock. Buy organic varieties of these crops to avoid GE produce.*